Best Climbs
Cascade Volcanoes

Climbers approaching the summit of Mount Hood.
PHOTO PETE KEANE/TIMBERLINE MOUNTAIN GUIDES

Best Climbs
Cascade Volcanoes

JEFF SMOOT

FALCONGUIDES

GUILFORD, CONNECTICUT
HELENA, MONTANA
AN IMPRINT OF GLOBE PEQUOT PRESS

FALCONGUIDES®

FalconGuides is an imprint of Globe Pequot Press.

Falcon, FalconGuides, and Outfit Your Mind are registered trademarks of Morris Book Publishing, LLC.

All interior photos by Jeff Smoot unless otherwise noted.

Maps © Morris Book Publishing, LLC
Topos by Sue Murray © Morris Book Publishing, LLC

Project editor: David Legere
Text design: Sheryl P. Kober
Layout: Sue Murray

Library of Congress Cataloging-in-Publication Data

Smoot, Jeff.
  Best climbs Cascade volcanoes / Jeff Smoot.
     p. cm.
  Includes bibliographical references and index.
  ISBN 978-0-7627-7796-9
  1. Mountaineering—Cascade Range—Guidebooks. 2. Cascade Range—Guide-
books. I. Title.
  GV199.42.C37S64 2012
  796.5220979—dc23

                                                         2012010766

Printed in the United States of America
10 9 8 7 6 5 4 3 2 1

WARNING

Climbing is a sport where you may be seriously injured or die. Read this before you use this book.

This guidebook is a compilation of unverified information gathered from many different climbers. The author cannot ensure the accuracy of any of the information in this book, including the topos and route descriptions, the difficulty ratings, and the protection ratings. These may be incorrect or misleading, as ratings of climbing difficulty and danger are always subjective and depend on the physical characteristics (for example, height), experience, technical ability, confidence, and physical fitness of the climber who supplied the rating. Additionally, climbers who achieve first ascents sometimes underrate the difficulty or danger of the climbing route. Therefore, be warned that you must exercise your own judgment on where a climbing route goes, its difficulty, and your ability to safely protect yourself from the risks of rock climbing. Examples of some of these risks are: falling due to technical difficulty or due to natural hazards such as holds breaking, falling rock, climbing equipment dropped by other climbers, hazards of weather and lightning, your own equipment failure, and failure or absence of fixed protection.

You should not depend on any information gleaned from this book for your personal safety; your safety depends on your own good judgment, based on experience and a realistic assessment of your climbing ability. If you have any doubt as to your ability to safely climb a route described in this book, do not attempt it.

The following are some ways to make your use of this book safer:

1. Consultation: You should consult with other climbers about the difficulty and danger of a particular climb prior to attempting it. Most local climbers are glad to give advice on routes in their area; we suggest that you contact locals to confirm ratings and safety of particular routes and to obtain first-hand information about a route chosen from this book.

2. Instruction: Most climbing areas have local climbing instructors and guides available. We recommend that you engage an instructor or guide to learn safety techniques and to become familiar with the routes and hazards of the areas described in this book. Even after you are proficient in climbing safely, occasional use of a guide is a safe way to raise your climbing standard and learn advanced techniques.

3. Fixed Protection: Some of the routes in this book may use bolts and pitons that are permanently placed in the rock. Because of variances in the manner of placement, weathering, metal fatigue, the quality of the metal used, and many other factors, these fixed protection pieces should always be considered suspect and should always be backed up by equipment that you place yourself. Never depend on a single piece of fixed protection for your safety, because you never can tell whether it will hold weight. In some cases, fixed protection may have been removed or is now missing. However, climbers should not always add new pieces of protection unless existing protection is faulty. Existing protection can be tested by an experienced climber and its strength determined. Climbers are strongly encouraged not to add bolts and drilled pitons to a route. They need to climb the route in the style of the first ascent party (or better) or choose a route within their ability—a route to which they do not have to add additional fixed anchors.

Be aware of the following specific potential hazards that could arise in using this book:

1. Incorrect Descriptions of Routes: If you climb a route and you have a doubt as to where it goes, you should not continue unless you are sure that you can go that way safely. Route descriptions and topos in this book could be inaccurate or misleading.

2. Incorrect Difficulty Rating: A route might be more difficult than the rating indicates. Do not be lulled into a false sense of security by the difficulty rating.

3. Incorrect Protection Rating: If you climb a route and you are unable to arrange adequate protection from the risk of falling through the use of fixed pitons or bolts and by placing your own protection devices, do not assume that there is adequate protection available higher just because the route protection rating indicates the route does not have an X or an R rating. Every route is potentially an X (a fall may be deadly), due to the inherent hazards of climbing—including, for example, failure or absence of fixed protection, your own equipment's failure, or improper use of climbing equipment.

There are no warranties, whether expressed or implied, that this guidebook is accurate or that the information contained in it is reliable. There are no warranties of fitness for a particular purpose or that this guide is merchantable. Your use of this book indicates your assumption of the risk that it may contain errors and is an acknowledgment of your own sole responsibility for your climbing safety.

Contents

Overview

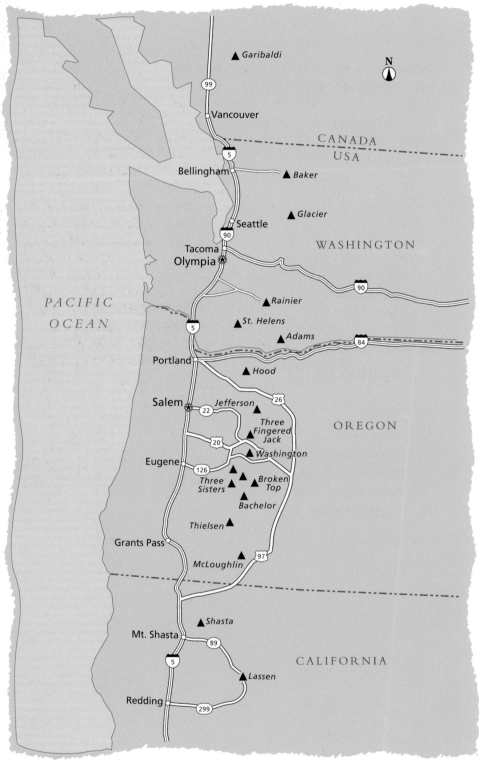

Preface

Fred Beckey wrote that his *Cascade Alpine Guide* intended "an equitable rather than selective coverage of peaks and routes." This author intends precisely the opposite, a selective rather than equitable coverage of climbing routes on the Pacific Northwest coast volcanoes. Although this guide will certainly not replace the many past, present, and future equitable or selective regional guides as the most thorough source of climbing route information, it should suffice for those wishing to climb the big peaks of the Cascade Range by one of the more popular or esteemed routes.

This guide was originally published in 1992 as *Summit Guide to the Cascade Volcanoes*. The second edition was published in 1999 as *Climbing the Cascade Volcanoes*, following the publisher's latest Climbing series of guidebooks. This third edition follows the trend as part of FalconGuide's new Best Climbs series. To that end, it has become even more of a select guide than the previous editions. Still, this is not a "Fifty Classic Climbs" of the Cascade volcanoes, nor is it a "peak bagger's" guide to only the easiest route up each Cascade volcano. But then, it is not an exhaustive treatment either. Hopefully this guide will provide sufficient information to get you where you want to go, provided where you want to go is to the summit of any of the major Cascade Range volcanic peaks by any one of their better routes.

Acknowledgments

If anything is true in guidebook writing, "It's not what you know but who you know." This guide is not solely the result of an individual effort by the author, but rather a compilation of efforts of many individuals. Without the assistance of others, whether in providing route information, photographs, reviewing the manuscript, or simply providing the name of someone with useful information or photographs, preparing this guide would have been an impossible task. I am greatly indebted to Eldon Altizer, Matt Arksey, Virginia Baker, Tom Bauman, Tom Bell, Alex Bertulis, Jim Blilie, Bob Bolton, Tim Boyer, James Bull, Jack Cameron, Riley Caton, Mark Dale, Bill Dengler, Nick Dodge, Steve Doty, Nancy Eberle, Phil Ershler, Bruce Fairley, Mark Gunlogson, Ed Hall, Brent Harris, Paul Hartl, Ken Henshaw, Dave Hirst, Pete Keane, Wally Kerchum, George Larsen, Lee Lau, Andrew Lavigne, Jeff Leisy, Darryl Lloyd, Royal Mannion, Christopher Mason, Dee Molenaar, Janice Naragon, Larry Nielson, Garry Olson, Jon Olson, Owen Purschwitz, Barbara Samora, Don Serl, Thomas Servatius, Ray Smutek, Steve Sorseth, Bill Soule, Matt Stamplis, Oliver Thomas, Richard Vance, Frank Vicen, Leif Voeltz, Mike Volk, Ron Warfield, Doug Weaver, Howard Weaver, Robert Webster, Jim Wickwire, Chris Wright, Margaret Yates, and Michael Zanger. Special thanks to Matt Keyser, who envisioned this guide but had the foresight to abandon it to me, and to Pat Gentry and Helen Vargas, for their invaluable proofreading and fact-finding efforts, and to my editor, John Burbidge, for his patience and the occasional kick in the rear. Great assistance was provided by personnel of the U.S. Geological Survey Ice and Climate Study Project, Mt. Baker-Snoqualmie National Forest, Gifford Pinchot National Forest, Mt. Hood National Forest, Shasta-Trinity National Forest, Washington Department of Recreation, Mount Rainier National Park, Lassen Volcanic National Park, Cascade Volcano Observatory, British Columbia Forest Service, and British Columbia Mountaineering Council. Thanks also to The Mountaineers and to the Northwest Interpretive Association for use of their excellent outdoor libraries. If I have forgotten anyone, I offer my sincerest apology.

Introduction

The volcanoes of the Cascade Range are magnets to the adventuresome populations who live nearby. Puget Sound lowlanders are treated to a panorama of mountains, but are drawn to the giants—Mounts Baker and Rainier. Columbia River Gorge and northwestern Oregon residents likewise hold Mount Hood in high esteem. Residents of central Oregon are treated to a splendid panorama of high volcanoes. Northern Californians cannot escape the dominating presence of Mount Shasta. These are the "power points," if you will, of the Pacific Northwest. Without going into the physical, mystical, psychological, and philosophical attractions of the big peaks, suffice it to say that millions visit the volcano parks and wilderness areas each year, and, like a rite of passage, thousands climb at least one of the Cascade volcanoes during their lifetime. For others, the lure of the high volcanoes does not end with one ascent, but becomes a lifelong obsession. Some return to the same mountain year after year; others climb each peak only once by the easiest route; some climb only the "classic" routes; and others climb whatever and whenever possible.

Due to the limited scope of this guide, many volcanic peaks within the Cascade Range have been omitted, including many "minor" summits, volcanic remnants, and a plethora of cinder cones. As a general rule, this guide covers only glaciated volcanic peaks and those rising above 10,000 feet. Exceptions to this rule have been made for a few lower volcanic peaks, such as Mount St. Helens, Mount Washington, Three Fingered Jack, Mount Thielsen, and Mount McLoughlin. These peaks were included because of their high visibility, popularity, or geological significance.

This guide is not intended to provide instruction for would-be mountain climbers. Those desiring to learn how to climb should consult other books and take a mountaineering instruction course before attempting to climb any route on a Cascade volcano, particularly those involving glacier travel or technical rock or ice climbing. (Mountaineering instruction books and climbing guide services are listed in the appendix for the reader's convenience.)

A warning for the unwary: While thousands of mountain ascents are safely accomplished each year, mountain climbing, and particularly glacier and volcano climbing, have inherent dangers that, although not always obvious, are always present. Many mountain accidents result from inexperienced climbers attempting routes that are too difficult for them, or from exercising poor judgment in the face of changing circumstances, and particularly by fatigue-induced error. However, many climbing accidents occur by chance, whether

Crispin Prahl on the Roman Wall, Mount Baker. Photo Jeremy Allyn Mountain Madness

due to unforeseen avalanches, rockfall, rapid weather changes, human frailty, and other objective hazards. Climbing accidents are usually avoidable with the use of good judgment developed through experience, but not always. There is no substitute for experience, not even a well-written guide. Most of the routes contained in this guide are no place for inexperienced climbers.

If this guide at times seems preoccupied with the hazards associated with mountaineering, it is because the author fears that nonclimbers, usually having inadequate experience or equipment, might buy this guide and head for the mountains. Considering that ill-equipped tourists sometimes head off from Paradise for the summit of Mount Rainier ("It seems so close!"), even though most turn back before they even reach Camp Muir, the possibility exists. "Tourist" climbers have died on Mount Rainier, Mount Hood, Mount Shasta, and elsewhere. A woman is reported to have reached the summit of Mount Hood wearing high heels. While this is an admirable accomplishment, it is also quite scary.

For nonclimbers reading this book who are inspired to climb these peaks, please, get professional help! Hire a guide service or take a climbing instruction course first.

Using This Guide

This guide does not presume to know every feature of every route on every volcano in the Cascade Range. Mountains—especially these mountains—change from season to season. Major rockfalls and mass wasting have occurred on Mount Adams, Mount Rainier, and Little Tahoma Peak during the past several decades. And, of course, Mount St. Helens bears little resemblance to the once graceful cone it was prior to its cataclysmic eruption in 1980. These are examples of large-scale changes that have occurred during recorded history; however, minor rockfalls, ice avalanches, or even weather or seasonal changes may alter the nature and course of a mountain route. These are not, after all, rock climbs on perfect Yosemite granite. A route that followed ice gullies one weekend may involve difficult technical climbing on frighteningly loose rock the next. A route that traversed snow-covered glaciers one month may be hideously crevassed or impassable the next. Changes can and do occur overnight. Snow slopes that are stable in the early morning can avalanche copiously in the afternoon. The inability to adjust to changing conditions can be hazardous, even deadly, to the uninitiated and unprepared.

As with any other climbing guide, the routes detailed here are approximate only and are based upon historical and popular usage, not correctness or exactness of line. There are no dotted lines to follow on the mountains; you have to pick the best and safest routes yourself.

All route descriptions and directions given here assume you are facing the mountain and/or your direction of travel. All distances, slope angles, ratings, and directions are approximate unless otherwise stated.

Each section of the guide has maps showing road and trail access to the mountains. You should not rely on these maps, photos, and drawings except to help guide you to your chosen mountain from the lowlands and show you the approximate line of ascent. The maps and drawings are not exact and cannot substitute for topographic maps, skilled compass use, and careful routefinding learned through experience. Camp and bivouac sites mentioned in the text and shown on maps and photographs are merely suggested or previously used sites, and, with the exception of designated wilderness campsites at which some modicum of comfort can be expected, they are not guaranteed to be safe or even comfortable.

With a few exceptions, the routes shown here are merely routes that have been climbed at least once before. These routes should not be deemed absolutely precise or correct. Numerous variations likely have been and will be climbed, whether for the sake of something different or to avoid hazards or obstacles, and all variations cannot possibly be listed here. On some routes each successive party climbs a slightly different variation of "the route," taking detours along the way to get around crevasses, avoid potential rockfall, or surmount a headwall. For most of the routes in this guide, there is no "correct" route; the route goes wherever you have to go to climb it as quickly and safely as possible under present conditions. Generally, where a route must climb a specific feature of the mountain, the route is described in more detail; when several possible variations exist, less detail is provided. Features and conditions change over time, and climbers must use their own judgment when deciding which route to climb.

On approaches, be aware that the density of the surrounding forests increases as one moves farther north. For approaches to Mount Baker, Glacier Peak, and other northern peaks, if you don't follow a precise course (i.e., the maintained forest service trail), you will become hopelessly lost or entangled. Stay on trails and climber's paths, or suffer the consequences. Farther south, the terrain opens up, allowing options for approaches and descents. Most routes have fairly well-established way trail and social trail approaches, and climbers should stick to those trails where possible to avoid doing additional damage to fragile subalpine terrain.

A large part of the climbing experience, as with any wilderness travel, is discovery and exploration. To that end, this guide won't reveal everything in minute detail. Hopefully users of this guide will get where they want to go, but won't miss out on the best part of the climbing experience—the adventure—in the process.

Difficulty Ratings

For the sake of simplicity, and without the intention of inventing yet another climbing rating system, this guide rates the general difficulty and seriousness of the volcano routes as follows:

0—No technical difficulty. Mostly hiking up easy to moderately steep snow and/or scree, with very minimal glacier travel, if any, and no technical rock. Should not require a rope during optimal conditions. Few unusual objective hazards to worry about. Experienced off-trail hikers and less-experienced climbers usually find these routes fairly simple and straightforward. Bring a rope, ice axe, crampons and helmet, except perhaps on routes that actually follow a trail. Examples: Paradise to Camp Muir (Rainier), South Slope (Adams), Monitor Ridge (St. Helens), North Ridge (Middle Sister), Green Lakes Route (South Sister).

1—Easy scrambling or glacier travel. May involve short rock scrambles, steeper snow, or basic glacier climbing. Few technical challenges or crevasses to be encountered during optimal conditions. Roping up is recommended on glacier portions of routes. Minimal commitment with minor exposure to hazards during optimal conditions. Bring a rope, ice axe, crampons, and helmet. Although crevasse hazard may be low on glacier portions of routes, crevasses or bergshrunds may be crossed, so be prepared to effect a crevasse rescue. Examples: Easton Glacier (Baker); Sitkum Glacier (Glacier Peak), Inter Glacier to Camp Schurman (Rainier), North Ridge (Adams), Prouty Glacier (South Sister), Avalanche Gulch (Shasta).

2—Moderate scrambling or glacier travel. More involved rock, snow/ice, and glacier climbing. Glaciers may have abundant crevasses that are not usually difficult to pass during optimal conditions, or possibly some Class 2 or 3 rock scrambling or steep snow or ice sections that generally will not require protection for an experienced leader. Roping up is highly recommended on glaciers and exposed rock sections; falls into crevasses are a definite risk. Climbers should have prior glacier and scrambling experience before trying these routes. Bring a rope, ice axe, crampons, helmet, and a few ice screws and/or rock pitons, and have crevasse rescue capability. Examples: Warren Glacier (Garibaldi); Coleman Glacier (Baker); Frostbite Ridge (Glacier); Emmons-Winthrop Glacier, Disappointment Cleaver (Rainier); Hogback, Eliot Glacier—Sunshine Route (Hood); Hotlum Glacier, Whitney Glacier (Shasta).

3—Moderate technical rock/ice climbing or glacier travel. Glaciers will be steeper with abundant crevasses that may be difficult to pass, and possibly some easy technical rock (Class 3 to Class 4, possibly easy Class 5) or steep ice sections that may require belaying. Greater commitment and exposure to hazards. Belayed climbing may be necessary in places, and roping up on glaciers is considered mandatory. Bring a rope, ice axe, crampons, helmet, and an assortment of ice screws and/or rock pitons, and have crevasse rescue capability. Examples: Atwell Peak Southeast Face (Garibaldi), North Ridge (Baker), Kautz Glacier (Rainier), Adams Glacier (Adams), Whitewater Glacier (Jefferson), South Ridge (North Sister), Casaval Ridge, Whitney Glacier Icefall (Shasta).

4—Difficult technical climbing or glacier travel. Steep or heavily crevassed glaciers including icefalls and ice cliffs, possibly having moderate technical rock (Class 4 up to mid-Class 5). Very committing and challenging, with great exposure to hazards. For very experienced climbers only. Bring a rope, ice axe and/or specialized ice tools, crampons, helmet, and a comprehensive rack of ice and/or rock protection; have crevasse rescue capability and be prepared for retreat or bivouac. Examples: Siberian Express (Garibaldi), Coleman Glacier Headwall (Baker), Liberty Ridge, Ptarmigan Ridge (Rainier), Eliot Glacier Headwall (Hood).

5—Technically extreme climbing. Routes with difficult and/or committing rock and/or ice climbing and very great exposure to objective hazards. Although considered "classics" by some, they tend to be "death routes" to others. For expert climbers and complete idiots only. Bring a rope, ice axe and/or specialized ice tools, crampons, helmet, and a comprehensive rack of ice and/or rock protection; have crevasse rescue capability and be prepared for retreat, bivouac, or rescue. Examples: Willis Wall, Curtis Ridge (Rainier), West Ridge (Little Tahoma), Victory Ridge (Adams), Yocum Ridge (Hood).

Grades

This guide also uses the commonly used Roman numeral grading system for technical routes. This system take various factors into account, including difficulty, routefinding, continuity, risk, and commitment. Like the technical ratings, these grades assume you are on route during good conditions and know what you are doing. Inexperienced climbers can easily have a Grade V experience on a Grade I route. The Roman numeral system, when used together with the system defined above, will give a very good impression of what to expect on a given technical route. It is a system for rating a route's seriousness and level of commitment, and may be generally defined as follows:

Grade I—Should take less than a few hours to climb technical portions of the route; little commitment, difficulty, or objective danger under optimal conditions. The entire route may take all day, but the technical climbing will not take very long and you can turn back fairly easily. Examples: North Ridge (Washington), South Ridge (Three Fingered Jack), Northeast Ridge (Thielsen), Hogback (Hood).

Grade II—Technical portions may take a few hours to half a day; increasing commitment, difficulty, and exposure to objective hazards. Retreat may not be especially difficult but possibly time consuming. Examples: South Ridge (North Sister), Whitney Glacier Icefall (Shasta).

Grade III—Expect to take at least half a day on technical portions of the route; moderate commitment and difficulty, and may have higher exposure to objective hazards. Retreat may be time consuming and difficult. Examples: North Face (Hood), Jefferson Park Glacier (Jefferson), Casaval Ridge (Shasta).

Grade IV—You could spend all day on technical portions of the route; very committing, technically difficult, and likely very objectively hazardous. Retreat may be very difficult and time consuming. Be prepared to bivouac if benighted or rescued if things go badly. Examples: Coleman Glacier Headwall (Baker), Mowich Face, Liberty Ridge (Rainier), Eliot Glacier Headwall (Hood).

Grade V—Technical portions of the route will take all day, and a bivouac is likely; may require extreme commitment, be technically demanding, or be greatly exposed to objective dangers. Retreat and even rescue could be difficult and dangerous. Examples: Willis Wall, Curtis Ridge (Rainier), Yocum Ridge (Hood).

Yosemite Decimal System

This guide uses the Yosemite Decimal System to rate technical rock sections. Climbers unfamiliar with this rating system are probably unfamiliar with the rigors of technical rock climbing and should stay off the routes in this book unless accompanied by an experienced leader. The difficulty level is represented as follows:

Class 1 and 2—Easy scrambling where the use of hands may or may not be required.

Class 3—Exposed scrambling that, while not especially difficult, may warrant the use of a rope for anyone who asks for one.

Class 4—Climbs where belays will likely be utilized on easy but highly exposed rock.

Class 5.0 through 5.5—Easy to moderate belayed technical rock climbing where intermediate protection will be placed.

Class 5.6 through 5.8—More difficult technical rock climbing where protection will be placed more frequently.

Class 5.9 and above—Very difficult technical rock climbing that requires a high level of fitness and technique.

Technical rock ratings presently go as high as 5.15; fortunately, there are no routes of that difficulty in this guide. In fact, you will be hard pressed to find an existing 5.8 route in this guide, and even more fortunate to survive a 5.8 lead on most Cascade volcanoes. Most of the rock climbing contained in this guide is on very poor-quality rock. Some of the rock will be fairly solid, some will be shattered, and some will have the consistency of dried mud. Climbing on snow or ice is preferable to rock on most of the Cascade volcanoes, so climb during the winter or early season on routes that otherwise would involve much loose rock scrambling or climbing. But, then, if hideously loose rock is your thing, enjoy!

Ice climbing in this guide will be rated using either the Alpine Ice (AI) or Water Ice (WI) Rating System. The Alpine Ice scale applies to any ice found on mountains, including glacier ice, while the Water Ice scale rates climbs on frozen waterfalls and drips, which is outside the scope of this guide, although there is water ice to be found on the Cascade Volcanoes under the right conditions. The ice-rating scales are summarized as follows:

AI1—Walking up gently angled ice in crampons; no tools needed to ascend.

AI2—Slightly steeper ice with short steps where an ice tool is needed to ascend.

AI3—Closer to vertical with longer ice steps, good rests, and protection.

AI4—Nearly vertical with good protection, but more strenuous due to fewer rests.

AI5—Vertical ice with no rests; protection is good but strenuous to place.

AI6—Consistently vertical, possibly with overhanging moves, technically difficult, with less protection or protection that is harder to arrange.

AI7—Vertical and overhanging ice with marginal protection; extreme technical difficulty requiring the highest level of strength and stamina.

Ice ratings are very subjective and depend on conditions. Generally, the average glacier slog is not even AI1; they may be referred to as "Easy" or "Moderate" glacier climbs. A climb up a steep ice chute or slope may be AI1 or AI2; a steeper ice cliff or face may be AI2 or AI3; and a vertical serac wall or ice cliff could be AI4 or AI5.

There is a rating system for mixed ice and rock climbing, which is beyond the scope of this guide, although there are some mixed routes on the Cascade volcanoes that could be rated using this scale. The problem with mixed climbing on these volcanoes is the same as with rock climbing: The rock is generally loose and broken, making it mostly unsuitable for any type of rock climbing. For this reason the mixed rating system is not used here. Extreme ice and mixed climbing does not exist on any of the Cascade volcanoes under "normal" conditions. However, this does not mean frozen waterfalls, vertical or overhanging ice cliffs, and mixed technical ice/rock pitches will not be encountered; it means they can usually be avoided via an easier variation for the sake of expediency and safety.

All ratings in this guide assume that the route is in perfect condition, with stable weather and snow or ice, and the climber is attempting to make the route as easy and as safe as possible by avoiding obvious difficulties and dangers and following the most reasonable line of ascent. Late-season ascents have increased difficulties and hazards (e.g., loose rock, rockfall). Winter and poor-weather ascents have additional difficulties and dangers (e.g., ice, increased avalanche danger, frostbite, storms, whiteouts, high winds). Any of these factors can render the rating used in this guide invalid.

Objective Hazards

Objective hazards are noted at the start of each climb description to indicate increased or unavoidable exposure to hazards that are regularly encountered on a given route. However, the absence of a warning in a route description doesn't mean avalanches, rockfall, or icefall never occur on a given route, or that nobody has ever been seriously injured or killed on a particular route, only that they are not frequent or regular occurrences under ordinary conditions. Nor does "death route" denote an actual fatality on a route (since, for example, no deaths have occurred on Willis Wall—yet). Also, calling a route a "dog route" doesn't mean a dog could actually climb the route, although you might be surprised—dogs are occasional visitors to many Cascade volcano summits.

This guide provides estimated climbing times for each route. These time estimates are calculated for an average party climbing at a steady pace from high camp to the summit, unless otherwise stated in the route description. Descent times will not be included except in a few instances. These estimated ascent times assume the party is up to the difficulties of the route and that they are encountering good climbing conditions. Weather, crevasses, poor snow, ice and rock conditions, slow climbers, and other factors may render these time estimates invalid. A strong climbing team may take much less time than the estimate provided for a given route, while another team may take more time. Don't try to "beat the clock," but if you are way behind schedule, don't press on into a forced bivouac or worse. Time estimates in this guide are fairly generous, assuming you will take longer than an average party.

These rating systems as used in this guide are to assist in keeping climbers on routes that are appropriate for them and letting them know what to expect on a given route, not to give an exact technical rating. Difficulty ratings assume perfect conditions and are provided merely to assist climbers in choosing appropriate routes for their perceived level of ability and experience; they are not intended as an indication of actual difficulty, safety, or as a guaranty of success.

Geology

Of the mountains of the Cascade Range, the volcanoes are the youngest. Geologists estimate the age of the oldest of these volcanoes is about 750,000 to 1 million years. A volcano is, strictly speaking, merely the vent through which ash, gas, and magma come to the surface, and the accumulation of erupted material. There are countless volcanic vents in the Cascade Range, including many cinder cones, plug domes, shield volcanoes, and stratovolcanoes.

All but one of the peaks included in this guide are of the stratovolcano variety. Stratovolcanoes are composite volcanoes, intermittently erupting and building, formed by various flows and ejections of differing materials occurring over a long span of time. Whereas shield volcanoes (such as Mauna Loa and Mauna Kea in Hawaii) consist solely of liquid basaltic flows, stratovolcanoes combine various materials (e.g., andesite, dacite, rhyolite, ash, tuff, basalt, and other assorted flows and ejections of pyroclastic materials) to build upward more rapidly by piling these distinct materials upon each other. The result is a

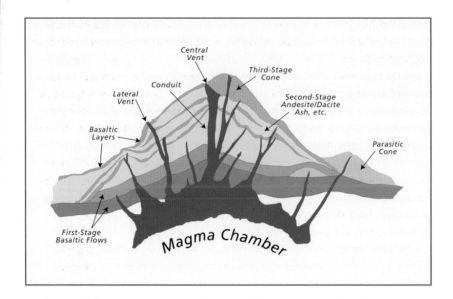

high, often uniformly shaped mass of varying consistency, as you might get if you built your own backyard volcano by piling up loose sand and gravel over a foundation of mud, rock, and concrete fragments.

Most volcano eruptions are comparatively mild, involving expulsion of steam and ash, but when a volcano is in an eruptive phase, anything can happen. Relatively recent eruptions of Redoubt Volcano in Alaska and Mount Pinatubo in the Philippines offer as sharp a contrast as Mount Baker's mid-1970s steam emissions and Mount St. Helens's 1980 decapitation. Needless to say, during any period of volcanic activity, it is best to stay off the volcanoes, not only those erupting but their neighbors too. Warming beneath glaciers triggers massive floods and mudslides, breaking glaciers apart. Earthquakes cause massive rockfalls, icefalls, or avalanches. Ash clouds bring lightning and low visibility, not to mention searing heat and suffocation. Usually, if there is a danger of eruption, the USDA Forest Service or National Park Service will issue an appropriate warning or close a given peak to climbing.

Based on data gleaned from the Mount St. Helens eruption cycle, geologists now feel confident that they can predict a major eruption, or at least give accurate warning of a potential eruption. However, volcano eruption predictions are about as useful as weather predictions. A good rule to follow is: If your mountain is blowing steam and ash, climb something else or stay home.

Lassen Peak is the only peak included in this guide that is not a stratovolcano. Lassen is a large plug dome built of fast-cooling, viscous dacite, which plugged its vent before any lateral flows could occur. However, Lassen's 1915 eruption proves it is capable of violence and destruction equal to any stratovolcano.

Native Indians witnessing volcanic activity on the great volcanoes have interpreted the eruptions as war-making among the spirits. Legends have this mountain hurling rocks at that mountain, with one mountain spirit prevailing over another. Mounts Rainier, Mazama, and Tehama have had similar stories told of their heads being knocked off during fierce combat with other peaks. A well-known myth tells of a jealous battle between Mounts Adams and Hood over Mount St. Helens, where the warriors showered each other with flaming rocks in a contest to win the fair maiden. Modern science has dispelled most myths about these fire mountains, although there are many unusual and creative modern myths, particularly about Mount Shasta.

There is little doubt that the volcanoes of the Cascade Range could each erupt again someday, perhaps violently. Baker, Rainier, Hood, and Shasta are very obviously still active volcanoes, as each has active vents, hot springs, and "hot rocks." They are merely sleeping, and should by no means be pronounced dead.

A discussion of the volcanic history of each peak is included in later individual chapters. Those wishing to learn more about the geological history and composition of these volcanoes may consult the references listed in the bibliography. For climbers, it is usually enough to know that the rock on these peaks is rarely as stable as an average cairn.

Volcanic Rock

Some of the more challenging routes on Cascade volcanoes have technical rock climbing sections, usually on unstable (i.e., rotten, crumbly, entirely untrustworthy) volcanic rock. Few climbers have anything good to say about it. Guidebook author Jeff Thomas described the rock on one Oregon volcano as having "the consistency of compacted graham crackers." Climber Ed Hall theorized that "the Oregon volcanoes are waiting to become Columbia River sandbars," explaining that "good rock is hard to find and, consequently, nontechnical routes can often be very hazardous due to rockfall or lack of secure hand and footholds." Technical routes are even more hazardous, for the same reasons.

There is no truly high-quality rock climbing to be found on any volcano summit route included in this guide. There is some fairly high-quality rock climbing on volcanic rock in the Cascades (e.g., Smith Rock), but on a majority of the Cascade volcano routes, as a general safety rule, avoid rock climbing whenever and however possible.

Glaciers

The volcanoes of the Pacific Northwest coast are home to the largest glaciers in the conterminous United States. Glaciers are formed when more snow accumulates during successive winters than melts away each summer. The resulting mass of snow builds up and compacts, and if there is sufficient slope and mass, the glacier is pulled down the mountainside by gravity. Glaciers are slow movers; objects lost in crevasses and interred in a glacier may be revealed at the terminus decades later.

The effects of glaciation on the Cascade volcanoes are obvious: The Carbon Glacier has worn out Willis Wall on Mount Rainier; glaciers have breached Mount Hood's and Glacier Peak's craters; and the Emmons, Winthrop, and Klickitat Glaciers are undercutting their retaining ridges, resulting in mass wasting on an enormous scale. Glaciers pick up rock debris, which speeds up the erosive process. They are transporters of tons of material, pushing, swallowing, or carrying debris for a slow ride down the mountain.

The most important glacial feature to climbers are crevasses. Crevasses are simply stress fractures in the ice, which represent the most common obstacle encountered on glaciers. Although glaciers are semi-flexible and can "bend" over, around, and through obstacles, they rarely do so without breaking. The more abrupt the turn or differential in glacier velocity, the more fractures will be formed. Crevasses most often form where the angle of descent (i.e., rate of descent) changes. If the angle is too severe, the glacier will likely break completely, sending huge chunks of ice avalanching down the peak and leaving "hanging" ice cliffs, such as those found atop Willis Wall on Mount Rainier and the Roman Headwall of Mount Baker. Undulations in the mountain's surface will cause an overriding glacier to buckle and crack. Glaciers squeezed through narrow corridors often shatter into nearly impassable, dangerous icefalls.

Negotiating crevasses can be very simple, or it can be extremely difficult. Lateral crevasses can usually be outflanked or crossed directly, depending upon length and width. Snow bridges sometimes offer a risky shortcut. Icefalls typically have seracs (ice blocks and towers) and jumbled crevasse patterns, which are much more difficult and hazardous to pass. Bergschrunds sometimes cannot be passed at all. In winter and early spring, crevasses may be filled by snowfall and avalanche debris. Some are merely bridged by cornices and snowfall, traps to be sprung on unsuspecting climbers.

Nearly every route in this guide, particularly on the northern and higher volcanoes, involves glacier travel. It is advisable to always rope up when traveling on glaciers, even when skiing. Just because you don't see crevasses doesn't mean they aren't there. Slips on glacier ice account for more climbing fatalities than falls into crevasses (and many falls into crevasses result at the end of a long, otherwise survivable slide), but hidden crevasses have swallowed up a great many unwary climbers. Being roped is not a guarantee that you won't be injured or killed slipping on ice or falling into a crevasse, but it can greatly diminish that likelihood. First-aid training and crevasse rescue skills are important for every member of your climbing team, because if the only person in your party who knows these skills is the one dangling unconscious in a crevasse, that climber is in trouble!

Because this is not a climbing instruction book, no instruction on glacier travel or rescue techniques—other than the above warnings—is contained in this guide. Snow and glacier travel and crevasse rescue techniques should be learned and practiced before attempting most of the routes in this guide.

Weather

Weather is not always poor in the Cascade Range, even if it sometimes seems that way. The Pacific Northwest coast's reputation for precipitation is not entirely unfounded, however. The lush rain forests of the Olympic Peninsula in Washington have the highest cumulative average rainfall in the nation. The slopes of Mount Rainier have seen world-record cumulative snowfalls.

In a nutshell, this is how Cascade mountain weather works: Warm, moist air blows in off the Pacific Ocean, squeezing moisture-laden clouds against the mountains. These clouds dump excess rain on the western slopes of the mountains, then dissipate as they pass over the Cascade crest. This warm, moist marine air condenses and freezes very rapidly when it hits a glaciated volcano, which accounts for the tremendous snowfall received each year by these peaks. Western slopes are often lush and heavily vegetated, while eastern slopes, protected by rain shadows, are usually less foliated.

It should be pointed out that the weather on the high, glaciated peaks of the Cascades can be remarkably different than lowland weather. High volcanoes "create their own weather," rising into the atmosphere and showing the effects of incoming weather patterns more dramatically than at lower elevations. Overall, the severity of the weather tends to increase as one moves north. Northern latitudes and differing weather patterns contribute to this phenomenon. Still, all the Cascade volcanoes experience severe storms each year, and these storms cannot always be predicted. Prepare yourself for the worst, including wind, rain, and snow, no matter what the weatherman says.

On the larger peaks, particularly Mounts Rainier and Shasta, lenticular cloud caps frequently form on or near the summit, sometimes obscuring the mountain's upper slopes. These clouds are formed when the expansive, warm marine air impacts the dense, cold mountain air. The clouds are usually accompanied by high winds and much moisture. Lenticular cloud caps sometimes disperse as quickly as they form, but more often they engulf a mountain in a raging storm with high winds, sometimes depositing several feet of snow in a few hours. Although it may be disappointing to turn back in the face of an approaching storm, it is better than continuing an ascent only to find that a full-on storm has settled in, leaving you stranded high on the mountain in high winds and extreme avalanche conditions. Indeed, one of Mount Rainier's greatest survival stories, and one of its most needless tragedies, occurred inside one such lenticular cloud. A father and son, who had come well prepared, dug in when they were enveloped by the storm during their descent. They were rescued several days later when the storm cleared, hungry but alive. Meanwhile, two experienced climbers set off from Camp Muir as the storm began to settle in on the summit. Despite warnings from guides and other climbers already descending the mountain because of the storm, they continued into the maelstrom. Sadly, and needlessly, they perished.

Winter climbers should go prepared for the worst weather imaginable. Fierce storms, with strong winds and large amounts of snowfall, often rage for several days on the high volcanoes, and can come without warning. Breaks between winter storms seldom last more than a few days. Plan winter climbs as you would a Himalayan expedition, because winter weather in the high Cascades isn't very much different than what you might find on Mount McKinley or Mount Everest.

That weather changes can occur suddenly and dramatically is well illustrated by a mining-era report of 100-plus-degree temperatures on the summit of Mount Adams in the afternoon followed within 12 hours by a storm with temperatures falling to 48 below zero. Just because it is sunny and calm doesn't mean it won't soon be freezing and blustery on any of the high volcanoes.

A majority of weather-related problems on the volcanoes occur when climbers are unable to find their way down out of a storm, or are trapped in a storm with no shelter. Whiteout conditions are frequent on all volcanoes, and are particularly problematic on featureless terrain, which means it is very easy to get lost in a whiteout on easier routes. Carry a compass and take bearings here and there, or wand your route on the ascent, so you can more easily find your way down if the weather deteriorates or visibility decreases. Be prepared to dig a snow cave or hide out in a crevasse if necessary for shelter from a storm.

Of all considerations of mountain travel in the Cascades, weather should be among the foremost to climbers. Weather has been the culprit, directly or indirectly, in many climbing deaths on the Cascade volcanoes. Prepare for the worst no matter what the weather report says. Check weather forecasts and avalanche conditions before you climb. Although the weatherman is not always right about good weather, when it comes to poor weather, considering your life may be in the bargain, you should give him the benefit of the doubt.

Preparation

Volcano climbing can be one of the most physically demanding and exhausting endeavors that a climber might undertake. The Cascade volcanoes will kick your butt if you aren't in shape, and probably will do so even if you are in shape. Climbers should be in good physical condition prior to attempting most of the routes included in this guide. A volcano climb is typically several long hours of trudging up and then down a steady incline at altitude. If you aren't in good shape, able to hike up a steep slope at an even pace for several hours with-

Not all climbing in the Cascade volcanoes is on snow and glaciers. Here, Joanne Deng nears the summit of Three Fingered Jack. Photo Matt Stamplis

out stopping, you shouldn't be climbing above 10,000 feet. You will only slow your companions down and increase your chances of becoming dangerously fatigued, which can lead to an accident, especially on the descent. Train for your climb (or climbing season) as you would for a marathon, because an ascent of a high volcano can be as strenuous if not more so. Whatever you do, don't make your companions drag you up the mountain because you aren't in shape (or down the mountain because you weren't). If you have any health problems that may be affected by very strenuous activity, consult with your physician before climbing.

Training for a big volcano climb can include running, cycling, stair climbing, or hiking. A combination of these is best, particularly emphasizing hill work, up and down, with a load. Start out easy and gradually increase until you are taking weekend hikes up long mountain trails with a heavy pack, simulating the kind of elevation gain and load you will be experiencing at altitude on the volcanoes. Spend some time at altitude just prior to tackling the higher volcanoes, to acclimatize prior to your ascent. Work your way up, climbing some of the lower volcanoes before tackling one of the higher volcanoes.

Experience, or lack thereof, is often an important factor in mountaineering accidents. Inexperienced and unprepared climbers often make fatal mistakes; experienced climbers usually know better. Inexperienced climbers should not climb on glaciers or at high elevations, no matter how easy the terrain. If you have no previous mountaineering experience, you should take a climbing instruction course or go on a guided climb prior to attempting any of these routes on your own. Climb nontechnical routes at first, gradually working up to more demanding routes as you gain technique, experience, and knowledge of your abilities and limitations. Practice rock, ice, self-arrest, and crevasse rescue techniques as often as possible so you know what to do when the time comes.

When to Climb

When you climb should be determined by several factors, including weather, snow and glacier conditions, trail conditions, permit requirements, and so forth. Generally climbing conditions are best between late May and July for most of the Cascade volcanoes. Before (and sometimes during) June, snow and weather may be less reliable, crevasse bridges more easily collapse, and trails and roads may still be snow covered; after July, rockfall hazard increases, snow slopes become more icy, and crevasses open up and become difficult or impassable. It is a trade-off as to whether you want a difficult approach but better climbing conditions or an easy approach with worse climbing conditions. During years of heavy snowpack, July and August may offer the best overall climbing conditions. This is not to say that climbing conditions may not be good during the rest of the year. Autumn is a popular season, although crevasses are wide open on many glaciers. Between October and April, climbs should be done only when weather and snow conditions are stable.

Of course, this means that more than half of all ascents of the volcanoes are made during late May, June, July, and August, so you'll be fighting crowds for elbow room on the summit and possibly waiting in line along the way on the dog routes.

This is all very generalized. Some routes require specific weather and snow conditions or else they are deadly; other routes are in shape all year except during poor weather or avalanche conditions. If you seek solitude, come between Monday and Friday to avoid the weekend crowds. The more remote your objective, the less likely you will find other climbers en route. It really all depends upon what you want out of your climbing experience.

Clothing and Equipment

Climbers using this guide should already know what kind of clothing and equipment to bring and how to use it. For those who don't, the following list is a good starting point, but you should consult the references listed in this guide and take a mountaineering instruction course from a qualified guide service. *Mountaineering: The Freedom of the Hills* (The Mountaineers) is perhaps the best overall comprehensive mountaineering instruction book available. This book contains instructions for nearly every aspect of mountain travel. However, once again, be warned that you can't learn how to climb by reading a book, even a good one. Take a climbing instruction course, complete a guided climb, do some easy glacier climbs, and perfect belaying, crevasse rescue, and ice-axe arrest techniques before trying to climb these mountains on your own.

The National Park Service has published a list of recommended clothing and equipment for all summit climbers on Mount Rainier. It is a comprehensive list, applicable to many volcano climbs, repeated here with some supplementation:

- Full-frame crampons
- Ice axe
- Helmet
- Lug-soled boots
- Sunglasses/goggles
- Wool/down/synthetic layers
- Water/windproof shell
- Mittens and gloves
- First-aid kit
- Sunburn preventive
- Rope (50m of 10mm diameter)
- Harness
- Carabiners (2 locking D)

- Prusik slings (3) or ascenders (2)
- Pitons/cams/ice screws
- Rescue pulleys
- Wands
- Map and compass
- Flashlight and/or headlamp
- Tent
- Sleeping bag
- Ensolite pad
- Water
- Stove/fuel
- Food

At a minimum you should bring an ice axe and crampons on any volcano climb, even easy climbs with only a little snow. Snow slopes can be treacherously icy. If steep snow, glacier travel, or ice climbing will be encountered, a rope is also a recommended minimum.

It's a good idea to bring a few ice screws, pickets, or dead man anchors on every route involving steep snow or ice travel, just in case they are needed. On more technical routes, bring more technical gear: on ice—ice screws, slings, carabiners, rigid-frame crampons; on rock—chocks, Friends, pitons, and so on. This guide will not make specific gear recommendations for any particular route. It is enough to say that climbers attempting technical routes should bring a comprehensive assortment of equipment appropriate for the task at hand and use their judgment and experience in its use. This guide assumes you already know how and where to use your equipment, and that if you don't, you will learn before you try a technical route. If you have never placed ice screws, you have no business climbing a route that may require their use. The same goes for any other route needing technical equipment. For that matter, if you don't have self-arrest, belay, and crevasse rescue skills, you shouldn't be climbing these mountains.

The point of bringing proper clothing is to keep yourself warm and dry in a hostile mountain environment. While it may be possible and enjoyable to climb these peaks in shorts and a T-shirt on perfect, warm, windless days, there have been many hypothermia deaths attributed to casual or inadequate clothing. Dress properly and prepare for the worst; your life may depend on it.

Sunscreen and sunglasses are vitally important when climbing the high volcanoes, so you don't burn up or go snow-blind while climbing on a sunny day at elevation. Consult your local climbing shop or guide service for their recommendations.

Wear a Helmet!

Climbers attempting any route that passes over, beneath, near, or through volcanic rock gullies and cliffs, and anywhere rockfall or icefall might occur, are advised to wear helmets. The rock on these peaks is mostly very poor and can disintegrate with little provocation. Icicles and ice chunks regularly pelt climbers without warning. Helmets are recommended on all climbs, but mostly on those with potential for rock or icefall. Granted, a helmet won't protect you from 2.6 million cubic yards of debris, but it might save your life if you get hit in the head by a more typical fist-size stone or chunk of ice. More often, helmets protect against head injury during falls on glaciers or down snow slopes. Hitting your head on the lip of a crevasse or a rock at the bottom of an otherwise harmless snow slope is more likely than getting hit by random rockfall. For this reason, even on easy snow routes, helmets are highly recommended.

Mountain Hazards

Mountaineering has numerous objective dangers, and routes described in this guide are not exceptions. Climbers venturing onto these mountains risk a plethora of hazards. Despite all the obvious, potential hazards of mountaineering, thousands of ascents are made each year without incident or injury. Climbers shouldn't be too smug about this, however, especially on the Cascade volcanoes. Even if you are very experienced and exercise perfect judgment, you may still get wiped out by an errant ice chunk. There are no guarantees of safety on these mountains, so proceed with caution and at your own risk.

Warnings in this guide are intended to let climbers know of dangers that are frequently encountered on given routes. Avalanches and rockfall can occur at any time on almost any route in this guide. However, some routes have especially high frequencies of these events during certain conditions. A list of potential mountain hazards could go on and on. To put it simply: Mountain climbing can be dangerous.

Unfortunately, no one can predict exactly which routes will be subject to rockfall, icefall, avalanches, or other natural occurrences, and even the weatherman cannot always predict the coming of a major storm. Climbers should be wary of these dangers at all times, and avoid them whenever possible. To climb certain routes, however, one must be willing to face these risks. Once again, this guidebook is no substitute for good judgment or experience. Take a mountaineering course, hire a guide, and build experience before you place yourself in a situation you are not prepared to face.

It is wise to check trail, weather, avalanche, and climbing conditions by calling ahead or checking on the Internet before your trip. Most NPS and forest service ranger district offices and websites can inform you of current conditions or special hazards.

If conditions become dangerous, for any reason, or you realize your chosen route is beyond your ability, don't be afraid to turn back. It is wiser to descend than to continue upward under questionable circumstances. You can come back another time. If you press on despite warning signs, you may not make it back. Your life is hopefully more important than reaching the summit of an icy heap of crumbly rocks. Think of it this way: There are thousands of mountains, but you have only one life.

Altitude Sickness

Altitude sickness is not an uncommon malady on the high volcanoes, particularly Mounts Rainier and Shasta. Lowlanders, going from sea level to over 10,000 feet during a 24-hour period without acclimatization, in a rush to get to the summit and back before work on Monday, are particularly susceptible.

While altitude sickness is usually regarded as a Himalayan malady, it can strike hikers and climbers at any elevation, and is not uncommon at even such lowly elevations as 8,000 feet. Without going into a prolonged discussion of the vagaries of HAPE (high-altitude pulmonary edema) and HACE (high-altitude cerebral edema), symptoms to watch for include headache, dizziness, nausea, vomiting, weakness, shortness of breath, blueness of lips, chills, insomnia, increased pulse and respiration, blurred vision, hallucinations, confusion, and disorientation. More serious are a tight chest, dry cough, noisy "bubbling" breathing, rapid pulse, frothy or blood-tinged sputum, severe headache, and convulsions. If you have a killer headache, can't recite the alphabet, and are carrying on a telepathic conversation with your ice axe, it may be time to turn around. But seriously, if you or any of your party experience or exhibit any of these symptoms, descend immediately, slow down to reduce demand for oxygen, and breathe deeper and faster (which may cause nausea and dizziness, but keep at it). In severe cases, give oxygen if available. The sooner you or your afflicted rope mate get to lower elevation, the faster the recovery time.

Like almost any other mountain hazard, prevention is easier than treatment. Acclimatize, increase fluid intake and carbohydrate consumption and decrease fats in your diet, avoid alcohol prior to your climb, and don't smoke or take anti-depressants. Eating a big lunch on the summit of a high volcano can easily induce nausea. Don't be embarrassed if you start puking on the summit of a volcano; you won't be the first. Just be sure to descend as quickly as is safe if you feel ill so nothing worse happens.

Hypothermia

Hypothermia is a genuine risk for all backcountry travelers, particularly volcano climbers. This often-fatal lowering of the body temperature is brought on by continued exposure to low temperatures, winds, and rain, usually a combination of all three. These conditions are all too frequently present on the Cascade volcanoes. Climbers venturing too far from the safety and comfort of shelter with inadequate clothing risk hypothermia. Wool clothing and modern synthetics, such as polypropylene, insulate even when wet, and are recommended. However, without a weather-resistant shell, any insulating clothing has limitations. Do everything possible to stay warm and dry, particularly during cold, rainy, and windy conditions.

Hypothermia's symptoms include fatigue, awkwardness, chills, lethargy, irritability, clumsiness, uncontrolled shivering, and slurred speech. Most victims don't realize they are hypothermic, and often will deny it to the end. Act quickly to save them. Stop, find shelter (erect a tent or dig a snow cave if you must), get the victim's wet clothes off, and get him or her into a sleeping bag (with somebody dry and warm if they appear to be seriously hypothermic, although decency permits wearing underwear for you modest rescuers). If you can't stop where you are, get down fast! Warm liquids should be given to conscious victims, but not to comatose ones. If the victim does not appear to recover, send someone for help immediately. The faster the victim's body temperature is raised, the better his or her chance of survival.

Like altitude sickness, prevention of hypothermia is easier than the cure. If you suspect you or one of your partners is becoming hypothermic, get to shelter quickly.

Winter Climbing

Despite the inherent hazards, winter ascents of the Cascade volcanoes are popular. Winter ascents can sometimes be made under perfect conditions with no more risk than a late spring or late fall ascent. Sometimes, though, winter climbs involve climbing conditions more akin to those experienced crossing Antarctica.

The major considerations for winter climbing are weather and snow conditions. Cascade weather is unpredictable enough during the summer; during the winter, fierce storms lasting several days at a time are not uncommon. Snowfall and high winds accompany these frigid storms, and whiteout conditions are frequent, particularly above timberline. Parties have become lost and pinned down for days by storms, and fatalities have occurred.

The National Park Service recommends the following equipment (in addition to the previous list) for winter climbers on Mount Rainier (again repeated with some supplementation):

- Extreme cold sleeping bag
- Down parka/pants/mitts
- Double boots
- Snowshoes or skis
- Expedition tent
- Snow shovel
- Extra wands (200 minimum)
- Extra food and fuel (2 days)
- Two-way radio/cell phone
- Altimeter/GPS unit
- Avalanche cords or transceivers
- Avalanche probes
- Additional ropes

Here are a few basic suggestions for winter climbing and avalanche avoidance:

- NEVER CLIMB ALONE!
- Check weather and avalanche conditions prior to every trip. Don't go out during poor weather or high avalanche danger. Avalanche hotlines:

British Columbia and Washington Cascades call (206) 526-6677; Oregon Cascades call (503) 808-2400; Mount Shasta call (530) 926-9613; National Weather Service call (206) 526-6087 (Washington), (503) 261-9246 (Oregon), (916) 976-3051 (California), or (540) 515-3700 (British Columbia). Or check the online weather and avalanche resources listed in the appendix.

- Register with park or wilderness rangers prior to your climb, and give a good indication of what route you are climbing and when you are expected back.
- Never travel during or immediately after a snowstorm. How long after is an often debated question, which is up to you and your better judgment.
- Carry avalanche cords (or better, avalanche transceivers), probe poles, and a collapsible snow shovel on all winter climbs.
- Avoid soft, steep snow slopes, leeward slopes, and obvious avalanche-prone slopes and gullies.
- Learn about avalanches and how to predict and avoid them. Also learn avalanche search and rescue techniques before your climb. Be prepared for a search and rescue, just in case. This means every member of your party should carry probe poles, a snow shovel, and an avalanche transceiver on all winter climbs.
- When crossing a suspect slope, expect to be buried, and prepare accordingly. Button up, put on mittens and a hat, loosen your pack and ski pole straps, and turn your avalanche transceiver to "transmit" mode (or tie on an avalanche cord). Only one person at a time should cross an avalanche slope, and everyone else should watch carefully.
- Climb above fracture lines and cornices, if possible.
- Potential avalanche paths should be used only if there is no other feasible route, and then only with extreme caution.
- When traveling above tree line in questionable weather, wand your route so you can find your way back if a storm sets in.
- Travel on ridgelines instead of open slopes whenever possible.
- During poor visibility, slow down and be alert for edges and cornices.
- Take enough food and fuel to last at least two extra days.
- Have someone at a base camp in communication with the climbing party via two-way radio, who can summon a rescue more quickly if there is trouble.

Frostbite is also a risk during winter and cold-weather ascents. Keeping your extremities warm, dry, and unconstricted is important. Overly tight boots (which reduce circulation) are a leading cause of frostbite.

Avalanches

Avalanches are another common, and more feared, hazard on the Cascade volcanoes and throughout the Cascade Range. Knowing how to predict avalanches, avoid avalanche-prone slopes, react correctly when caught in an avalanche, and perform avalanche rescue are important skills for all who venture into avalanche country.

Avalanches can range from minor snow sloughs to huge slabs capable of great damage. A high volume of snowfall, wind-accumulated snow, and rapidly changing weather patterns on the Cascade volcanoes account for particularly high avalanche danger during certain conditions. Warm, wet weather or a rapidly rising temperature with accompanying wind are common warning signs of avalanche danger, and during such weather, questionable snow slopes should be avoided. During unstable snow conditions, almost anything can trigger an avalanche. Watch for shifts in wind direction, freezing rain, and rising temperatures, and stay off unstable slopes. When in doubt, stay away from any suspected avalanche slopes. Climbers should have training and experience in spotting and avoiding dangerous avalanche conditions and with avalanche rescue techniques before they venture onto these mountains, particularly in winter and spring. Avoiding potential avalanche slopes is the best way to avoid getting caught in an avalanche.

If you are caught in an avalanche, do everything you can to stay on top of the sliding snow. Discard all equipment and use a swimming motion to keep on the surface of the avalanche. If you can't stay on top and become buried, close your mouth and eyes and cover your face with your arms. This will help create an air space. As the snow stops sliding, try to enlarge your air space before the snow solidifies, which is usually instantaneous. If you have time, and if you can tell which way is up (spit to check), dig furiously toward the surface. If you are lucky, you can get an arm out and create an air hole, which may permit you to be found and rescued more quickly. If you can't get out yourself, relax and wait. Conserve your air by staying calm and breathing slowly. Chances of survival are reduced by more than 50 percent 30 minutes after burial, so the more you can do to conserve your precious air, the better your chances of survival. Because of avalanche danger alone, it is very unwise to climb by yourself in winter and spring. Parties of three are a recommended minimum for safety.

If a companion is buried in an avalanche, don't panic! Watch and make a note of the last place you saw the victim. After making sure all surviving members are safe, make a visual search of the entire avalanche area for clues. This is where avalanche transceivers come in handy. Mark areas where you last saw the victim, and begin your search. If you can't locate anything, start probing in accumulation areas first, using an avalanche probe, ski pole, or ice axe, in that order of preference, as avalanche victims are buried about 4 feet deep, on average. Be careful, but be fast! Don't stop looking until help arrives. If you are the only person around, you are the victim's only chance for survival. Unless reliable help is less than 15 minutes away, you must do your best to find the victim immediately.

Reading an avalanche book and taking an avalanche safety course are good ideas before you venture into the Cascade Range during winter.

Four levels of avalanche danger are usually given by reporting agencies:

Low hazard—Mostly stable snow exists and avalanches are unlikely (but still possible) except in isolated pockets on steep, snow-covered open slopes and gullies. Backcountry travel is generally safe in areas with low hazard.

Moderate hazard—Areas of unstable snow exist and avalanches are possible on steep, snow-covered open slopes and gullies. Backcountry travelers should use caution in areas with moderate hazard.

High hazard—Mostly unstable snow exists and avalanches are likely on steep, snow-covered open slopes and gullies. Backcountry travel is not recommended except in avalanche-free areas.

Extreme hazard—Widespread areas of unstable snow exist and avalanches are certain on steep, snow-covered open slopes and gullies. Backcountry travel is not recommended except in avalanche-free areas. Backcountry travel should be avoided. (Even auto travel should be avoided, if possible.)

Sky Sjue on the summit of Atwell Peak.
Photo Lee Lau

Just as this guide cannot provide mountaineering instruction, it also cannot provide a thorough lesson on avalanche safety, snow travel, navigation, or winter mountaineering survival strategies. Winter climbers should learn about preventing frostbite and hypothermia, be familiar with avalanche prediction and rescue, and know how to prepare for winter travel before they find themselves lost in a blizzard or buried neck-deep in wet snow.

Ski Mountaineering

Ski ascents and descents and snowboard descents of many of the Cascade volcanoes have become more popular. During winter and spring, skis are often necessary to approach the volcanoes. Some volcano routes can be ascended fairly easily by experienced, properly equipped skiers. Skiing offers a much faster means of descent for those who have mastered the necessary skills, but it does have additional risks for those who have not. Volcano skiing and snowboarding have lately become ends in themselves rather than merely means of transportation. Some climb the volcanoes just to ski or board down for the fun of it. Many glaciers offer thrilling downhill runs of many thousands of feet, even miles, but with all the attendant risks of glacier travel amplified by the dynamics and speed of skiing.

If you plan on making a ski descent, remember that roping up on glaciers is still advisable. Skiing can cut your descent time greatly, turning a mindless downhill trudge into a joyful run. But at speed you might not see a crevasse coming until you are upon it.

Extreme ski mountaineering's risks are very great. Those with proper experience, equipment, and conditioning for ski mountaineering (not to mention a good dose of fortitude) may proceed and enjoy when the conditions are just right; like climbers, those without are cautioned to get proper experience, equipment, and conditioning before they endanger themselves foolishly.

No-Trace Ethic

Because of the popularity of the Cascade volcanoes, many popular trails, campsites, and climbing routes are showing signs of overuse. No-Trace use of the wilderness areas of the Cascade Range is urged by the National Park Service and USDA Forest Service. Here are some simple suggestions to help minimize your impact on the mountain environment:

- Travel in small groups to do less damage to meadows and campsites.
- Use a stove for cooking, and bring a tent rather than relying on scarce natural resources. Campfires are not permitted in most wilderness areas in Washington, Oregon, and California.

- Use pit toilets or practice accepted human waste disposal practices (such as not eliminating waste near water sources and packing it out in plastic bags).
- Plan your actions so as to make the least impact on the environment.
- Stay on trails, even when muddy, to avoid sidecutting or erosion, and don't take shortcuts on switchbacks.
- Tread gently on vegetation, which is often fragile on high mountain slopes.
- Hike on snow or talus whenever possible, rather than causing unnecessary erosion on pumice slopes and vegetation.
- Choose stable sites for camps and rest stops, rather than fragile vegetation.
- Use existing campsites rather than creating new ones.
- Camp on snow instead of bare ground whenever possible.
- Don't construct rock windbreaks or clear bare ground areas of rocks or vegetation for any reason.
- Avoid having leftover food, so as not to attract wildlife to your camp.
- Don't bring your pets with you.
- Pack out your trash.

Litter and human waste disposal used to be major problems on many of the Cascade volcanoes. NPS and FS now provide plastic bags ("blue bags") for human waste disposal at most ranger stations and many climbing route trailheads. Putting any refuse into crevasses, or burying it in snow or soil or under rocks is not acceptable. Use pit toilets and trash containers where available, or else pack it out, particularly in high-use areas. If you are on a remote, infrequently traveled route, you might be okay leaving your byproduct out in the open, where wind and sun will decompose it. But on crowded routes, unless you want to drag your rope through it, it is best to use a well-sealed plastic bag to pack it out and dispose of it properly.

Wilderness Permit Requirements

Many of the wilderness areas included in this guide, including Mount Shasta Wilderness and Mount Rainier National Park, have established quotas on the number of persons who may occupy certain campsites and who may climb certain routes. Permit systems have been implemented at most other wilderness areas. These measures, though occasionally restrictive, are meant to help reduce the harm humans have done and continue to do to these fragile mountain environments. National Park Service and USDA Forest Service Wilderness

Management Plans have established "limits of acceptable change" for certain high-use areas. When an area exceeds the limits of acceptable change, access is often restricted. Examples of areas where human use has had significant adverse impact are Lake Helen on Mount Shasta, Jefferson Park on Mount Jefferson, Green Lakes, South Sister Climbers' Trail, and Camps Muir, Schurman, and Hazard on Mount Rainier, to name a few. The more popular the corridor of travel, the more likely it will be overused and abused, not only by climbers but by other wilderness visitors as well.

Climbers have been singled out by those who monitor human wilderness activity as a type of wilderness user who cares very little about most overuse issues. Climbers, it is reasoned, are goal oriented, seeking only to reach the summit of a mountain by whatever means, and are therefore less inclined to be concerned with human impacts on the wilderness. This is not true of all climbers, but is regarded by wilderness management agencies as a fair statement of climbers in general. Climbers are not any better or worse than the majority of other wilderness users, but we can help to dispel this attitude by spreading out onto less-traveled routes and areas where adverse impacts are less severe, and doing what we can to lessen our impact in sensitive areas. When you have climbed the standard non-technical route on Mount Shasta, for example, turn your attention to the other routes on the mountain. The fewer trips up heavily impacted routes, the less likely future restrictions will be imposed.

Climbing permits are required for Mounts Rainier, Shasta, St. Helens, and Adams. Some permits may be obtained in advance; others are issued on a first-come, first-served basis. Permit requirements change from time to time. It is recommended that you check with the NPS or forest service prior to your visit, just in case a new permit requirement has been imposed. Permit information is available online.

To Report Climbing Accidents
In most areas, to report a climbing accident or other emergency, dial 911. Cell phones are the usual method of reporting accidents and summoning rescues, but they don't work everywhere in the mountains, especially if not fully charged before you start your climb. If you cannot contact a 911 operator, dial "0" and ask for the emergency dispatch operator or county sheriff. The county sheriff is responsible for coordinating mountain rescue operations in most areas, except in national parks and some wilderness areas.

Map Legend

==<70>==	Interstate	✕	Airfield
==(191)==	US Highway	⟩ʗ	Bridge
==(279)==	State Highway	⌂	Building
———————	Local Road	⛺	Campground
= = = = =	Unpaved Road	❶	Climbing Area
⊢—⊢—⊣	Railroad	•—•	Gate
——PCT——	Pacific Coast Trail	🅿	Parking
--[WT]--	Wonderland Trail	⌣⌢	Pass/Saddle
....	Off-Trail Route	▲	Peak
～～	Waterway	■	Point of Interest
⟋ᵒ	Spring	🏢	Ranger Station
⬭	Lake/Reservoir	🎿	Ski Area
⬚	Glacier	○	Town
⌐ ¬ Boundary	National Forest/ State Park Boundary	🔳	Viewpoint
		🔳	Visitor Center

British Columbia

Mount Garibaldi

1.

Mount Garibaldi

The northernmost volcano included in this guide is British Columbia's Mount Garibaldi (8,787 feet/2,678 meters). To be absolutely correct, Garibaldi is not considered part of the Cascade Range, but part of the Coast Mountains of British Columbia. It is included as a Cascade volcano here even though it lies well north of the Fraser River, the customary dividing line between the two ranges. In *Fire and Ice,* Stephen Harris writes: "Garibaldi and other volcanoes in the Coast Mountains may be structurally related and represent a northern extension of the same geologic system." Geologically speaking, Garibaldi is definitely part of the Cascade volcano chain, which in fact extends farther north through Mounts Cayley and Meager to peaks in the southwestern Waddington Range and near Mount Silverthrone. Thus Garibaldi can with clear conscience be included among the Cascade volcanoes, even if technically it is not a Cascade volcano.

One of the lowest in elevation of the Pacific Coast stratovolcanoes, Garibaldi is not the highest peak in Garibaldi Provincial Park, nor is it the highest volcanic peak in Canada (that honor goes to Mount Edziza (9,144

feet/2,787 meters) in northwestern British Columbia). However, it stands out alone in the typical manner of Cascade volcanoes, whereas most other Canadian volcanic peaks are hidden within higher subranges of the Coast Mountains of British Columbia. It is a singular, striking mountain, the centerpiece of one of British Columbia's finest provincial parks.

Garibaldi, one of the youngest Pacific Rim volcanoes, has the distinction of being the only volcano included in this guide that erupted through a glacial ice sheet. According to available evidence, Garibaldi volcano was once actually supported by an ice age glacier. The wasting of the ice, it is theorized, caused the summit cone to collapse toward the west. This collapse would certainly explain why Garibaldi's rock is entirely untrustworthy. Its ridges and faces are shattered, and rocks regularly rumble down the mountain's flanks without apparent provocation. Because Mount Garibaldi is composed of unstable rock, climbing routes keep mostly to the glaciers and snow slopes, which are abundant in winter and spring, but which become "boggy" and then usually vanish after June or July in

Garibaldi Peak

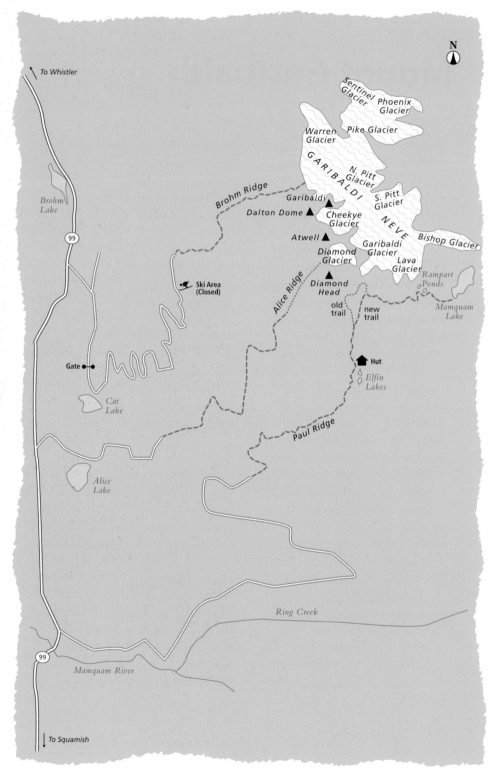

N

To Whistler

Brohm Lake

99

Brohm Ridge

Ski Area (Closed)

Gate

Cat Lake

Alice Lake

99

Mamquam River

To Squamish

Sentinel Glacier

Phoenix Glacier

Warren Glacier

Pike Glacier

GARIBALDI

N. Pitt Glacier

S. Pitt Glacier

NEVE

Garibaldi

Dalton Dome ▲

Cheekye Glacier

Atwell ▲

Garibaldi Glacier

Bishop Glacier

Lava Glacier

Diamond Glacier

Alice Ridge

Diamond Head ▲

old trail

new trail

Rampart Ponds

Mamquam Lake

Hut

Elfin Lakes

Paul Ridge

Ring Creek

most years. After the snow melts, crevasses and bergschrunds can pose difficulty and danger, and rockfall is an ever-present hazard. For this reason, early-season, cold-weather snow ascents are recommended for most routes up Garibaldi, and technical rock climbing is pretty much out of the question.

Garibaldi has three distinct summits: Garibaldi, the true summit, Dalton Dome (8,638 feet/2,633 meters), a domelike shoulder to the west, and Atwell Peak (8,596 feet/2,620 meters), a pointed summit on the southwest (also known as Diamond Head). Its eastern flank is smothered by the Garibaldi Neve, a broad glacial sheet containing at least ten individually named glaciers. The Neve is a popular ski destination, particularly in spring, and provides open access to many climbing routes until late summer. Winter ski camping on the Neve is common, but high winds are not uncommon, so most winter skiers and climbers wisely protect campsites by digging into the snow or constructing snow walls or igloos for shelter.

Mount Garibaldi's first recorded ascent was in 1907 by a mob (A. Dalton, W. Dalton, Atwell King, T. Pattison, J. Trorey, and G. Warren). Its first winter ascent came in 1943, also by a crowd (Vernon Brink, R. McLellan, H. Parliament, J. Rattenburg, and F. Roots).

Winter ascents of Garibaldi are reasonably popular, because the very loose nature of the volcano's rock makes snow and ice climbing much preferable and the mountain is in close proximity to a major highway. However, Garibaldi's routes can have high avalanche danger in winter and spring. It is a trade-off between whether you prefer rockfall or avalanche hazard. Ideal climbing conditions on Garibaldi can occur anytime during the winter (December to March), although ascents of less rockfall-prone routes are routinely made well into the summer. For a winter ascent, climbers should wait for a very cold spell following a brief warming period. With stable weather under such conditions, snow has settled, rocks are frozen in place, snow and ice offer secure climbing, crevasses are covered, and avalanche danger is low. Such conditions occur once or twice (three times at most) during most winters in the Coast Mountains, so good luck trying to plan for them! When such conditions arrive, you must pack and go instantly—the good weather probably won't last long. Otherwise, wait until late spring or summer, when weather is more reliable, and take your chances with loose rock and crevasses.

Winter and early-season climbing parties commonly approach on skis; in later season, skiing across the Neve is possible but not much easier than walking. By June or July, when most ascents are made, skis are rarely used.

All amenities are available in nearby Squamish. For additional information regarding access, road conditions, maps, and recreation opportunities, contact Squamish Forest District, 42000 Loggers Lane, Squamish, BC V0N 3G0; (604) 898-2100; www.for.gov.bc.ca/dsq/. The BC Parks website is also helpful at www .env.gov.bc.ca/bcparks/explore/park pgs/garibaldi/. To report a climbing accident or other emergency, call 911.

Elfin Lakes Approach

Garibaldi and Atwell's southern routes are commonly approached from Elfin Lakes via Paul Ridge Trail. To reach Paul Ridge Trail, turn off Provincial Highway 99 about 2 miles/4 kilometers north of Squamish onto Mamquam Road. A 10-mile/16-kilometer drive up a good gravel road leads to the trailhead parking lot. Hike the trail over Paul Ridge to Elfin Lakes (the hut there is currently available on a first-come, first-in basis with a nightly fee, subject to change without notice). In winter a marked ski route may be followed to Elfin Lakes Hut to avoid avalanche danger on the trail route. If you plan to stay in the hut, call (604) 898-3678 or visit www.env.gov.bc.ca/bcparks for current information.

From the lakes, continue along the trail northward toward Opal Cone and Mamquam Lake until cairns mark the way to the Neve. In winter and early season this stretch of trail is avalanche prone, in which case the approach more commonly used is a traverse over the gap between Columnar Peak and the Gargoyles, then north to a saddle between these peaks and Diamond Head. From here a northeasterly traverse joins the former route. Alternatively, some climbers approach via a tributary of Ring Creek or along side slopes and ridges to the Diamond Glacier, which is traversed to the saddle accessing the upper Neve. Your route of choice and prevailing conditions will dictate your approach route.

Alice Ridge Approach

Signs lead from Highway 99 to Alice Park, where jeep roads lead up switchbacks onto Alice Ridge. A trail leads to the saddle dividing Diamond Head and the Gargoyles. From here, continue northeast, as for the Elfin Lakes approach, traversing onto the Neve. Some parties camp at the saddle dividing Diamond Head from the Gargoyles.

Brohm Ridge Approach

North from the Alice Park turnoff, and just before Brohm Lake is reached, an unmarked road curves back south and up to Cat Lake. Drive 3 miles/4.8 kilometers to a gate, just past a fork to the north. The gate is locked at 5 p.m. on Friday evenings and not reopened until Sunday evening. After 5 p.m. Friday the gatekeeper will let you out but not in (except in an emergency). So, if you want to drive in, come early on or before Friday. Otherwise, walk from the gate (last resort), or try the

Garibaldi Peak–Elfin Lakes Approach

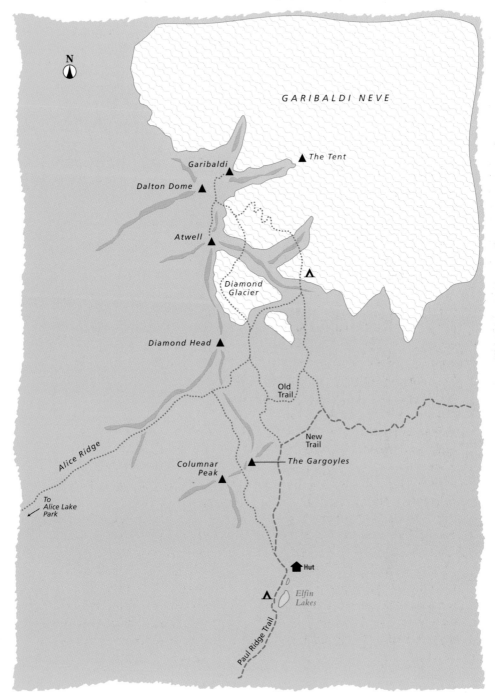

Garibaldi Peak–Brohm Ridge Approach

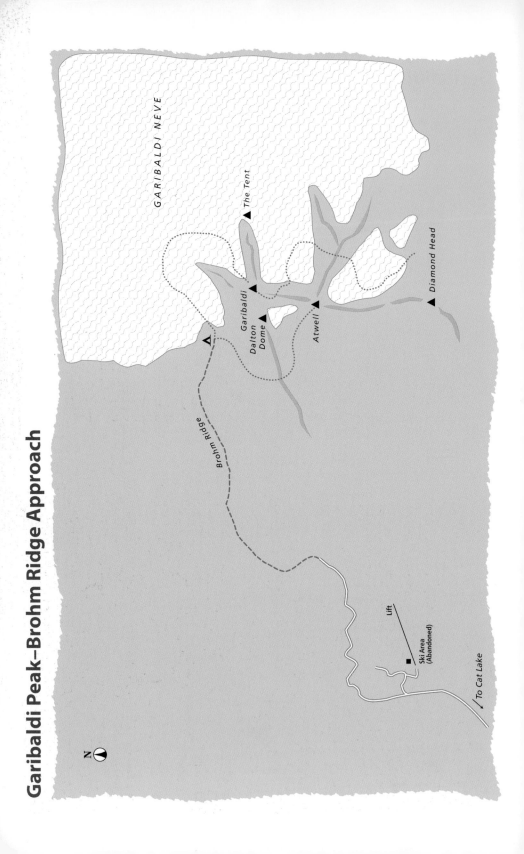

tougher Brohm Ridge jeep road. If you get past the gate in time, continue driving up the rough road as far as you can make it. The road passes an abandoned ski area. From road's end, hike up Brohm Ridge to the Neve. Camp at the cabin about halfway along Brohm Ridge, or anywhere on the Neve. In winter this area is heavily used by snowmobilers.

GARIBALDI SUMMIT

Garibaldi is the true summit, a rocky horn situated a bit north of Atwell and northeast of Dalton Dome. It has two customary routes, although it can be reached directly from either of the other summits. The East Face is most conveniently approached from Alice Ridge or Elfin Lakes and the Northeast Face from Brohm Ridge, but it is straightforward to cross below The Tent from one route to the other.

1. East Face
Difficulty rating: 2
Grade: II
Class: 3–4
Time to summit: 6 hours
Objective hazards: Moderately prone to avalanching, exposed to icefall and rockfall, very loose rock on summit pinnacle

This is the usual route up Garibaldi because it is the shortest. A common approach is via Elfin Lakes and Garibaldi Neve, although Alice Ridge is an equally feasible approach. Cross the Neve and ascend toward the Garibaldi-Atwell saddle, staying left (west) of The Tent formation (a popular winter ski

Garibaldi—East Face

Garibaldi Summit

Diamond Glacier

The Tent

1

PHOTO ANDREW LAVIGNE/ALAVIGNE.NET

destination). Crevasses in the icefall here are sometimes difficult to pass, and there is avalanche danger during ripe snow conditions. A less crevassed and popular option is to approach via Diamond Glacier to a saddle in the moraine ridge at the foot of Atwell's Southeast Buttress, then traverse the upper Neve and ascend a final steep slope to the saddle.

From the saddle, proceed up the diminutive Cheekye Glacier toward the rocky summit of Garibaldi. The final ascent is up exposed, shattered rock, with attendant rockfall hazard. The climbing is not terribly difficult if you stay on route, but it is extremely loose and exposed in places. Pick the path of least resistance and take care not to knock rocks onto your companions. Helmets are definitely advised.

Descent: Most parties descend via the route of ascent. It is possible to descend via the Warren Glacier route.

2. Northeast Face—Warren Glacier
Difficulty rating: 2
Grade: II
Class: 3–4
Time to summit: 6 hours
Objective hazards: Moderately prone to avalanching and exposed to rockfall below summit pinnacle

This was the route of the first ascent; it is a straightforward glacier ascent

Garibaldi—Summit Detail

Summit

1

PHOTO ANDREW LAVIGNE/ALAVIGNE.NET

Garibaldi—Warren Glacier

Garibaldi Summit

Dalton Dome

The Tent

North Face
Route

Warren Glacier

2

Garibaldi Neve

PHOTO NICOLAS POTIRON

often done on skis by parties traversing the Garibaldi Neve.

Approach as for the East Face onto the Neve, then cross the Warren Glacier and climb to a point more or less directly southeast of Garibaldi. Ascend the moderate snow and glacier slopes to the headwall. Passing the bergschrund may be difficult; you may have to outflank it via the rotten ridges to the east or north. Once beyond that obstacle, ascend broken rock or snow to the summit.

Descent: Most parties descend via the route of ascent; ski descents are popular. It is possible to descend via the East Face route, but not advised unless you have previously climbed that route and know your way down the exposed, loose face.

ATWELL PEAK (DIAMOND HEAD)

Atwell Peak (8,569 feet/2,620 meters) is the sharp southwest summit of Garibaldi, which is popularly known as Diamond Head. This summit was first reached by A. Armistead, Basil Darling, J. Davies, Frank Hewton, and Allan Morkill in 1911. Early-season ascents are recommended so snow and ice can be climbed instead of loose rock. Atwell's ridges are sharp and exposed, its faces steep, loose, and avalanche prone, and its summit ridge quite rotten. Still, it is a popular ascent, particularly in winter and early spring. It is not recommended that you try Atwell without snow or ice covering the rocks. Then again, Atwell's couloirs are notorious avalanche chutes after heavy snowfall

Atwell Peak—North Ridge

Atwell Peak

3

Siberian
Express

North Ridge

7

6

Armenian
Express

Garibaldi-Atwell
Saddle

PHOTO ANDRE CHARLAND

and on warm spring days. Helmets are highly recommended.

3. North Ridge
Difficulty rating: 3
Grade: III
Class: 4–5
Time to summit: 6 hours
Objective hazards: Highly exposed climbing on loose rock or snow, prone to avalanching, cornices on summit ridge

This is the usual route up Atwell Peak, climbing the distinct ridge from the Garibaldi-Atwell saddle to the summit. It is a straightforward climb, with little routefinding difficulty, but is exposed and committing.

Approach as for the East Face route up Garibaldi to the saddle. From the saddle, ascend the short, exposed, shattered ridge to Atwell's rotten summit. The ridge is distinctly alpine in character and attractive in appearance, especially when snow covered, but it is steep and avalanche prone, and has very loose rock. Winter ascents are not uncommon, but be mindful of avalanche hazard and cornices all along the ridge.

Descent: Most parties descend via one of the Southeast Face couloirs, which offers a more direct and expeditious descent, although descending the route of ascent is also straightforward. If you plan to descend via the Southeast Face, scout out your descent line on the approach.

4. Southeast Face
Difficulty rating: 3
Grade: II
Class: 3–4, AI1–2
Time to summit: 6 hours
Objective hazards: Highly prone to avalanching and exposed to rockfall, cornices on summit ridge

The Southeast Face rises directly above Diamond Glacier. The rock is rotten on the face and is not at all recommended in late season, but it's a popular winter and early-season snow ascent, especially with the extreme ski crowd. It is also the usual route of descent from the other Atwell summit routes.

Approach via Alice Ridge or Elfin Lakes to Diamond Glacier and pick your route. The face is composed of steep, shattered rock divided by distinct couloirs (at least two of which have been descended on skis). The leftmost major couloir in particular offers a direct route to a point immediately south of the summit, which is a more or less direct descent route

Atwell Peak—Southeast Face

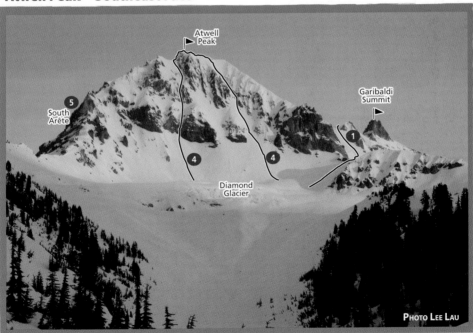

PHOTO LEE LAU

for other routes on Atwell when it is snow filled and rockfall isn't copious. There is often a short, icy section at about mid-height. If you find the couloirs in prime condition (stable snow and iced over with rocks frozen in place), this is an enjoyable and straightforward snow and ice climb. In less than optimal conditions, it can be a rockfall or avalanche funnel. Beware of cornices on the summit ridge.

Descent: Most parties descend via the route of ascent. It is also possible to descend via the North Ridge. Extreme skiers sometimes descend one of the Northwest Face couloirs, although this is not recommended.

5. South Arête

Difficulty rating: 5
Grade: IV
Class: 4–5, AI3–4
Time to summit: 6–8 hours
Objective hazards: Unprotected climbing on rime ice and loose rock, cornices on summit ridge

The South Arête is one of Atwell's most popular testpieces, a technical route ascending the obvious and highly exposed arête dividing the southeast and southwest faces, leading directly to Atwell's summit. This route has gained popularity as a winter ascent, but it should only be climbed when in optimal condition.

Atwell Peak—Northwest Face

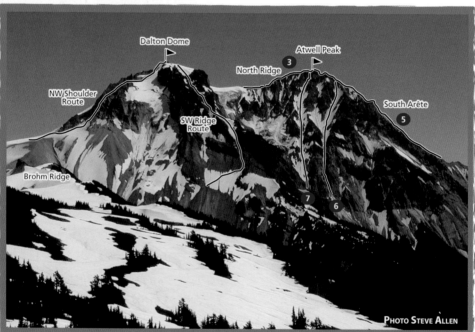

PHOTO STEVE ALLEN

The entire route is steep and airy, providing enjoyable climbing when in good condition.

Approach from Elfin Lakes or Alice Ridge to the base of the arête and ascend more or less directly up the arête. The route passes two rock bands along the ridge via Class 4–5 climbing. The final steep section often consists of unprotectable steep snow and rime ice over frighteningly rotten rock. The route is best climbed during a cold spell when snow and ice are stable and cover loose rock. It is not recommended after early spring, although it has been climbed as late as June. When the route is out of condition, avoid it. Protection may be difficult or untrustworthy, and rockfall will be copious.

Descent: Most parties descend via either of the Southeast Face couloirs or the North Ridge route.

NORTHWEST FACE

This 3,280-foot/1,000-meter face has two semipopular routes and possibilities for a few others, but high avalanche and rockfall danger makes it an unwise choice except in perfect winter conditions. The face is approached from Brohm Ridge below the western flanks of Dalton Dome. From the head of Brohm Ridge, traverse southward around the southeast ridge of Dalton Dome. This traverse is subject to considerable rockfall and icefall danger from Dalton Dome. In optimal conditions, the couloirs are excellent climbs. They are also sought-after ski descent

routes with the extreme ski crowd, so watch out!

6. Armenian Express
Difficulty rating: 5
Grade: V
Class: 4–5, AI2–3
Time to summit: 12–16 hours
Objective hazards: Highly prone to avalanching and exposed to rockfall

Another of Atwell's testpieces, this route climbs the major couloir on the far right of the Northwest Face. It was climbed solo on the first ascent, and a summit bivouac was required.

Ascend the couloir until loose rock forces a traverse onto the south ridge just below the summit. The route becomes quite steep and loose near the summit and has high avalanche, icefall, and rockfall danger. It should not be attempted except under optimal winter climbing conditions.

Descent: Most parties descend via one of the Southeast Face couloirs. The North Ridge route is also an option, but if you've made it up the Northwest Face, a descent via the Southeast Face should be no problem and much more expeditious.

7. Siberian Express
Difficulty rating: 5
Grade: V
Class: 4–5, AI2–3
Time to summit: 12–16 hours
Objective hazards: Highly prone to avalanching and exposed to rockfall

Yet another of Atwell's testpieces, this route climbs the huge central couloir up the Northwest Face to the notch just north of Atwell's summit. The route was first climbed in a single 21-hour effort (including descent).

Ascend the couloir directly to the summit ridge. The climbing is mostly over moderately angled snow and ice, with a very steep finish. The route has high avalanche and icefall danger, plus loose rock, and is very exposed and committing. This challenging winter route would be a poor choice during any other season. Make sure the route is well frozen to minimize rockfall danger, and climb only during stable snow and weather conditions. A retreat or rescue could be very difficult.

Descent: Most parties descend via one of the Southeast Face couloirs or the North Ridge route.

DALTON DOME

Dalton Dome (8,638 feet/2,633 meters) is the blunt summit southwest of Garibaldi summit. Its first ascent was made by the 1907 mob during the first ascent of Garibaldi. It is often combined with an ascent of Garibaldi, usually from the Garibaldi-Atwell saddle. Dalton Dome has a few routes, none of which is very popular due to extremely poor rock. A few of these routes are shown on the photo topo and described here briefly for reference.

The Northwest Shoulder route is not highly recommended, but it is the most direct independent summit route on Dalton Dome. Approach via Brohm Ridge to the base of the Northwest Shoulder. Ascend snow or loose rock up and right (south) of the shoulder proper, then up loose rock to easier snow slopes leading to the summit ridge. Grade II, Class 4.

The Southwest Ridge is a semi-popular winter route when in condition. Approach via a snow/scree traverse from Brohm Ridge beneath the West Face to gain the ridge, then ascend Class 3–4 rock and snow to the summit. Grade III, Class 3–4.

The North Face (not shown) ascends the Warren Glacier headwall on the far right side, crossing the bergschrund to gain the face, then climbing shattered rock and steep snow to a slight rib that gains the Northwest Shoulder, which then leads to the summit. This route features remarkably unstable rock and is not recommended any more than the other routes up Dalton Dome. Grade III, Class 4–5.

Descent: Descents from Dalton Dome are best made via the East Face route on Garibaldi, descending from the Garibaldi-Atwell saddle to Diamond Glacier, or over the top of the Garibaldi summit down the Warren Glacier and across the Neve back to Brohm Ridge.

Washington

Mount Baker
Photo Jason Broman/Mountain Madness

2.

Mount Baker

Mount Baker (10,778 feet/3,285 meters), the "northern sentinel" of the Cascade Range, is one of the iciest of the Cascade volcanoes, having 44 square miles of ice spread out among its twelve glaciers (by comparison, Mount Rainier has only 35 square miles of ice). Standing a short distance south of the Canadian border, only about 50 miles from Bellingham Bay and a few miles south of the 49th Parallel, Mount Baker is a dominating presence from any northern Puget Sound vantage. Its stark white glaciers are clearly visible from Seattle, and on a clear day you can see it from Mount Rainier's summit, more than 100 miles away.

Mount Baker was "discovered" in 1792 by Captain Vancouver's first mate, Joseph Baker, for whom it was named. On that voyage Baker had claimed the first ascent of Hawaii's giant volcano, Mauna Kea, but apparently did not consider climbing Baker. It is suspected by many historians that Juan de Fuca sighted the peak in 1592. However, the first recorded mention of the mountain was in 1790 by Manuel Quimper, a Spanish navigator, who named it La Gran Montaña de Carmelo. Long before

Quimper or Baker's sightings, local Nooksack tribesmen and other indigenous natives knew the mountain as Koma-Kulshan (meaning Wounded Mountain or Damaged Mountain or Steep White Mountain or White Shining Mountain or Great White Watcher, or any of several other translations depending upon your reference). According to one native legend, an angry god struck down the mountain with a lightning bolt, wounding or breaking the great peak, causing it to "bleed" molten rock, which was undoubtedly the best explanation of a volcanic event that could be mustered by the superstitious inhabitants of the mountain's foothills.

Mount Baker volcano was active during the mid-1970s, when Sherman Crater broke open and began spewing steam and ash clouds—minor compared with Mount St. Helens in 1980, but of great concern to local residents, particularly those living below Baker Lake. The peak has settled down a bit, but seismic activity beneath the mountain continues. Thermal vents in the vicinity of the peak have been considered as a source of geothermal energy. Obviously, Mount Baker is not finished.

There is little doubt among geologists that it could erupt again in the not-too-distant future. The mountain was supposedly more precipitous prior to the mid-1800s, but a summit "slump" or partial collapse is thought by some geologists to have occurred (the result of some kind of seismic activity within the mountain), giving Grant Peak its more rounded appearance. Like other volcanoes in this guide, Mount Baker's rock is bad if not worse, and Mount Baker's flanks are slowly becoming moraines and sand bars. Among Mount Baker's sub-summits are Sherman Peak, a sharp point rising directly above the Sherman Crater, and the Black Buttes, known individually as Colfax Peak (the east butte, nearest the summit) and Lincoln Peak, standing as the crumbly remains of a former crater rim of Mount Baker; the Deming Glacier now occupies that obstructed vent. There are routes to the summits of the Black Buttes, but none is recommended.

Mount Baker was first climbed in 1868 by Edmund T. Coleman, David Ogilvy, Thomas Stratton, and John Tennant. Coleman, an English librarian living in Victoria, BC, had made two previous attempts to climb the mountain, and was devoted to the task. His detailed journals and artworks provide a remarkable glimpse of early climbing attempts on Mount Baker. Coleman was a member of Mount Rainier's first ascent party, but

Climbers on Easton Glacier, Mount Baker.
PHOTO JASON BROMAN/MOUNTAIN MADNESS

did not complete the ascent with Hazard and Van Trump.

Of further historical interest are the Mount Baker "marathons," which began in 1911 and ended in 1913. The marathons were essentially a race from Bellingham to the summit of Mount Baker and back to Bellingham, involving car or train travel and many miles of trail running. After one contestant fell into a crevasse, and due to growing fear of a worse accident, the event was discontinued. The Mount Baker Marathon has been revived as the modern Ski-to-Sea Race, which begins at the Mount Baker ski area and involves downhill and cross-country skiing, running, bicycling, canoeing or kayaking, and sailing to Marine Park in Bellingham.

Climbers should be particularly wary of crevasses on Mount Baker, which seem more numerous than on any other Cascade volcano. Hidden crevasses swallow up dozens of climbers each year; luckily, most of them are pulled out without serious injury. Early-season climbers especially should beware of crevasses, even if none are visible. Even in late season, crevasses can surprise you. Amazingly, considering all the people who had climbed Mount Baker unroped prior to that year, the first known crevasse-related death on Mount Baker occurred in 1913.

Because Mount Baker receives an annual average of over 50 feet of snow, avalanches are also a very real danger, even on gentle slopes and during the summer months. This danger is compounded by warm, wet weather, which allows heavy snow to accumulate. Snow followed by warm, rainy weather (common on Mount Baker) spells certain avalanche conditions. A July 1939 avalanche high on the Deming Glacier killed six people, an event repeated more than once since. The volume of snowfall here is a fair indicator that Mount Baker has very poor climbing weather during much of the year. In winter it gets the brunt of arctic air masses coming down from Alaska, and these frigid air masses colliding with the marine air blowing north up Puget Sound and east through the Strait of Juan de Fuca is responsible for high winds, storms, clouds, and snowfall. A winter ascent of Mount Baker can therefore be a very serious undertaking. Of course, the high snow accumulation feeds the glaciers and keeps the mountain white all year, which makes it a very attractive ski climb.

In 1984, 132,200 acres were added to the National Wilderness System, which created the Mount Baker Wilderness. As a wilderness within the definition of the Wilderness Act of 1964, no motorized travel is permitted (except for a pie-wedge portion of the Easton Glacier, a privilege occasionally abused by snowmobilers who cross the saddle onto the Coleman Glacier). This has

Mount Baker–Vicinity Map

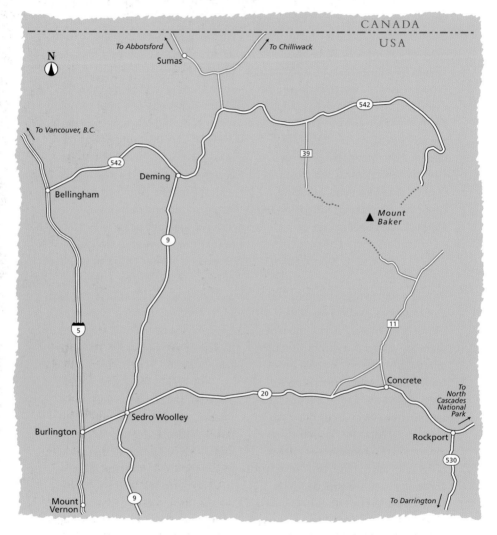

Mount Baker Trail

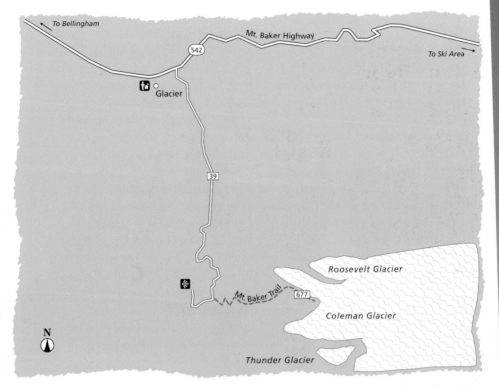

To Bellingham

Mt. Baker Highway

542

To Ski Area

Glacier

39

Roosevelt Glacier

Mt. Baker Trail   677

Coleman Glacier

N

Thunder Glacier

preserved Mount Baker's immediate slopes from the threat of logging and other commercialization and exploitation, and is a long-overdue tribute to a beautiful mountain.

Permits may someday be required for entry into the Mount Baker Wilderness, but as of this printing are not. Blue bags (for waste disposal) are available from USDA Forest Services offices. A regional Northwest Forest Pass is required for trailhead parking. For current information about permits or access, contact Mt. Baker Ranger District, 810 SR 20, Sedro Woolley, WA 98284, (206) 856-5700; Glacier Public Service Center, 10091 Mt. Baker Hwy., Glacier, WA 98244, (206) 599-2714; Outdoor Recreation Information Center, Seattle REI Building, 222 Yale Ave. North, Seattle, WA 98109-5429, (206) 223-1944; or Mount Baker Climbing Home Page, www.fs.fed.us/r6/mbs/recreation/mtn_climbing/index.shtml.

1. Coleman-Upper Deming Glacier
Difficulty rating: 2
Grade: II
Class: N/A
Time to summit: 6 hours
Objective hazards: Moderately prone to avalanching and exposed to rockfall, glacier is heavily crevassed

This was the approximate line of the original route climbed on Mount Baker in 1868 by Edmund Coleman and party, and remains the most popular route to the summit of Mount Baker, probably because it has the shortest approach hike.

The route is approached via the Heliotrope Ridge Trail 677 (also known as Mount Baker Trail), which is commonly used to approach the north-side routes. To reach the trailhead, take WA 542 east from Bellingham to about 1 mile past the Glacier Public Service Center (about 33 miles from I-5) and turn right (south) on FR 39. Drive about 8 miles on FR 39, just past where the road leaves pavement for gravel, to the trailhead, on the left. Two miles of hiking lead to the former site of Kulshan Cabin, at timberline. (The cabin was torn down shortly after the area was granted wilderness status.)

From the cabin site, continue up the trail for about 0.5 mile and take a right up the Hog's Back, a lateral moraine. The Coleman Glacier sits about 6,000 feet. In early season, when the high trail is still covered in snow, it may be difficult to tell when you have reached the glacier, making roping up early a wise choice because there are crevasses lurking everywhere. A variation approach

Mount Baker—Coleman Glacier

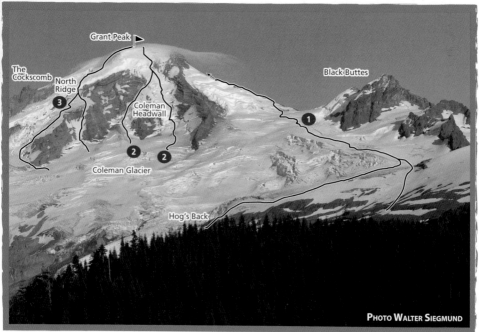

PHOTO WALTER SIEGMUND

is to leave the trail just above the cabin site and head straight up snow and moraine slopes to the western flank of the glacier, which avoids some of the crevasses encountered on the Hog's Back approach. It is possible to camp where Kulshan Cabin used to be, a nice flat spot that is too low for most parties except on crowded weekends. Most parties camp either at the top of the Hog's Back (also often crowded) or below the Black Buttes at about 9,000 feet on the Coleman Glacier (popular with small, unguided parties and, alas, also sometimes crowded). If camping on the glacier, remember that there are crevasses lurking about and use caution.

From wherever you camp, ascend the right flank of the glacier (usually fewer crevasses farther west), bearing toward and then beneath the Black Buttes, to the saddle between Colfax Peak and Grant Peak. From the saddle, proceed upward via a pumice ridge, staying right of the Roman Wall, and continue straight up the headwall toward the summit dome, bearing right as you near the summit.

Beware of hidden crevasses, and stay roped on the descent until you are certain you are off the glacier. The Roman Wall has avalanched several times even in late season, so pay attention to snow conditions in all seasons. Rock and ice bombardment from the Black Buttes is an occasional hazard.

Descent: Descend via the route of ascent.

2. Coleman Glacier Headwall
Difficulty rating: 4
Grade: IV
Class: 4–5 depending on variation, AI2–3
Time to summit: 9 hours
Objective hazards: Highly prone to avalanching and exposed to rockfall and icefall, glacier is heavily crevassed

The Coleman Headwall rises some 2,000 feet above the Coleman Glacier and is consistently steep, averaging over a 40-degree angle, with ice cliffs hanging menacingly above much of the face. This is a committing and challenging climb, and quite popular despite its intimidating nature.

Approach as for the Coleman Glacier route to the Hog's Back, then traverse the glacier as crevasses permit to the base of the central portion of the headwall. Crevasse conditions approaching the headwall are often a determining factor in a successful ascent; in some seasons the glacier is so badly crevassed that reaching the headwall is a near impossible task. In late season a bergschrund sometimes prevents access to the face. When the bergschrund is impassable, determined parties have crossed the lower Roman Nose to gain the headwall.

Ascend the most feasible route up the headwall, following steep ice on either side of the lower rock bands, or one of many possible variations passing obstacles on the headwall, including steep ice, rock bands, crevasses, and ice cliffs. Passing the upper ice cliffs can be troublesome, but there is usually a feasible route that avoids ascending the ice cliffs directly. Numerous variations have been climbed, so no route is given precedence here. Pick the line that looks safest and most feasible or challenging, depending on your mood and route conditions. All involve similar climbing over continuously steep snow, ice, and rock bands, with similar exposure and risks of avalanches and falling rock and ice. Certain variations have greater exposure to falling ice, especially if ice cliff seracs are loaded. The headwall should be well frozen during any attempt to minimize

exposure to rockfall and snow slides. A couple of sharp ice tools and a good selection of ice screws/pitons are recommended.

Descent: Descend via the Coleman-Upper Deming Glacier route.

3. North Ridge
Difficulty rating: 3
Grade: III
Class: AI3
Time to summit: 10 hours
Objective hazards: Highly prone to avalanching and exposed to icefall, glacier is heavily crevassed

The North Ridge route is regarded as a Mount Baker classic. All things considered, it is perhaps the finest route on Mount Baker, although some consider

Coleman Glacier Headwall/North Ridge

Photo Brian Lawrence

the Coleman Glacier Headwall the better outing for more serious climbers.

Approach as for the Coleman Glacier route to the Hog's Back, then traverse the Coleman Glacier laterally as crevasses permit to the base of the ridge—if you can. The directness of your approach to the ridge will be dictated by prevailing crevasse patterns. At times crevasses and the bergschrund may completely bar access to the ridge.

Assuming you reach the ridge, ascend snow and ice slopes closely right, on the headwall side of the ridge, to gain the North Ridge proper. A few obstacles along the ridge, including an ice cliff, lead to easier climbing to the summit.

The ice cliff may involve a short- to medium-length belayed pitch on ice varying between 45- and 60-degrees with incredible exposure. The ice cliff may sometimes be skirted, as conditions permit, although many parties look forward to the challenge of ascending the ice cliff as directly as possible. The condition of the ice cliff varies, so be prepared for anything, including retreat. From the top of the ice cliff, most parties veer leftward to avoid summit dome crevasses on their way to the summit. Ice tools and ice screws are essential.

Descent: Descend via the Coleman-Upper Deming Glacier route.

Mount Baker–Southern Approaches

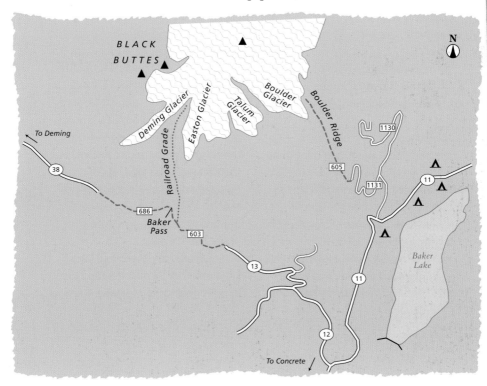

Mount Baker—Easton Glacier

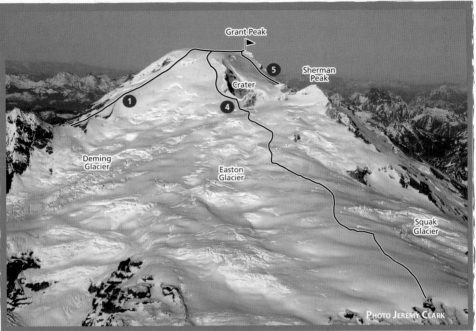

Grant Peak

5

Sherman Peak

Crater

1

4

Deming Glacier

Easton Glacier

Squak Glacier

PHOTO JEREMY CLARK

4. Easton Glacier
Difficulty rating: 1
Grade: II
Class: N/A
Time to summit: 4 hours
Objective hazards: Moderately prone to avalanching, crevasses

The Easton Glacier flows southwesterly from the summit, and is the more gentle alternative to the Coleman Glacier, providing a direct and relatively hazard-free ascent to the summit—except for the abundant crevasses and avalanche-prone slopes. It is a popular route, especially with guided parties.

Approach via Park Butte Trail 603 (also known as Baker Pass Trail).

To reach the trailhead, follow WA 20 east from the Mount Baker Ranger District office in Sedro-Woolley for 16 miles to milepost 82. Turn left (north) on Baker Lake Highway (FR 11). After 12 miles, turn left on FR 12. Drive 3.6 miles to a junction with FR 13; stay to the right and follow FR 13 for 5.3 miles to the trailhead at road's end. Overnight campsites are available at the trailhead. This trail was once recognized as one of the most abused trails in North America. It is very important that you minimize your impact in this area.

Hike up Park Butte Trail 603, staying left at the first junction (Scott Paul Trail 603.1) to Morovitz Meadow,

Mount Baker—Easton Glacier

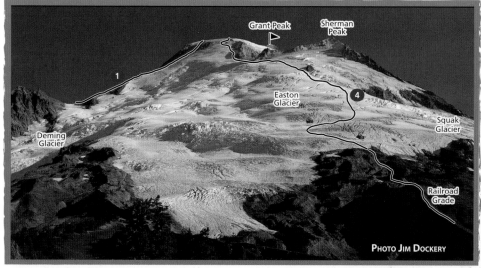

PHOTO JIM DOCKERY

where the trail forks. Take the right fork up Railroad Grade Trail 603.2, which leads about 1.5 miles up the Railroad Grade moraine to the edge of the Easton Glacier. Camping is available at Cathedral Camp near Morovitz Meadow, Railroad Camp about 0.5 mile up the moraine, or High Camp at the top of the moraine. Camp on permanent snow or established bivouac sites; don't camp in Morovitz Meadow. Campsites are limited; if there are no established campsites available, camp on the glacier as snow and crevasse conditions permit.

From the head of the Railroad Grade, ascend the glacier wherever there appear to be the fewest crevasses. Some parties bear left toward the Coleman-Deming saddle; others right toward the crater before

turning to the summit. Both routes converge at the headwall just below the summit dome. This route is shorter and less demanding than the Coleman-Upper Deming Glacier route, and is a popular ski ascent and descent. Rope up—there are plenty of crevasses. The glacier is usually less crevassed on the west side, but most parties climb the east side, trending across upper Squak Glacier to the crater gap. The final headwall can be avalanche prone; pay attention to snow conditions on the ascent and descent.

Be aware that the trail and climbing route lie within the Mt. Baker National Recreation Area, which is open to snowmobile use during approximately December to June each winter and spring (dependent on snow depth). If you are planning a winter

Mount Baker—Boulder Glacier

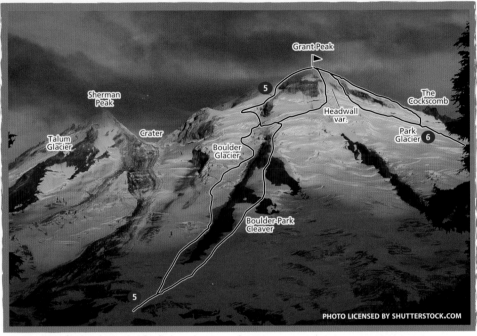

ascent on this side, don't be surprised to have some noisy company.

Descent: Descend via the route of ascent.

5. Boulder Glacier
Difficulty rating: 2
Grade: II or III
Class: 2–3, AI2 (headwall)
Time to summit: 6 hours
Objective hazards: Moderately prone to avalanching, threat of lahars below crater

This route ascends the Boulder Glacier or the Boulder-Park Cleaver more steeply and directly to the summit. Although less traveled and less popular than the Coleman or Easton Glacier routes, it is a good, moderate glacier climb with several possible variations.

Approach via Boulder Ridge Trail 605. To reach the trail, follow WA 20 east from the Mount Baker Ranger District office in Sedro-Woolley for 16 miles to milepost 82. Turn left (north) on Baker Lake Highway (FR 11) and continue for 18 miles. After passing Boulder Creek Campground and crossing Boulder Creek, turn left on FR 1130. Drive for about 1 mile to the junction with FR 1131 and turn left. Continue for 4.1 miles to the trailhead.

Hike Boulder Ridge Trail 605 about 2.1 miles to its end in a small meadow. From there a boot path continues through brush and forest to a moraine, where a short scramble gains Boulder Ridge. Continue hiking up the ridge to the glacier. Bivouac at one of several possible sites along the ridge.

There are several possible climbing routes from high camp. The Boulder-Park Cleaver is crevasse free and thus more popular than ascending the glaciers on either side. Climb the cleaver as directly as possible, ascending firn slopes just right of the cleaver when forced right, staying mindful of lurking crevasses the farther you stray from the cleaver. You can climb Boulder Glacier directly, but with greater exposure to avalanches, possible mudflows from the crater, and crevasses. And you can stay right of the cleaver, ascending Park Glacier, which may be more time consuming due to crevasses. Above the cleaver, angle leftward onto the Boulder Glacier headwall, above Sherman Crater, which leads to the summit. The slope steepens near the top, providing some challenging snow or ice climbing; some parties belay the final pitches when icy.

A steep and challenging finish is to climb the Park Glacier headwall from the head of the cleaver. It may be very difficult to pass the bergschrund, and the 60-degree snow/ice slope above the bergschrund may be difficult to protect. Bring ice tools and ice screws/pitons, and be prepared to belay the steepest pitches. Grade III.

Descent: Most parties descend via the regular Boulder Glacier route via the cleaver. It is also possible to descend the Easton Glacier route with arranged transportation.

6. Park Glacier
Difficulty rating: 3
Grade: III
Class: 3–4, AI1 or AI2 (headwall)
Time to summit: 8 hours
Objective hazards: Highly prone to avalanching and exposed to rockfall

This route was pioneered by the legendary Joe Morovitz in 1892, solo, using a rifle butt to hack steps in the ice. It is recommended that modern parties rope up on the glacier and use crampons and ice axes instead of rifles. It is a long route, all things considered, and not particularly popular, but certainly a challenging route for those wanting to get off the beaten track.

Ptarmigan Ridge Trail 682.1 is commonly used to approach routes on the northeast side of Mount Baker. Drive WA 542 (Mount Baker Highway) from Bellingham to its end at Artist Point to reach the trailhead, at the northwest side of the parking area. Follow Chain Lakes Trail 682 about 1 mile to a junction. Take the left fork on Ptarmigan Ridge Trail 683, which leads another 3 miles to the base of Coleman Pinnacle, then another 1 mile to Camp Kiser. The trail is rocky and steep, and can be difficult to follow in poor weather. From Camp Kiser, cross Sholes Glacier and upper Landes Cleaver to reach the Rainbow Glacier, and

Mount Baker–Ptarmigan Ridge Approach

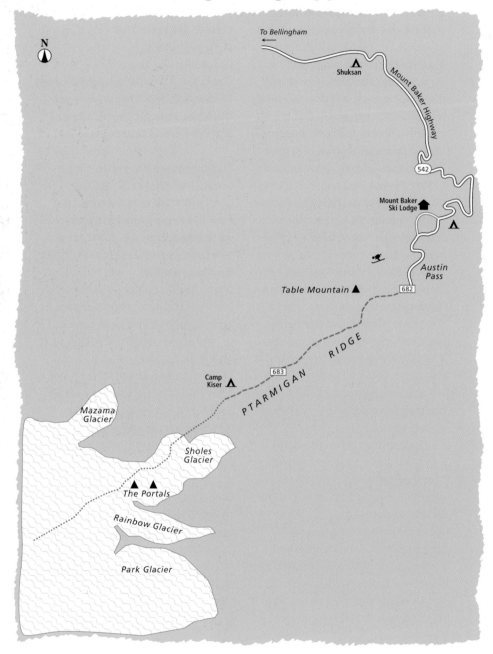

Mount Baker—Park Glacier

Sherman Peak

The Cockscomb

5

6

Park Glacier

Boulder Glacier

continue in the direction of whichever route you are climbing. Start early from Camp Kiser or bivouac higher, as the routes beginning from here are quite long. All approaches involve glacier travel, so rope up as necessary.

It is also possible to approach this route via a traverse of the Coleman and Roosevelt Glaciers from Heliotrope Ridge, which is said to be shorter in distance but involves more crevasse problems. All approaches are long, so get an early start whichever way you come.

From high camp, ascend the Park Glacier to a 40-degree snow/ice slope (or headwall), which is usually passed on the far right flank, close to

the Cockscomb rock formation (with attendant rockfall hazard). Some parties climb directly through the upper headwall. The steep headwall leading directly to Grant Peak has also been climbed. These routes involve difficult-to-protect snow and ice up a 50- to 60-degree slope. Passing the bergschrund can be difficult. Beware of avalanches, and watch for cornices above the headwall. All in all, this is a fairly serious route, particularly if you tackle one of the headwalls. Ice tools and ice screws/pitons are helpful.

Descent: Descend via the route of ascent or the Easton Glacier or Coleman Glacier routes with arranged transportation.

Glacier Peak

PHOTO PAUL HARTL

3.

Glacier Peak

Tucked away within the interior of the Cascade Range of central Washington, Glacier Peak (10,541 feet/3,213 meters) is the most remote of the peaks included in this book. Indeed, no road penetrates within 8 miles of the mountain, many approach hikes are over 10 miles long, and from Puget Sound the peak barely stands out from lesser surrounding mountains. If you didn't know better, you would not guess it was one of Washington's high volcanoes. Nevertheless, Glacier Peak, at 10,541 feet, is one of the Cascade giants, highly visible from nearly all points along the Washington Cascade crest. Local Indians knew the mountain as Dakobed (one translation says Great Parent) and Takomed or Takobud, a generic term meaning White Mountain.

Like Garibaldi, Glacier Peak is a heavily glaciated, significantly eroded dacite volcano. The mountain has a long history of building and explosive eruptions, the last major eruption occurring at least 12,000 years ago. That eruption, though not as violent as the 1980 eruption of Mount St. Helens, did manage to deposit volcanic ash as far away as Alberta and spewed debris over a wide area to

the southeast. There is no evidence of significant eruptions since that time—except for the extrusion of Disappointment Peak, a dacite plug—but hot springs near the base of the peak are a sign that volcanic forces are still at work beneath the mountain. At least one geologist considers Glacier Peak the least likely of the Washington volcanoes to erupt in the future; others are not so certain.

The volume of glacial ice and the composition of Glacier Peak have resulted in very heavy erosion. The summit crater has been worn away to a gentle saddle (Crater Gap) between the Scimitar Glacier on the west and the Chocolate Glacier on the east. Sections of the crater rim still exist in the summit formation and on several craggy points to the north. There is evidence to suggest that the mountain was once a bit higher than its present altitude; however, it is thought that the eruption 12,000 years ago, or earlier eruptions, and not glaciation alone, lowered the elevation of Glacier Peak.

Glacier Peak was first climbed in 1898, long after the first ascents of every other nontechnical Cascade volcano, when Thomas Gerdine, a

U.S. Geological Survey surveyor, and four others, made an ascent to place a survey marker at the summit. Professor I. C. Russel climbed Glacier Peak later that year. In 1906, A. L. Cool and C. E. Rusk climbed what is now known as the Cool Glacier. A Mountaineers club reconnaissance team ascended the Cool–Chocolate Cleaver in 1910. Many of the early ascents were made from the south or southeast, mostly via the Disappointment Peak route.

Because of its remoteness and its unassuming skyline presence when viewed from the lowlands, Glacier Peak is not as popular an ascent as most of the other Cascade volcanoes. It is enjoyable, however, and mostly private except on the popular weekend routes. Glacier Peak is regarded

Glacier Peak–West Side Approaches

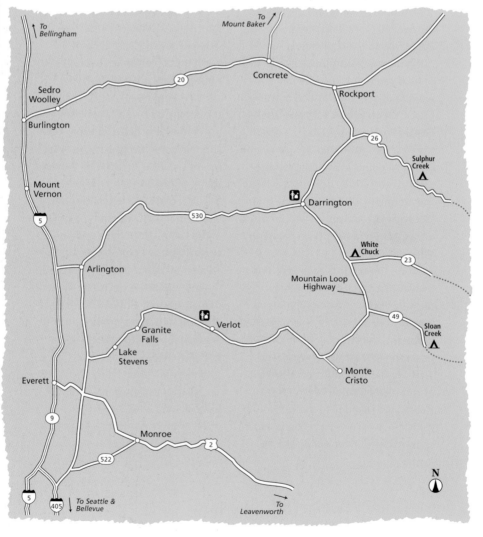

as an easy climb by most, but it has had its share of accidents and fatalities due to falls, crevasses, and poor weather, and should not be taken lightly, especially considering its remoteness. Climbers must be self-sufficient on Glacier Peak, perhaps more so than on some of the other Cascade volcanoes, where rescues are typically more forthcoming.

The mountain is the centerpiece of the Glacier Peak Wilderness, established in 1964 with the passage of the Wilderness Act. Permits are no longer required for overnight visits. Flood-damaged roads and trails have led to longer approach hikes, which has reduced the number of visitors to Glacier Peak. Check current road and trail conditions and access prior to your

Glacier Peak–West Side Trails

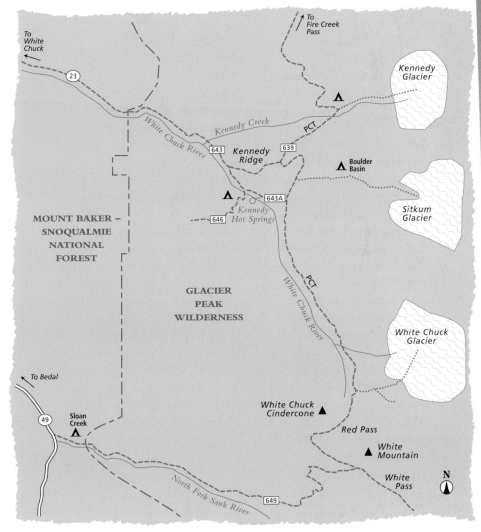

climb. Information may be obtained from Darrington Ranger District, 1405 Emmens St., Darrington, WA 98241, (206) 436-1155; Outdoor Recreation Information Center, Seattle REI Building, 222 Yale Ave. North, Seattle, WA 98109-5429; (206) 470-4060.

White Chuck Trail Approach

The customary approach for west-side routes on Glacier Peak is via White Chuck Trail 643 to Kennedy Hot Springs. This approach was compromised by floods in 2003, 2006, and 2007, and is now a much longer hike than it used to be. As of 2010 repairs are in progress. The route description below is based on planned repairs to the road, extension of the trail following the decommissioned road, and current trail conditions. Check with the Darrington Ranger District office for current road and trail conditions and accessibility.

Drive WA 530 to Darrington and obtain permits at the Darrington Ranger District office (just north of downtown Darrington). Follow Mountain Loop Highway south from Darrington about 9 miles to a bridge crossing the Sauk River. Once across the river, take White Chuck Road (FR 23) east about 5 miles to the new White Chuck Trailhead. Hike the trail about 10 miles to the Kennedy Hot Springs junction, following 5 miles of decommissioned road and another 5 miles of trail.

To approach Sitkum Glacier and Disappointment Peak routes from the Kennedy Hot Springs junction, follow Upper White Chuck Trail 643A, which forks left and switchbacks steeply up the wooded ridge from the hot springs trail junction. In about 2 miles Trail 643A meets the Pacific Crest Trail (PCT). Go left (north) 0.3 mile to reach the climber's trail to Sitkum Glacier; go right (south) about 5 miles to access White Chuck Glacier.

Note: Kennedy Hot Springs was wiped out by floods in October 2003. The old soaking pool is buried under rocks and debris.

1. Sitkum Glacier
Difficulty rating: 1
Grade: II
Class: 2
Time to summit: 4–6 hours
Objective hazards: Moderately prone to avalanching and mild exposure to rockfall

Sitkum Glacier was formerly the most popular route on Glacier Peak, if for no other reason than the fact that it had a relatively short approach drive and hike (by Glacier Peak standards). Unfortunately, flooding has washed out the roads and lengthened the approach hike considerably.

The climber's trail from the PCT is a steep boot path that reaches Boulder Basin, the customary climber's camp in a small basin near the toe of the northern lobe of Sitkum Glacier. Protect your food from hungry marmots here, who have taken a liking to

Glacier Park—Sitkum Glacier

Rabbit Ears

Frostbite
Ridge

Disappointment
Peak

7

2

8

1

Sitkum
Glacier

Scimitar
Glacier

Boulder
Basin

PHOTO **USFS/**JEFF LEISY

climber's food. Some parties prefer to camp higher up, at the toe of the glacier, to get a head start. Some make a round-trip from a base camp at Kennedy Hot Springs, but this makes for a long day of climbing (although climbers have been known to make a one-day round-trip ascent from Seattle, at least prior to all of the flood damage and increased approach hike distance). Boulder Basin is a heavily used base camp and has suffered some adverse impacts, most notably improperly disposed human waste. There is a pit toilet here, but before July it is buried in snow. Parties bivouacking here in early season should be mindful of this problem and take

measures to minimize it, including using blue bags.

From the basin, several routes are possible. In general, continue directly up to the terminus of Sitkum Glacier and then ascend the glacier, staying on the left flank of the lower lobe (the right flank is more heavily crevassed) and avoiding mid-height crevasses, then traverse the upper lobe to a saddle above Sitkum Spire (which has reportedly been climbed despite its rotten appearance). From the saddle the route continues up snow or pumice on the ridge, or just left of the ridge on Scimitar Glacier, to the summit.

Other variations from Boulder Basin are possible, climbing ice and snow gullies or scree ridges farther right. These variations are not often done because they have higher rockfall hazard and take 2 or 3 hours longer than the normal route to the summit and back.

Descent: Descend via the route of ascent.

2. South Ridge—
Disappointment Peak
Difficulty rating: 1
Grade: II
Class: 1
Time to summit: 6–8 hours
Objective hazards: Moderately prone to avalanching and mild expo-sure to rockfall

This was the route of the first ascent of Glacier Peak, and is used by modern parties wanting to avoid significant

glacier travel and the crowds on Sitkum Glacier. It is quite long and remote and not very popular, although it may be the shortest route to the summit (via North Fork Sauk River Trail) depending on the condition of White Chuck Trail. It offers an excellent winter ski ascent and descent route for those so inclined.

The shortest approach is via North Fork Sauk River Trail 649 from Sloan Creek Campground, just off FR 49, about 8.2 miles to White Pass (versus 15 miles one-way from the new White Chuck trailhead). Any way you come, it is a long way in to White Chuck Glacier. Although the route has been climbed car-to-car in a long day, plan on taking at least two to three days via any route.

Traverse the usually (but not always) uncrevassed White Chuck

Glacier Peak—Disappointment Peak

PHOTO BOB BOLTON

Glacier or the gentle ridge crest northeaster to a gap (Glacier Gap), then continue more or less directly north up the crest, via snow or pumice slopes, to the summit of Disappointment Peak (9,755 feet/2,973 meters). From Disappointment Peak, drop down to a saddle and climb a final snow or pumice slope to the summit. In early season, with snow cover, this is pretty easy going, and the route makes a nice ski ascent and descent in winter and spring under good conditions. Later, when the route involves scree hiking, the last 500 feet to the summit are steep, loose, and scary.

An easier alternative, but one requiring roping up for crevasses, is a traverse around Disappointment Peak on the east side, crossing upper Gerdine and Cool Glaciers to reach the saddle.

Descent: Descend via the route of ascent.

Buck Creek Pass Approach

Buck Creek Pass Trail 1513 offers the shortest approach to Glacier Peak from the east side. From Lake Wenatchee, drive west to Chiwawa River Road (FR 62). Drive past Fish Lake and continue north past Phelps Creek Campground to Trinity, about 24 miles from Lake Wenatchee. An abandoned road leads a distance beyond Trinity; the trail begins there. Buck Creek Pass Trail 1513 forks off

Glacier Peak–Buck Creek Pass Approach

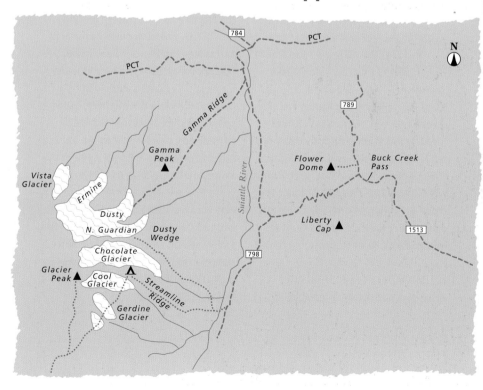

Glacier Peak—East Side

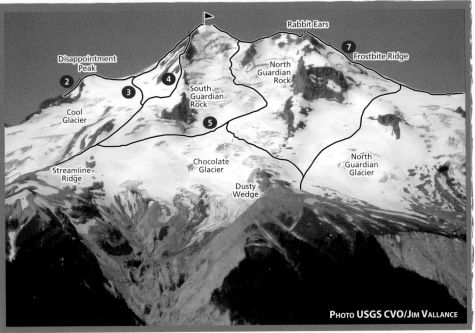

Disappointment Peak

Rabbit Ears

7 Frostbite Ridge

North Guardian Rock

2

4

South Guardian Rock

3

Cool Glacier

5

Chocolate Glacier

North Guardian Glacier

Streamline Ridge

Dusty Wedge

PHOTO **USGS CVO/JIM VALLANCE**

after 1.5 miles. Take the left fork about 8 miles to Buck Creek Pass, with fine views of Glacier Peak. Drop into the Suiattle River drainage via Triad Trail 792 another 3 miles to reach Upper Suiattle River Trail 798 about 3.5 miles from its end. Climbing routes are described from this junction. Unfortunately, there is no bridge crossing the Upper Suiattle River at the Triad Trail junction. Parties coming this way will have to find a logjam or fallen log crossing, if there is one. The crossing can be very difficult, dangerous, or impossible. Climbers, being ingenious fools, usually find a way.

If the Buck Creek or Suiattle River approaches are infeasible, it is possible to approach this route via the North Fork Sauk River Trail and the PCT, by crossing over Glacier Gap and traversing the Gerdine Glacier. The approach from the west is faster for west-side parties, considering all factors including driving time, but is more complex and a waste of time considering you can get to the summit and down via another route in the same amount of time it takes to traverse to the east side of the mountain. Any way you come, expect to take at least all day on your approach, which will invariably involve poorly maintained roads, washed-out bridges, log crossings, and bushwhacking unless the route is snow covered.

3. Cool Glacier
Difficulty rating: 1
Grade: II
Class: 2–3, easy glacier
Time to summit: 6–8 hours
Objective hazards: Moderately prone to avalanching and mildly exposed to rockfall

The Cool Glacier descends south-easter from the Disappointment Peak saddle. It is named for A. L. Cool, who made its first ascent in 1906 with Claude E. Rusk. Rusk originally named this the Chocolate Glacier. The major difficulty of the route is the approach.

Assuming you are approaching from the Triad Trail junction, hike south until just across Chocolate Creek. A hard-to-find way trail leads up Chocolate Creek Basin, from where bushwhacking provides access to Streamline Ridge, the gentle ridge between the termini of the Cool and Chocolate Glaciers. The route is straightforward from Streamline Ridge, ascending Cool Glacier toward the Disappointment Peak saddle as crevasses permit, then snow or pumice slopes to the summit as for the Disappointment Peak route. The ascent to the summit may seem anticlimactic compared to the challenges of the approach hike.

Descent: Parties coming from the west side can descend via the route of ascent, the Disappointment Cleaver, or Sitkum Glacier routes. Those coming from the east should descend the route of ascent.

4. Chocolate–Cool Cleaver
Difficulty rating: 2
Grade: II
Class: 2–3, easy glacier
Time to summit: 5–6 hours
Objective hazards: Moderately prone to avalanching, dangerous to descend during low visibility

This route climbs the cleaver dividing Chocolate and Cool Glaciers. Approach as for the Cool Glacier route to Streamline Ridge or more directly via the Disappointment Cleaver variation traversing Gerdine Glacier to Cool Glacier. Whichever way you approach, ascend from Cool Glacier above South Guardian Rock to gain the cleaver, then ascend the cleaver directly to the summit. No routefinding difficulty here, other than on the approach. In late season, without snow cover, this route is not recommended.

If you use this route as a descent route, be careful to leave the cleaver well above South Guardian Rock, which is very steep on its north and east sides. This is not advised as a descent route during poor visibility, as walking off the edge is a distinct possibility. If you plan to descend the cleaver, wand the exit point from the ridge on the way up so you don't miss it on the way down. Or better, if visibility is an issue, descend to the Disappointment Peak saddle and down the Cool Glacier back to Streamline Ridge.

Descent: Descend via the route of ascent or the Cool Glacier route.

Again, descending the cleaver during poor visibility is not recommended.

5. Chocolate Glacier
Difficulty rating: 2
Grade: II
Class: N/A
Time to summit: 6–8 hours
Objective hazards: Moderately prone to avalanching and mildly exposed to rockfall

The Chocolate Glacier descends east from the crater gap in a broad crevassed flow. Rusk originally called this the Cool Glacier; somehow the names were reversed. The standard and recommended approach to this route is via Streamline Ridge as for Cool Glacier, although it is possible to cross over from White Chuck Glacier. As with other east-side routes on Glacier Peak, the approach will be the most challenging part of the climb.

From Streamline Ridge, traverse the glacier north beneath South Guardian Rock and continue angling toward North Guardian Rock, then cut back and ascend the broad glacier as crevasses allow to the crater gap. Crevasses are abundant, but corridors usually allow reasonable passage until late season.

Descent: Most parties descend via the Chocolate–Cool Cleaver or Cool Glacier routes. Because of the risks associated with descending the cleaver too late or in poor visibility, the Cool Glacier descent is recommended.

Suiattle River Approaches
Approach via Suiattle River Trail 798 and the PCT to Gamma Ridge Trail 791. The Upper Suiattle River is the usual approach for north-side routes on Glacier Peak. About 6 miles north of Darrington on WA 530, just north of where the highway crosses the Sauk River, take Suiattle River Road (FR 26), which leads along the Suiattle River about 25 miles to Sulphur Creek Campground. This road has been washed out several times and as of 2010 was closed at about the 12-mile mark due to flood damage, with repairs pending. Check current road and trail conditions and access prior to using this approach. If the road is open, drive to Sulphur Creek Campground; in another 1 mile is the Suiattle River Trailhead.

6. Gamma Ridge—Dusty Glacier
Difficulty rating: 2
Grade: II
Class: 3
Time to summit: 6–8 hours
Objective hazards: Moderately prone to avalanching and mildly exposed to rockfall

A fine route ascending the Dusty Glacier on the northeast side of Glacier Peak. This route, like others on Glacier Peak, is not as popular as it deserves to be due to approach difficulties.

Hike Suiattle River Trail 784 about 9 miles to a junction with Image Lake/Miner's Ridge Trail 785. You can

Glacier Peak–Suiattle River Approaches

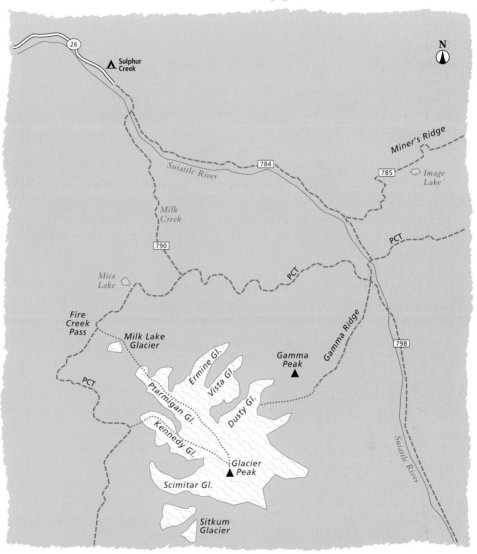

approach other east-side routes (such as Cool and Chocolate Glaciers) by continuing along the Upper Suiattle River Trail 798 an additional 7 miles to the Chocolate Creek junction, rather than approaching from Buck Creek Pass; this approach saves driving time if coming from Puget Sound but is a longer hike, especially if Suiattle River Road is closed to vehicle traffic.

Glacier Peak—Northeast Side

PHOTO PAUL HARTL

To climb the Dusty Glacier route, hike Gamma Ridge Trail 791 to its end and continue cross-country up Gamma Ridge to reach the Dusty Glacier well above its terminus. Traverse and ascend the glacier as crevasses permit to reach Frostbite Ridge, which is followed to the summit. Many variations are possible, depending upon crevasse conditions; all reach Frostbite Ridge eventually.

Descent: Descend via the route of ascent or the Chocolate–Cool Cleaver or Cool Glacier routes.

7. Frostbite Ridge

Difficulty rating: 2
Grade: II
Class: 4
Time to summit: 6–8 hours
Objective hazards: Moderately prone to avalanching and mildly exposed to rockfall

While this route is named Frostbite Ridge, its only difference from many of the preceding routes is how you approach the ridge. Frostbite Ridge is an interesting climb that is deservingly popular albeit infrequently climbed due to approach difficulties.

The usual approach for Frostbite Ridge and Kennedy Glacier begins

Glacier Peak—Northwest Side

Rabbit Ears

Sitkum
Glacier

Dusty
Glacier

Gamma Ermine
Ridge Glacier

Kennedy Scimitar Boulder
Glacier Glacier Basin

Vista
Glacier

Kennedy
Peak

PHOTO PAUL HARTL

via White Chuck Trail 643 as for the Sitkum Glacier route approach. At about 5 miles from the old trailhead (or about 10 miles from the new trailhead), turn up Kennedy Ridge Trail 639 and follow it about 2 miles to the PCT. Continue another 2 miles northeast on the PCT to upper Kennedy Ridge, from where a climber's trail leads to Kennedy Glacier. There are campsites at the trail junction and along the upper ridge and nearer the glacier terminus.

The Frostbite Ridge route has several variations. You can climb Kennedy Glacier partway and traverse to the Ptarmigan Glacier gap; stay high on Kennedy Ridge, skirting around

Kennedy Peak on the north side via Ptarmigan Glacier; or gain Frostbite Ridge directly from Kennedy Glacier via an obvious saddle (shortest, most popular route). Another possibility is to hike the PCT north toward Fire Creek Pass to access Ptarmigan Glacier. Approaching via the PCT from the Suiattle River may be shorter; check with the forest service before committing to an approach route.

Once you reach Frostbite Ridge proper, continue up the ridge crest (or just east), which attains its maximum angle about 20 feet below the Rabbit Ears formation high on the ridge. Pass through the Rabbit Ears and downclimb Class 3–4 rock to a notch.

A short, vertical snow step is usually encountered here. Continue across the crater rim to the summit.

Descent: If you approached via White Chuck, descend via the Sitkum Glacier route. If via Suiattle, descend the route or some variation of it.

8. Kennedy Glacier
Difficulty rating: 2
Grade: II
Class: 3
Time to summit: 6–8 hours
Objective hazards: Moderately prone to avalanching and exposed to rockfall

Another of Glacier Peak's popular routes is Kennedy Glacier, more rugged than Sitkum Glacier but equally accessible and said to be more enjoyable. Approach as for Frostbite Ridge, then climb the Kennedy Glacier as directly as possible. The route is moderately crevassed, but usually very straightforward during good conditions. A variation reported in Cascade Alpine Guide climbs the south arm of the Kennedy Glacier directly to the summit ridge, and appears to be steeper and more challenging than the usual glacier route.

Descent: Descend via the route of ascent or the Sitkum Glacier route.

4.

Mount Rainier

Mount Rainier (14,411 feet/4,392 meters) is arguably the King of the Cascade volcanoes. Certainly the other peaks have their charms, but Rainier stands supreme in the hearts and minds of nearly all who view it from near or afar. It is the highest volcano in the conterminous United States. The mountain was for many years measured at 14,410 feet, but in 1988 a new satellite measurement added just over 1 foot to that height. Either way, Rainier is still the highest. It is visible from more than 100 miles distant from almost any high vantage in south-central Washington and north-central Oregon, but is best known by its profile from Seattle, as depicted on Rainier Beer labels. The uniqueness and grandeur of Mount Rainier and its surrounding peaks and forests was recognized early enough that the area was preserved by the establishment of the present national park on March 2, 1899.

Because of its height, and due to its proximity to the Pacific Ocean (only about 100 miles distant), Mount Rainier truly creates its own weather. Rising high into the thinning atmosphere, Mount Rainier stands directly in the path of prevailing moisture-laden marine winds, which results in some unusual weather that seems unique to the mountain, including lenticular cloud "halos" or "caps" that sometimes settle on the summit of the mountain for several days while the remainder of the sky is clear. This proximity to wet marine air accounts for the high volume of snowfall on Mount Rainier. Indeed, Paradise, on the mountain's southern slope at 5,400 feet, has had world-record snow depths, and Paradise Inn is frequently buried up to its three-story roof (early summer guests commonly enter the inn via a snow tunnel). The weather can be quite unpredictable. "Perfect" days often become cold, windy, and cloudy with little warning. Winter and spring storms frequently deposit several feet of new wet snow on the mountain, and winds can reach extremely high velocity at any time of year.

Mount Rainier's glacier system, consisting of twenty-six major glaciers covering over 35 square miles, is the largest single-mountain glacier system in the United States outside of Alaska (although statistically Mount Baker is reported to have a greater mass of ice within its twelve glaciers).

However, Mount Rainier's mantle of ice belies its fiery origins. Geologists speculate that Mount Rainier volcano once rose to a height of over 16,000 feet. A subsequent violent eruption, possibly similar to that of neighboring Mount St. Helens in 1980, or a caldera collapse as occurred with Mounts Mazama and Tehama, reduced the summit cone, leaving a wide crater that later erupted to form the present cone and two smaller craters that now make up the summit of Mount Rainier.

Mount Rainier has been predominately dormant during recorded history, but it is by no means extinct. The fumaroles that warmed Stevens and Van Trump on their first ascent of the peak in 1870 still spew steam from the summit-crater firn caves. Heat fluctuations within the mountain sometimes cause the melting of glacial ice and the heating of mudlike volcanic rock, producing devastating mudflows. Indeed, mudflows have been singled out by geologists as the greatest volcanic threat to nearby lowland populations. The Osceola Mudflow of about 6,000 years ago buried what are present-day Enumclaw and Puyallup under a thick layer of volcanic concrete. More recently the Nisqually, Kautz, and South Tahoma Glaciers have discharged mudflows and outburst floods. Lahar warning systems are in place on the mountain and down into its lowland river valleys.

More than 4,000 people climb Mount Rainier each year (a record

Crossing a snow bridge on the Emmons Glacier route

7,432 climbers summited in 1999), and almost twice that number attempt the mountain. About 30 percent of these climbers are guided to the top. Most ascents are via the "dog routes" of Disappointment Cleaver and Emmons-Winthrop Glacier. Often after a spell of good weather, climbers can follow deep snow trenches left by dozens of preceding parties like trails, all the way to the summit of Mount Rainier. For those seeking a bit more adventure than this, avoiding Camp Muir and the two routes above is advisable. These routes have dangers and challenges, but are as different from most other routes on Rainier as modern freeways are to country roads.

Because of its prominence and attractiveness to lowlanders, Mount Rainier has been the site of many climbing accidents and fatalities. Mount Rainier is not more dangerous than the other peaks, but because more climbers visit Mount Rainier, the chances of an accident are greater. Each year, it seems, at least a few people are killed on Mount Rainier. For those wishing to learn the details of these accidents, an in-depth accounting of all known fatalities on Mount Rainier is contained in Dee Molenaar's *The Challenge of Rainier.* Read this before you attempt to climb Mount Rainier; you might learn something that could save you from repeating someone else's mistakes.

Many deaths on Mount Rainier can be attributed solely to inexperience and folly. Mount Rainier is no place for unguided, inexperienced climbers. Also, physical conditioning can play a major role in climbing safety. Climbers should be in good physical shape before attempting the climb, as fatigue and sickness can lead to injury or death at high elevations.

Climbers planning to go higher than 10,000 feet or onto any glaciers are required to purchase a Mount Rainier Climbing Pass, which is available in advance by mail or fax, or in person when registering at the Paradise Climbing Information Center, Jackson Visitor Center, White River

Wilderness Information Center, Longmire Wilderness Information Center, or Carbon River Ranger Station, in season. Call or visit the national park website for current fee information. Passes purchased in November and December are valid for the following year. Valid photo ID is required upon registration. Climbers are also required to check out upon completion of their climb or attempt.

Climbing campsite reservations may be made in advance, except at the Camp Muir shelter, which is available on a first-come, first-served basis. There is a campsite reservation fee, in addition to the climbing pass fee. Camping is allowed only on permanent snow or ice, or on bare ground areas previously used as campsites. Clearing new tent sites on rocky or snow-free areas is prohibited.

Solo travel above high camps or anywhere on glaciers is not permitted except with prior written permission from the National Park Service superintendent. A Solo Climb Request Form is available online or by mail.

Anyone younger than eighteen years of age must have written permission of a parent or legal guardian before climbing above normal high camps.

Engaging in any business in park areas except in accordance with the provisions of a permit, contract, or other written agreement is prohibited. Leading or participating in an unauthorized guided climb of Mount Rainier is illegal.

Because of the number of climbers attempting Mount Rainier each year (more than 10,000 annually), refuse and waste disposal is a problem. Please pack out all refuse whether biodegradable or not. Climbers are required to use blue bags for human waste disposal where toilets are not available. Blue bags are available from Climbing Information Centers and Wilderness Information Centers including Paradise, Longmire, White River, and Carbon River, and at high camps including Camp Muir and Camp Schurman. Blue bags should be disposed of in labeled collection barrels at Camp Muir, Camp Schurman, Paradise Comfort Station, White River Campground, Ipsut Campground, and Westside Road. Do not drop used blue bags in trash cans!

A number of guide services lead summit climbs of Mount Rainier. If you want to hire a guide, do so early, as trips fill quickly. For information, contact Alpine Ascents International, (206) 378-1927; International Mountain Guides LLC, (360) 569-2609; or Rainier Mountaineering, Inc., (360) 569-2227.

For further information about climbing Mount Rainier, contact Mount Rainier National Park, 55210 238th Ave. East, Ashford, WA 98304, (360) 569-2211; Mount Rainier Climbing Rangers, (360) 569-6009; www.nps.gov/mora/planyourvisit/climbing.htm; or Mount Rainier Blogspot, http://mountrainierclimbing.blogspot.com.

Mount Rainier National Park

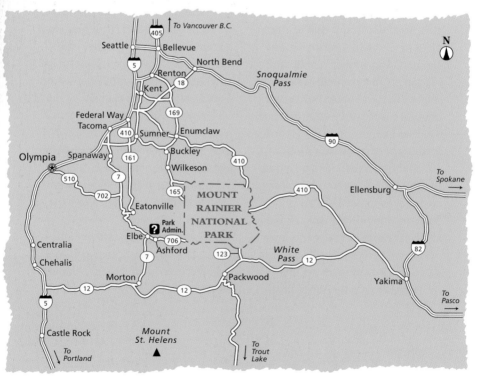

The author gratefully acknowledges the acquiescence of Dee Molenaar in granting permission to use
information from his book, *The Challenge of Rainier,* and the assistance of
the NPS, in preparing this chapter.

Camp Muir Approach

Routes on Mount Rainier's east side
are approached via Camp Muir from
Paradise, including Nisqually Icefall
and Ice Cliff, Gibraltar Ledge, and
the Disappointment Cleaver route.
Camp Muir, elevation 10,080 feet, was
named for John Muir, who, recogniz-
ing the presence of light pumice on

Mount Rainier–South Side

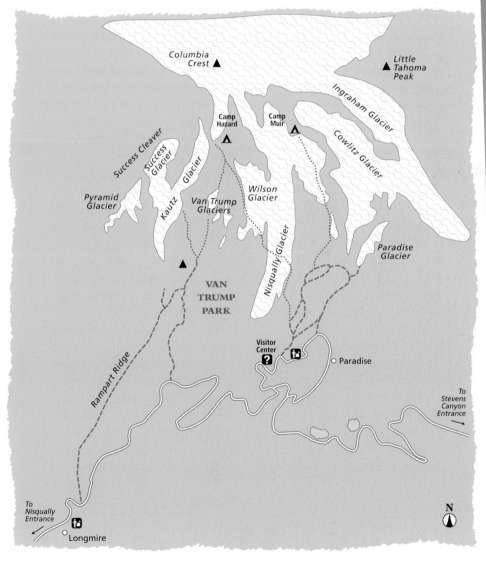

the ground as an indication of shelter from the wind, selected the site during his 1888 ascent of the mountain. An ascent to Camp Muir is a popular day's outing, either as conditioning for a later ascent of Rainier or as a destination in its own right. Camp Muir is typically overcrowded. The NPS permits only one hundred people per night at Camp Muir, and reservations are not accepted for the public shelter, which is available on a first-come, first-in basis. Toilet facilities are in place here—use them!

The ascent to Camp Muir begins from Paradise parking lot via Panorama Point Trail, which is paved part of the way. From the Panorama Point Junction, follow Pebble Creek to trail's end, where a climber's trail continues to Muir Snowfield. Ascend the snowfield toward Moon Rocks, then to the saddle occupied by Camp Muir. Crevasses sometimes lurk here, particularly closer to Nisqually Glacier, so beware! The route is usually easy to follow, particularly on sunny weekends, but during poor weather it is easy to become lost, particularly on the descent. Climbers and especially skiers have become disoriented on the descent from Camp Muir; a few have vanished altogether. Compass bearings during the ascent may save routefinding troubles on the way down. There are also some particularly avalanche-prone slopes between Paradise and Camp Muir, especially on either side of Panorama Point. A "hike"

to Camp Muir has all the hazards of an ascent of many other Cascade volcanoes; pay attention to your route and conditions and you should be fine.

1. Disappointment Cleaver— Ingraham Glacier
Difficulty rating: 2
Grade: III
Class: 2–3
Time to summit: 6–8 hours
Objective hazards: Moderately prone to avalanching and exposed to rockfall and icefall, heavily crevassed

Disappointment Cleaver (also known as the guide route, RMI route, dog route and D.C.) is presently the most frequently traveled route on Mount Rainier. More than half of all annual ascents of Mount Rainier are made by this route, as it is the usual guided route. Non-guided climbers are urged to avoid this route on summer weekends to avoid crowds and alleviate overcrowding at Camp Muir and Ingraham Flats.

The usual route traverses the Cowlitz Glacier laterally from Camp Muir to Cathedral Gap, continuing across a shelf of the Ingraham Glacier to reach Disappointment Cleaver, which is climbed (snow early season, Class 2–3 loose rock later) or skirted on the right (as crevasses permit). From the cleaver's head, continue via Ingraham Glacier to the east crater rim (the "summit" for some parties too tired to cross the crater), then

Mount Rainier—Camp Muir Routes

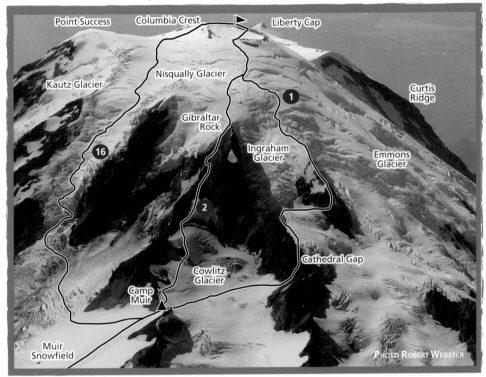

Point Success Columbia Crest Liberty Cap

Kautz Glacier Nisqually Glacier Curtis Ridge

1

Gibraltar Rock

Ingraham Glacier Emmons Glacier

16

2

Cathedral Gap

Cowlitz Glacier

Camp Muir

Muir Snowfield

PHOTO ROBERT WEBSTER

across to Columbia Crest. Unless you are breaking trail up the mountain, simply follow along in everyone else's footsteps. A veritable snow trail sometimes can be followed most of the way to the top.

Although this is sometimes referred to as a "dog route," Disappointment Cleaver is long and committing with some unavoidable objective hazards. This route has icefall hazard below Disappointment Cleaver and rockfall danger on the cleaver. Take care to avoid kicking rocks down on other climbers.

Avalanche danger is often high in early season, on the glaciers and on the cleaver. Falls into crevasses are not uncommon. Accidents and fatalities on this route have occurred due to icefall, rockfall, avalanches, falling into crevasses, slipping on ice while downclimbing and glissading, and getting caught in bad weather. Despite its reputation as an easy walk-up, don't take this or any other route on Rainier lightly, especially in less than favorable conditions.

Descent: Nearly all parties descend via the route of ascent.

A descent of the Fuhrer Finger is another option, offering a faster descent to Paradise, but is more avalanche prone.

2. Gibraltar Ledge
Difficulty rating: 3
Grade: II
Class: 4
Time to summit: 6 hours
Objective hazards: Highly exposed to rockfall and icefall

> This route is not recommended. At its best it presents danger that cannot be avoided by foresight or skill.
>
> —Joseph Hazard, 1911

This route is included as an alternative to Disappointment Cleaver but is not especially popular or recommended. Gibraltar Ledge was the route most often used in early ascents of Mount Rainier, including the first confirmed ascent in 1870, and was very popular until 1936, when a large hunk of the ledge fell away. The route was not climbed again until 1948, and has not quite regained its former popularity. Although some climbers insist that this route is safe ("under the right conditions"), and it is the most direct route to the summit, Gibraltar Ledge is an objectively hazardous route, subject to random rockfall and icefall, and is not highly recommended. Ascend

very early so you can, with luck, avoid being pelted by rocks or large icicles on your descent.

Ascend from Camp Muir to the left edge of Gibraltar Rock's east face. Traverse a wide ledge on the south side until you are forced to rappel or downclimb to a lower shelf, then traverse along the base of the wall to snow/ice gullies that regain the upper portion of the ledge. Continue along the upper ledge to the top of Gibraltar Rock, then up the glaciers more or less directly to the summit crater. Regaining the upper ledge during the descent is usually accomplished with a fixed rope; if one is not already fixed, consider fixing a rope to safeguard your return to Camp Muir.

Descent: Most parties descend via a different route due to increasing rock and icefall risk later in the day. The Disappointment Cleaver route is the usual option.

3. Emmons-Winthrop Glacier
Difficulty rating: 2
Grade: II
Class: 2–3
Time to summit: 6–8 hours
Objective hazards: Moderately prone to avalanching, heavily crevassed

This is presently the second most popular route on Mount Rainier, frequently guided, though it is merely a long glacier trudge under ordinary conditions. The route was possibly ascended in 1855, definitely in 1884.

Mount Rainier–Camp Schurman Approach

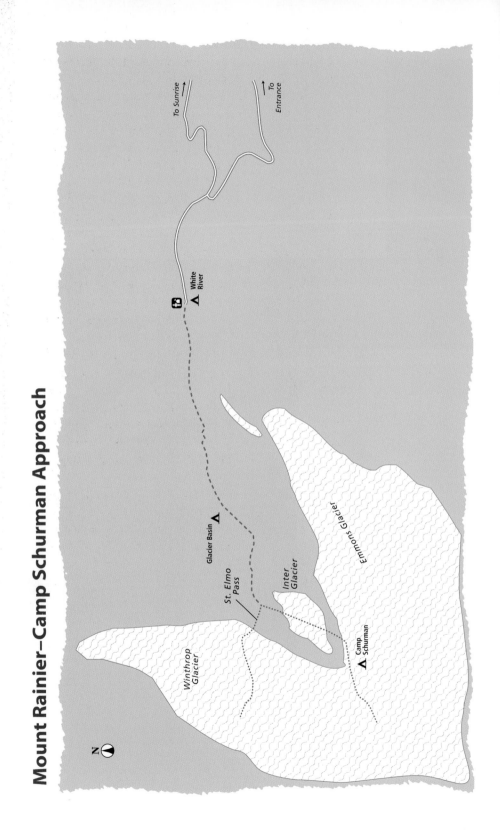

Approach via White River Campground and the Glacier Basin Trail. From trail's end, continue up a climber's path to the terminus of the Inter Glacier. Ascend the glacier (rope up, there are crevasses) obliquely left to the gap between Mount Ruth and Steamboat Prow, the site of formerly popular Camp Curtis. From here, either descend briefly to the Emmons Glacier and ascend the glacier alongside Steamboat Prow to reach Camp Schurman, or continue to the head of Inter Glacier to a point just left of the summit of Steamboat Prow and descend Class 2–3 gullies to Camp Schurman. Camp Schurman sits at 9,440 feet at the head of Steamboat Prow, where it cleaves the Emmons and Winthrop Glaciers. The NPS presently permits only thirty-five climbers per night at Camp Schurman (including Emmons Flats). Camp Schurman has a climber's hut (for emergency use only) equipped with a radio, toilets (use them!), and a number of rock windbreaks and other existing campsites. High winds have stolen more than one tent here. Many climbers prefer to camp about 300 to 500 feet above Camp Schurman on the glacier (Emmons Flats), to get an earlier start and avoid the crowds below.

From Camp Schurman, climb up and slightly left on the Emmons Glacier to enter The Corridor, a usually unbroken pathway between crevasses that ends at about the halfway point to the summit. Continue up the glacier as crevasses permit. The final obstacle, the bergschrund, may usually be passed on either end. In late season this may require considerable traversing.

There are few extraordinary dangers on this route, besides those normally encountered on long glacier climbs. Accidents and fatalities on this route have resulted from slips and falls on ice while descending or glissading, falls into crevasses, avalanches, and weather. The majority of fatalities have involved climbers dragged down the glacier or into crevasses by rope mates. Fatigue-induced error is the usual culprit here, as on many other long volcano climbs.

Descent: Descend via the route of ascent, which is the standard descent for Liberty Ridge and other north-side routes approached from White River.

Mount Rainier–Carbon Glacier & Ptarmigan Ridge Approaches

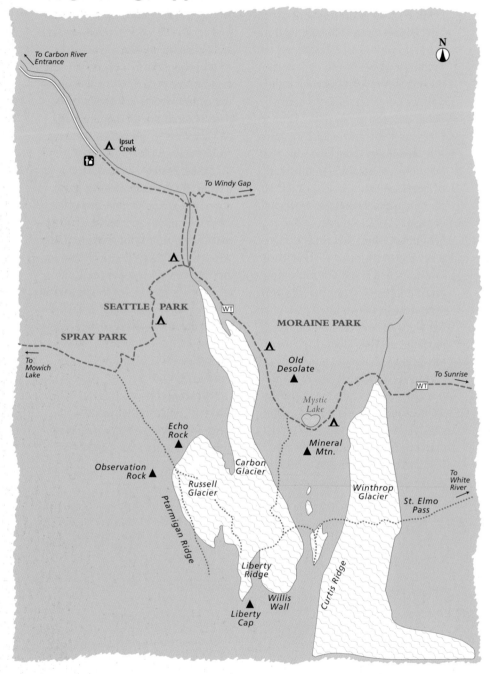

N

To Carbon River Entrance

Ipsut Creek

To Windy Gap

SEATTLE PARK

SPRAY PARK

To Mowich Lake

WT

MORAINE PARK

Old Desolate

To Sunrise

WT

Mystic Lake

Echo Rock

Carbon Glacier

Mineral Mtn.

Observation Rock

Russell Glacier

Winthrop Glacier

To White River

St. Elmo Pass

Ptarmigan Ridge

Curtis Ridge

Liberty Ridge

Willis Wall

Liberty Cap

4. Liberty Ridge
Difficulty rating: 3
Grade: IV
Class: 3–5 depending on route taken, AI2–3
Time to summit: 10–12 hours
Objective hazards: Highly prone to avalanching and exposed to rockfall and icefall

Liberty Ridge is the most popular north face route on Mount Rainier. In fact, it is the only north face route on Mount Rainier that is at all recommended. Other north face routes—particularly those on the menacing 4,000-foot-high Willis Wall—consist of steep, loose rock overshadowed by 300-foot-high ice cliffs that regularly cut loose huge ice avalanches, scouring the face clean. While several ascents of the north faces of Mount Rainier have been made without reported incident, this can only be attributed to the speed and skill of the climbing parties as much as dumb luck. Liberty Ridge is the exception. It is a narrow ridge that cleaves the north face in two, providing a relatively safe haven from the rockfall and icefall that threaten Willis Wall and Liberty Wall to either side. The route is included in *Fifty Classic Climbs of North America,* which has significantly added to its popularity. First ascended by Jim Borrow, Arnie Campbell,

Climbers approaching Liberty Ridge on Mount Rainier. PHOTO LICENSED BY SHUTTERSTOCK.COM

Mount Rainier—Liberty Ridge

Liberty Cap

Liberty Cap Glacier

Willis Wall

Thumb
Rock

4

Carbon Glacier

and Ome Daiber in 1935, it was not repeated for twenty years. It is now a trade route, regularly receiving dozens of ascents each year, mostly without incident, although it is a serious route demanding respect even under the best conditions.

The usual approach is via St. Elmo Pass, then across Curtis Ridge and the Carbon Glacier to the toe of Liberty Ridge. St. Elmo Pass is the saddle dividing The Wedge from Burroughs Mountain. Approach via White River Campground and the Glacier Basin Trail. From trail's end, scramble over St. Elmo Pass and cross the Winthrop Glacier. In late season, this may not be feasible due to rockfall debris on the glacier. In early season, snow cover prevents problems of this sort. Continue across Curtis Ridge onto the Carbon Glacier and traverse to the base of Liberty Ridge. It is possible that ice avalanches coming down Willis Wall could wipe out a party crossing the glacier, but the climbing route is far enough down that this hasn't happened yet.

Some parties approach Liberty Ridge via Moraine Park, although this is a bit longer than crossing St. Elmo Pass. To approach via Moraine Park, begin from Ipsut Creek Campground and hike the Wonderland Trail into Moraine Park. From just below the saddle, where the trail drops to Mystic Lake, continue cross-country through Moraine Park to a bivouac site above the upper Carbon Glacier at about 8,000 feet (some stone windbreaks here—don't build any more!). From here the glacier is easily accessible. A bergschrund may form after August, which prevents easy access to Liberty Ridge.

From the toe of the ridge, ascend snow/ice slopes right of the ridge crest, crossing over rock steps in places, or approximately along the ridge crest but sometimes crossing over depending on route conditions, to Thumb Rock at about 11,000 feet (usual campsite; keep it sanitary, please). Alternate approaches climb snow/ice slopes right (west) of the ridge proper during stable snow conditions. Continue rightward up an ice gully or farther right via open ice slopes to the top of the final rocks (Black Pyramid) and the Liberty Cap Glacier. Continue to Liberty Cap. The most difficult portion of the route often is passing the bergschrund at about 13,000 feet, which can vary each year from steep snow to one or two pitches of steep ice. Ice tools and ice screws are recommended; belaying may be required during icy conditions.

Liberty Ridge is best done in early season, before crevasses on Carbon Glacier become difficult and while much of the loose rock is snow and ice covered. The route is long and more serious than many parties anticipate. Perhaps due to its "classic" status, it has lured many an unsuspecting climber to his demise. This route has rockfall danger and serious avalanche conditions after fresh snowfall. Early-season ascents during cold weather may offer the best snow and ice conditions; late-season ascents involve more loose rock and rockfall exposure.

Descent: Some parties have descended Liberty Ridge, but most prefer descending via the less exposed Emmons-Winthrop Glacier route, or even over the top down Disappointment Cleaver or Fuhrer Finger to Paradise.

5. Ptarmigan Ridge
Difficulty rating: 4
Grade: IV
Class: 3–5 depending on route taken, AI2
Time to summit: 10–12 hours
Objective hazards: Highly prone to avalanching and exposed to rockfall and icefall

Ptarmigan Ridge is a lesser classic route compared with Liberty Ridge, but still a classic! It was first ascended by Wolf Bauer and Jack Hossack in 1935, a few weeks before Liberty Ridge was first climbed. Considering all factors including alpine nature, continuity of line, commitment, and difficulty, it is one of the most distinctive routes up Mount Rainier.

Parties climbing Ptarmigan Ridge almost always use the Spray Park approach. From Mowich Lake, hike to Spray Park either via the Wonderland Trail connector or the shorter cross-country route over Knapsack Pass.

Hike the Wonderland Trail up through Spray Park, leaving the trail at its highest point, and follow a climber's trail and snow slopes to the toe of the Flett Glacier (campsites here), then ascend to the col between Echo Rock and Observation Rock to reach the Russell Glacier. Continue on Russell Glacier just below (east of) the crest of Ptarmigan Ridge and around the left side of Point 10,310 to a bivouac site at the notch just beyond the high point. Russell Glacier is crevassed; roping up is advised.

The original ascent climbed ice slopes and ledges more or less directly above the bivouac site, with attendant rockfall hazard and difficult (for 1935) ice climbing. The second ascent party found an easier way. From camp, drop west onto the North Mowich Glacier and traverse beneath the rock buttress to a prominent snow/ice corridor leading left between the rock bands (rockfall hazard) back toward the ridge proper. Ascend continuous snow and ice slopes to a prominent rock buttress that forces the route either left or right. Stay left, ascending Liberty Cap Glacier as crevasses permit to Liberty Cap. There are several pitches of steep ice and some rock scrambling. Belaying the steepest sections is advised. Bring ice tools, ice screws, and rock protection.

A route variation goes right at the rock buttress onto upper Mowich Face and finishes via the

North Mowich Glacier Icefall route through the rock band. A later variation traversed under the Liberty Cap Glacier ice cliff. While more direct, this variation is much more objectively dangerous. Another variation passes the imposing ice cliff directly, via a fracture on the right side. When the cliff is "in shape," two or three pitches of steep (70 degrees) ice are the norm. Most climbers will wisely avoid it.

This route is quite committing and difficult in places. It is exposed to rockfall and should not be attempted except during periods when loose rock is likely held in place by solid snow and ice. The ice cliff variations have that additional hazard.

Descent: Descents are usually made via another route, usually Emmons-Winthrop Glacier, or by carrying over the top to Paradise via the Disappointment Cleaver or Fuhrer Finger routes.

MOWICH FACE

Mowich Face is the steep wall on the northwest flank of Mount Rainier, between Ptarmigan and Sunset Ridges, narrowing at a shoulder of Liberty Cap at about 13,600 feet. The face is consistently steep (about 40 to 50 degrees) and, like Willis Wall, has hanging ice cliffs and a propensity for rockfall, though not in the same degree as its north face counterpart.

Routes on Mowich Face are commonly approached via Klapatche Park to St. Andrews Lake, where a climber's trail leads up Puyallup Cleaver to where one can traverse the Puyallup and South Mowich Glaciers to reach the base of the wall. Some parties have approached via Colonnade Ridge from Sunset Park; however, this is longer than most modern climbers care to walk on the approach. One could also approach via Ptarmigan Ridge, descending the North Mowich Glacier to the base of Mowich Face. Bivouacs are customarily made on one of the several rock ridges and nunataks (rock islands surrounded by glacial ice) immediately below the face. Descents are usually made via the Tahoma Glacier route or Sickle variation after a summit stop atop Liberty Cap. Those who continue to Columbia Crest more often descend to Camp Muir or via Fuhrer Finger to Paradise.

All routes on the Mowich Face should only be attempted during periods of snow and rock stability. The period between mid-June and mid-July is the best time to attempt the ascent. Hanging ice and loose rock contribute to this face's difficulty and danger. Mowich Face is not considered as dangerous as Willis Wall, but if conditions aren't right, it can be just as perilous.

Bring ice screws and helmets for all routes on Mowich Face, and pitons for those with rock pitches. Retreat from high on the face would be difficult, so come prepared.

Mount Rainier—Mowich Face

Liberty Cap

Liberty Ridge

Ptarmigan Ridge

Liberty Cap Glacier

Willis Wall

Point 10,310

North Mowich Glacier

Mowich Face

Sunset Ridge

10

5

6

7

8

9

Edmunds Glacier

PHOTO TODD STAHLECKER

6. North Mowich Glacier Icefall
Difficulty rating: 4
Grade: IV
Class: 5.7 or A1 reported, AI2–3
Time to summit: 10–12 hours
Objective hazards: Highly prone to avalanching and exposed to rockfall and icefall, difficult rock climbing on loose rock to exit face

This is the left (northern) route up Mowich Face. It skirts the leftmost headwall by climbing on or beside a steep icefall.

From a nunatak between the North Mowich and Edmunds Glaciers, attain the headwall and icefall. Several mid-face rock bands are passed

as far left as possible, or over the icefall as some parties have done, to where consistently steep snow and ice leads to the final cliff. Passing the cliff gives access to upper Ptarmigan Ridge. Over time the final rock band has become a very formidable cliff. It is doubtful that an easy or safe route can be found to overcome this obstacle as it presently exists. A direct finish variation has been climbed, which passes the rock band farther right (loose 5.7 or aid reported), then skirts below an ice cliff. Bring a selection of rock protection in addition to ice tools and ice screws.

If you are unable to pass the final rock band, a retreat can possibly be made down and left, joining Ptarmigan Ridge. Traversing right to finish as for the Headwall or Central Routes is another possibility, but with substantial risk of rock and icefall. Be prepared to bivouac.

Descent: Most parties descend via another route, usually Emmons-Winthrop Glacier or Disappointment Cleaver, although the Tahoma Glacier route is an option if you don't have arranged transportation.

7. North Mowich Glacier Headwall
Difficulty rating: 4
Grade: IV
Class: 4–5, AI2
Time to summit: 10–12 hours
Objective hazards: Highly prone to avalanching and exposed to rockfall and icefall

This route climbs the left flank of Mowich Face, right of the icefall. From the rock island between the North Mowich and Edmunds Glaciers, ascend to the head of the North Mowich Glacier. Continue directly up the headwall, passing several rock bands, then up steep snow and ice slopes to the final cliffs. The original party traversed right, around the summit cliffs to the upper shoulder of Liberty Cap. A direct finish has been done, climbing straight up and traversing under the ice cliff to reach the shoulder of Liberty Cap. Be prepared to bivouac.

Descent: Most parties descend via another route, usually

Emmons-Winthrop Glacier or Disappointment Cleaver, although the Tahoma Glacier route is an option if you don't have arranged transportation.

8. Mowich Face Central Route
Difficulty rating: 4
Grade: III
Class: 3–4, AI2
Time to summit: 8–10 hours
Objective hazards: Highly prone to avalanching and exposed to rockfall and icefall

This route climbs the central portion of Mowich Face. The route passes several mid-face rock bands, then traverses beneath higher rock bands, which are passed via one of several possible routes. In late season, if a direct route is impassable or dangerous, outflanking the final rock bands is a possible but time-consuming alternative.

9. Edmunds Glacier Headwall
Difficulty rating: 3
Grade: III
Class: 3–4, AI2
Time to summit: 8–10 hours
Objective hazards: Highly prone to avalanching and exposed to icefall

This was the route of the first ascent of Mowich Face, and is the most direct. Ascend snow and ice slopes directly from the head of Edmunds Glacier to join Sunset Ridge. The route is mostly protected from rockfall, but has avalanche and icefall danger in places.

Descent: Most parties descend via another route, usually Emmons-Winthrop Glacier or Disappointment Cleaver, although the Tahoma Glacier or Sunset Ridge routes are options if you don't have arranged transportation.

10. Sunset Ridge
Difficulty rating: 3
Grade: III
Class: 3
Time to summit: 10–12 hours
Objective hazards: Moderately prone to avalanching and exposed to rockfall

This prominent ridge flanks Mowich Face on the right. The route is long, and will take most parties a full day from high camp, but it will almost certainly not be crowded.

From the head of Colonnade Ridge, traverse the South Mowich Glacier to the cleaver separating South Mowich and Edmunds Glaciers. The primary route ascends left of the actual ridge crest via prominent snow/ice slopes and snow gullies (rockfall hazard) to reach the ridge proper. A popular rest stop is atop a rotten rock formation jutting west at about 11,800 feet. Traverse on rotten rock along the crest, or via snow/ice slopes below the crest (faster when snow conditions are good but more exposed), to reach the upper slopes. Continue to Liberty Cap or Columbia Crest.

Descent: Descend via the route of ascent or the Tahoma Glacier or Sickle routes. Some parties carry over the top to Paradise via Disappointment Cleaver or Fuhrer Finger.

11. Tahoma Glacier
Difficulty rating: 2
Grade: II
Class: 3
Time to summit: 8–10 hours
Objective hazards: Highly prone to avalanching and exposed to rockfall and icefall, heavily crevassed

One of the six glaciers descending from Mount Rainier's summit plateau, the Tahoma Glacier flows through a narrow gap between Sunset Amphitheater and Tahoma Cleaver on the mountain's west side. This is the most popular west-side route, as it is the least technically demanding and most direct.

Approach via Westside Road and Klapatche Park Trail. Drive up Westside Road as far as permitted (road has been closed due to flood damage for several years and may never reopen), then hike or mountain bike (if permitted) up the road to the South Puyallup River. Hike in 1 mile to the Wonderland Trail and 3 miles to St. Andrews Lake to meet the climber's trail leading up Puyallup Cleaver past Tokaloo Spire. Continue up the cleaver and avoid an impassable rock buttress on the left via the Puyallup Glacier. Regain the cleaver at a saddle near 9,000 feet,

Mount Rainier—Tahoma Glacier

PHOTO LICENSED BY SHUTTERSTOCK.COM

which is the customary bivouac site with a few stone wind shelters.

Puyallup Cleaver is suffering from overuse by climbing and cross-country hiking parties. Smaller parties are recommended in order to lessen impact here. Use established campsites only, or camp on snow or ice.

From the bivouac, continue up the Puyallup Glacier left of the cleaver's crest to where the cleaver fades and the slope drops off steeply toward the Tahoma Glacier. Traverse to the central portion of the narrowing glacier and ascend more or less directly to the summit plateau. Note that ice cliffs forming on the upper right side of the Tahoma Glacier, where it flows from the summit ice cap, pose an increasing threat of icefall here. Venturing too close to Tahoma Cleaver will subject you to rockfall.

Descent: Most parties descend via the route of ascent. The Sickle, on the glacier's left side, is commonly used as a descent route in early season. The Sickle descent continues directly over crumbly St. Andrews Rocks, but sometimes around the north side when crevasses permit. Alternatively, carry over the top to Paradise via Disappointment Cleaver or Fuhrer Finger.

12. Success Cleaver
Difficulty rating: 3
Grade: III
Class: 3–4
Time to summit: 10–12 hours
Objective hazards: Loose, mixed rock/snow scrambling with attendant rockfall exposure

Success Cleaver is the long ridge descending from Point Success on the mountain's southwest side. This is the only route up Mount Rainier that involves no glacier travel (as far as Point Success at least), but it has loose rock and is a very long climb. Its name is no guarantee of success.

The usual approach is via Success Divide. Approach either from Long-mire or Tahoma Creek Trail to Indian Henry's Hunting Ground. Hike to Mirror Lakes, then skirt Pyramid Peak on its left side to reach Success Divide. Comfortable bivouac sites are found at several places along the divide.

From there, traverse around the left side of Pyramid Peak onto lower Success Cleaver. Ascend cinder slopes on the cleaver's crest until forced down and right onto the Success Glacier headwall. Continue up snow or ice slopes leading between rock bands to about where the cleaver merges with Kautz Cleaver and continue to Point Success. Alternatively, some parties have traversed left across the upper South Tahoma headwall to gain the summit plateau, rather than climbing through the rock bands leading to Kautz Cleaver (not recommended in late season). In late season this route becomes very tedious, with loose rock and some snow/ice problems.

Descent: Descents are most often via another route, such as Kautz Glacier, although it is possible to descend the cleaver.

13. Kautz Glacier Headwall
Difficulty rating: 3
Grade: III
Class: 3–4, AI2
Time to summit: 8–10 hours
Objective hazards: Highly prone to avalanching and exposed to rockfall

This increasingly popular route climbs the steep headwall above the lower portion of the Kautz Glacier, immediately right of the Kautz Cleaver.

Approach via Van Trump Park Trail and the Van Trump Glaciers, although a longer approach may be used along the ridge crest above Mildred Point. Ascend the Wapowety Cleaver to about 10,000 feet instead of crossing onto the glacier earlier. Alternatively, approach via Kautz Glacier and descend from Camp Hazard. Most parties bivouac on the Kautz Cleaver (several good sites) and cross the Kautz Glacier on the morning of their ascent. Stay on snow as much as possible to minimize your impact in this sensitive area. Do not construct new campsites on bare ground.

Mount Rainier—Kautz Glacier

Columbia Crest

Point Success Kautz
Headwall

Kautz
Glacier

Gibraltar
Rock
1

2

Disappointment
Cleaver

Cathedral
Gap

12

16

Camp
Muir

Success
Cleaver

Kautz
Cleaver

The
Turtle

Nisqually
Glacier

Muir
Snowfield

Wapowety
Cleaver

13

Wilson
Glacier

Success
Cleaver

14

15

PHOTO ROBERT WEBSTER

However you approach, traverse the glacier and ascend the snow finger up the headwall to where rock bands must be passed (or avoided) to reach Point Success. There are no special difficulties on this route when there is sufficient firm snow to allow climbers to pass the rock bands. It is a steep climb, prone to avalanching at times, and has occasional rockfall, but is said to be very enjoyable by those who have climbed it during optimal conditions.

Descend: Most parties descend via the Kautz Glacier route. Alternatively, carry over the top to Paradise via Fuhrer Finger or Disappointment Cleaver.

14. Kautz Glacier
Difficulty rating: 3
Grade: III
Class: 2, AI2
Time to summit: 6–8 hours
Objective hazards: Moderately prone to avalanching and exposed to icefall

This route was the approximate line attempted by August V. Kautz in 1857. Kautz and party are credited with ascending up to nearly 13,000 feet. The route was frequently used by guided parties after the collapse of Gibraltar Ledge in 1936, until the Disappointment Cleaver route gained popularity.

From Paradise, ascend Skyline Trail to Glacier Vista and descend to the Nisqually Glacier. Cross the glacier as crevasses allow to gain a prominent gully dividing cliffs on the other side. Ascend this gully to the left edge of the Wilson Glacier. Continue up and left along the glacier's edge, ascending snowfields (several possibilities) on the east side of Wapowety Cleaver to Camp Hazard. The camp is merely a flat spot on the ridge, a relatively safe haven from ice avalanches. It is named for early explorer and writer Joseph Hazard, and not because it is in a precarious position, although it has steep slopes on all sides. It is possible to reach Camp Hazard from Van Trump Park, but this involves more distance and elevation gain than the approach from Paradise and is not as popular. Camp Hazard has had sanitation problems. Do your part to minimize impacts in this area.

From Camp Hazard, descend slightly onto the Kautz Glacier, skirt the ice cliff area, and climb a steep ice chute connecting the lower and upper Kautz Glacier. The route under the ice cliff is not usually unsafe, but move fast anyway. Ice screws are recommended for the chute, which can be tricky, especially on the way down. Continue as conditions permit to the summit plateau. A large crevasse above 12,000 feet may require skirting onto the west side after July.

Depending upon conditions, it may be possible to climb over the ice cliff and rappel over the cliff on the descent. However, be on guard against falling ice. This option may save time, but it is more risky. The ice cliff was easily climbed in the early 1940s, but has increasingly become a very imposing wall.

Descent: Descend via the route of ascent. Alternatively, carry over the top to Paradise via Disappointment Cleaver or Fuhrer Finger.

15. Fuhrer Finger
Difficulty rating: 2
Grade: II
Class: N/A
Time to summit: 4–6 hours
Objective hazards: Highly prone to avalanching and exposed to rockfall

This is considered the fastest route to the summit of Mount Rainier, and has been climbed in a one-day round-trip from Paradise several times. It was first climbed by guides Hans and Heinie Fuhrer, with Joseph Hazard and others, in 1920. In August 1934 park ranger Bill Butler made a round-trip from Paradise to the summit in 11 hours, 20 minutes (a time that has since been beaten by several others. Although time records are not officially kept and are frowned upon by park officials, the current "record" is under 5 hours for a round-trip car-to-car ascent).

Ascend from Paradise across the Nisqually Glacier and to the left side of the Wilson Glacier, or ascend the

Mount Rainier—South Side

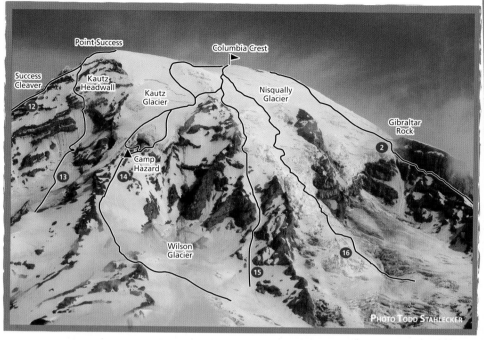

Point Success

Columbia Crest

Success Cleaver

Kautz Headwall

Kautz Glacier

Nisqually Glacier

Gibraltar Rock

12

2

Camp Hazard

13

14

Wilson Glacier

16

15

PHOTO TODD STAHLECKER

Nisqually Glacier to where you can traverse directly across to the base of the finger (less avalanche-prone approach for early season). Continue into the obvious snow finger on the right side of the upper Wilson Glacier and up to the upper Nisqually Glacier. From the top of the finger, ascend along the upper left margin of the Nisqually Glacier, or directly if feasible.

Beware of killer avalanches down the chute, especially in late spring. Rockfall is likely, and after August the Fuhrer Finger becomes unsafe.

Descent: Descend via the route of ascent or the Disappointment Cleaver or Kautz Glacier routes.

Glissading down the chute is popular, but not recommended for safety reasons.

16. Nisqually Glacier Icefall
Difficulty rating: 3
Grade: III
Class: AI2–3
Time to summit: 8–10 hours
Objective hazards: Highly exposed to rockfall and icefall

This route ascends the steep and heavily fractured Nisqually Glacier as it is squeezed down from the summit ice plateau in a narrow icefall. It is a challenging route, with steep snow and ice climbing over and around crevasses and seracs.

Traverse down and left (southwest) from Camp Muir to the center of the Nisqually Glacier and ascend the icefall as directly as is feasible. The exact route will depend on serac and crevasse conditions. This route has significant icefall and rockfall danger, particularly while passing below the ice cliff and Gibraltar Chute, and while below the icefall. Several large rockfalls occurred here in 2011, and the cleavers on either side of the icefall are seriously unstable and prone to further wasting. Nevertheless, this route remains popular, no doubt because of its menacing nature and easy accessibility. Be prepared for anything, including belayed ice climbing up seracs and ice cliffs. Ice tools, ice screws, and helmets are recommended.

Descent: Descend via the Disappointment Cleaver or Fuhrer Finger routes.

LITTLE TAHOMA PEAK

Little Tahoma Peak is a craggy remnant of the once higher Mount

Little Tahoma Peak.
PHOTO ROBERT WEBSTER

Little Tahoma Peak–Approaches

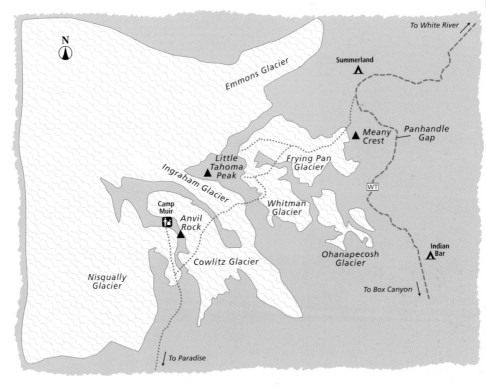

Rainier/Tahoma volcano. It is largely unstable and is being undercut by glaciers on both sides, particularly by the Emmons Glacier. In 1963 a massive rockfall occurred on the peak's northwest face, scattering debris on the glacier below and obliterating the only route climbed on that face so far.

Although a mere satellite peak of Mount Rainier, Little Tahoma, at 11,138 feet/3,395 meters, stands taller than most of the summits in the Cascade Range. It is a popular ascent, mostly because of its elevation, and offers a challenge for climbers of all abilities, even though the standard route is "only Class 2." Little Tahoma is not recommended for inexperienced climbers or scramblers because it requires glacier travel and has very loose rock, especially on the summit formation, which is so loose that most balk at climbing the last few feet to the top. The slopes of the Fryingpan and Whitman Glaciers are popular with telemark skiers.

Little Tahoma Peak and Mount Rainier

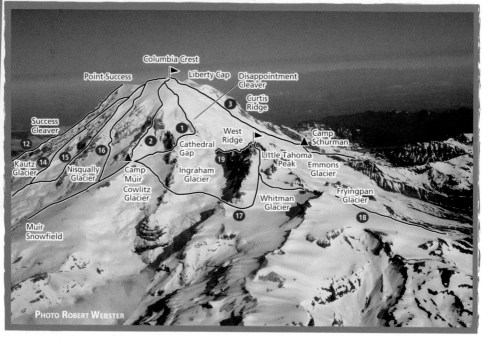

Columbia Crest
Point Success
Liberty Cap
Disappointment Cleaver
Curtis Ridge
3
Success Cleaver
1
West Ridge
Camp Schurman
12
2
Cathedral Gap
Little Tahoma Peak
Emmons Glacier
Kautz Glacier
14
15
16
19
Nisqually Glacier
Camp Muir
Ingraham Glacier
Fryingpan Glacier
Cowlitz Glacier
Whitman Glacier
17
18
Muir Snowfield

PHOTO ROBERT WEBSTER

A climbing permit is required for ascents of Little Tahoma Peak. Roping up on the glaciers is strongly advised.

17. Whitman Glacier
Difficulty rating: 2
Grade: II
Class: 3–4
Time to summit: 6 hours
Objective hazards: Moderately prone to avalanching and exposed to rockfall, extremely loose rock on summit pinnacle

This was the route of the first ascent of Little Tahoma, made by J. B. Flett and H. H. Garrison in 1895. The route may be approached by either of two variations. This variation begins from Camp Muir, traverses the Cowlitz Glacier to a divide below Cathedral Gap, and continues across the Ingraham Glacier to the Whitman Glacier via a broad gap in the east ridge of Little Tahoma. Ascend Whitman Glacier to its head, then climb snow or loose rock to a short traverse left across a divide to a gully leading to a notch. The summit is reached by a final short traverse and scramble. The last few feet to the summit are very loose and frighteningly exposed, and although not technically difficult, most climbers

Little Tahoma Peak Fryingpan Glacier

Gibraltar Rock

Ingraham Glacier

Disappointment Cleaver

North Face

Ingraham Flats

West Ridge

Emmons Glacier

K's Spire

18

Fryingpan Glacier

PHOTO TODD STAHLECKER

forgo the actual summit out of fear for their lives.

Descent: Descend via the route of ascent.

18. Fryingpan Glacier
Difficulty rating: 2
Grade: II
Class: 3–4
Time to summit: 6 hours
Objective hazards: Moderately prone to avalanching and exposed to rockfall, extremely loose rock on summit pinnacle

Most parties climbing Little Tahoma Peak approach from Summerland via the Wonderland Trail, continuing to Meany Crest and crossing the Fryingpan Glacier to a notch in Whitman Crest. From the notch, the route descends onto the Whitman Glacier and joins the route coming from Camp Muir.

Descent: Descend via the route of ascent.

19. West Ridge
Difficulty rating: 5
Grade: V
Class: 5.7, WI5+ reported
Time to summit: 10–12 hours
Objective hazards: Extremely loose rock and unreliable ice, exposed to rockfall and icefall

The spiny west ridge of Little Tahoma was for many years considered the last unclimbed natural line on Mount Rainier. Early attempts were thwarted by unstable, difficult rock. The first ascent was made during full winter conditions to avoid the worst of the loose rock, climbing frozen snow and water ice to pass the rotten rock, but still encountered difficult rock sections and rockfall. This route is similar in character to Yocum Ridge on Mount Hood, but more technically difficult.

The route is most easily approached via Cathedral Gap from Camp Muir. Ascend the ridge as conditions dictate. The route does not stay on the crest, but traverses around a majority of the gendarmes. It may involve technical rock climbing (up to 5.7 reported) and water ice climbing (up to WI6). Expect loose rock and poorly protected ice, with rockfall and icefall.

Descent: Descend via whichever of the other easier routes leads you back to your car. No one has descended the West Ridge so far; perhaps try it on a snowboard?

5.

Mount Adams

The third highest of the Cascade volcanoes, Mount Adams (12,276 feet/3,742 meters) rises above the rounded foothills of the eastern Cascade Range, much farther east than its neighboring volcanoes (which is probably why it's known as "Washington's forgotten volcano"). Adams is the second-largest volcano of the Cascade Range, about one-third larger than Mount Rainier. It is not a precipitous peak, but a broad dacite dome.

The mountain was observed by Lewis and Clark's expedition in 1805 and was mistaken for St. Helens. Later explorers and cartographers frequently confused the two mountains. In 1839 the mountain was officially named for President John Adams as part of Hall Kelley's "President's Range" scheme to rename all the volcanoes down the coast after U.S. presidents. The plan had limited success, as Adams apparently was the only peak named under this scheme, and this by a cartographer's error. Although botanist David Douglas was said to have climbed the mountain shortly after his arrival in the region in 1825, the first ascent of Mount Adams is credited to an 1854 party, including A. G. Aiken, E. J. Allen, Andrew Birge,

and B. F. Shaw. For a time there was a manned lookout cabin atop Mount Adams, which was built with the help of horse and mule pack trains. The remains of the lookout still stand, supported by a mass of old snow inside the frame. For a brief time a sulphur mine operated at the summit, but soon proved to be unprofitable.

Mount Adams is not typical of the Cascade volcanoes. It lacks the symmetry of Hood and Shasta and the abruptness of Rainier. It stands so far east of the Cascade crest that it is readily visible only from the summits of nearby volcanoes and the Hood River Gorge region. Although believed to have erupted from a single vent, several lateral eruptions high on the main cone have spread the mountain out. Adams was originally thought to be a long ridge composed of several cones that erupted at different times to produce the large mass that is the mountain today, and not a mountain extruded from a single vent or cone, which has been more recently theorized. Although a single-vent volcano will typically produce a more uniform, symmetrical volcanic shape, such as St. Helens or Hood, this apparently was not the case with Mount Adams.

Climbers ascending the Adams Glacier on Mount Adams. Photo Jason Broman/Mountain Madness

The mountain is believed to have begun forming about half a million years ago, with the most recent cone building within the last 25,000 years. Geologists suspect that the mountain is almost entirely composed of dark andesite, which is a bit more resistant to erosion than other volcanic materials. The mountain has displayed little evidence of its volcanic birth during the past 200 years, other than its summit fumaroles, but there have been other geological events, most notably large rockfalls similar to that which occurred on Mount Rainier's Russell Cliff in 1989. Mass wasting from the south side of The Castle occurred in October 1997 on Adams, when an estimated 1 to 5 million cubic meters of rock avalanched onto the Klickitat Glacier. Continued volcanic activity is thought unlikely, but Mount Adams is very prone to future rockfalls and mudslides.

Like other Cascade volcanoes, the rock of Mount Adams is usually rotten or unstable. Few routes climb over any significant rock obstacle, but stick to snow and ice as much as possible anyway, and for good reason. Rockfall is a hazard on many of Mount Adams's routes, particularly its headwalls, where nearly every climbing party has dodged significant rockfall.

Most headwall routes on Mount Adams remain infrequently repeated, also for good reason. Future climbers may become desperate enough to attempt to climb the several rotten headwalls of Mount Adams, but let us hope they have more sense.

Climbing Mount Adams requires a Cascade Volcano Pass, which can be ordered ahead of time by mail, purchased during regular office hours from the Mount Adams Ranger Station in Trout Lake or Cowlitz Valley Ranger Station in Randle, or from self-issuing stations at Mount Adams Ranger Station or Killen Creek Trailhead. Passes are required when traveling above 7,000 feet between June 1 and September 30. The cost depends on the day of the week you are climbing. If you will be on the mountain on Friday through Sunday, you need a weekend pass. An annual pass good for unlimited climbs of Mount Adams during the calendar year of purchase is available. If you have a Cascade Volcano Pass, you do not need a Northwest Forest Pass to park at the trailhead, but you still need to display the parking stub from your climbing pass inside your vehicle when parked at the trailhead. Check the Gifford Pinchot National Forest website for current Cascade Volcano Pass requirements, cost, and availability.

Mount Adams is situated partially within the Mount Adams Wilderness and partially within the Yakama

South Washington–Vicinity

Mount Adams–Southern Approaches

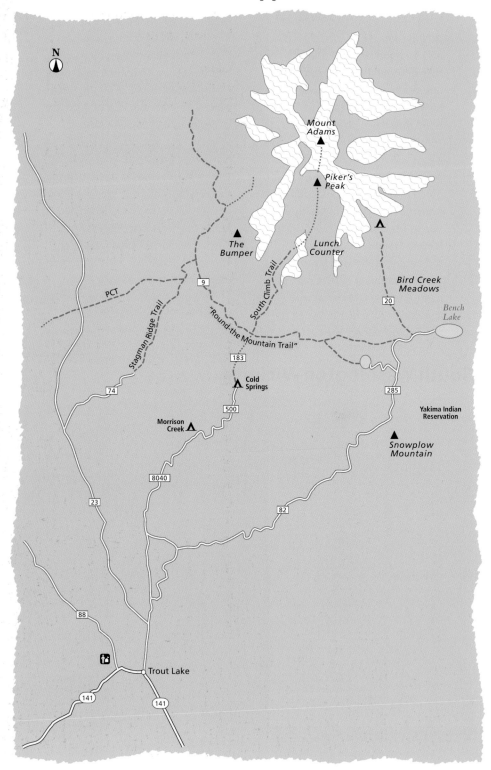

N

Mount Adams

Piker's Peak

The Bumper

Lunch Counter

Bird Creek Meadows

PCT

9

Stagman Ridge Trail

South Climb Trail

"Round-the-Mountain Trail"

183

20

Bench Lake

74

285

500

Cold Springs

Yakima Indian Reservation

Morrison Creek

Snowplow Mountain

8040

23

82

88

141

141

Trout Lake

Indian Reservation. A Yakama Reservation Tract-D tribal-use permit is needed if you climb on the southeast side of Mount Adams starting from Bird Creek Meadows, which includes Mazama Glacier, Klickitat Glacier, The Castle, and Rusk Glacier Headwall. This permit can be obtained from the Mount Adams Ranger Station in Trout Lake and must be displayed on your dash when parked at Bird Creek Meadows Trailhead. If you are not an enrolled member of the Yakama Nation, your climbing season is limited to July 1 to October 1.

For information about access and permits, contact Mount Adams Ranger District, 2455 Hwy. 141, Trout Lake, WA 98650; (509) 395-3400; www.fs.fed.us/gpnf/recreation/mount-adams.

1. South Spur (South Climb)
Difficulty rating: 0
Grade: II
Class: N/A
Time to summit: 6–8 hours
Objective hazards: Moderately prone to avalanching and occasional rockfall

> You are a piker if you think this is the summit. Don't crab, the mountain was here first.
> —Inscription on rock at false summit (Piker's Peak)

The South Spur is the most popular and least technical route on the mountain. Mules made the ascent on a regular basis during the mining era, transporting supplies up and sulphur down the mountain.

Mount Adams—South Spur

Pikers Peak
The Castle
SW Chute
Mazama Glacier
Lunch Counter
Crescent Glacier
South Climb Trail

PHOTO BOB WEBSTER

The South Spur route is commonly approached from Cold Springs Campground, which is reached from Trout Lake via FR 8040 (the turnoff is well marked as Mount Adams Recreation Area; follow the signs). Mazama Glacier can also be reached from this campground, although most parties prefer the shorter and more direct route from Bird Creek Meadows. The last 3 miles of road beyond Morrison Creek Campground is rough and narrow; drive carefully. If the road is washed out or closed, you will have to hike farther.

Drive to the end of FR 8040-500 to the South Climb Trail 183 trailhead. Hike up South Climb Trail to its intersection with Round-the-Mountain Trail 9, then continue upward on Trail 183, which is maintained to about 8,000 feet. Flank the Crescent Glacier on the left, ascending to the Lunch Counter at about 9,000 feet. An alternate approach to the Lunch Counter is to hike Round-the-Mountain Trail 9 east to gain McDonald Ridge, which is traversed directly north to reach the Lunch Counter. Some parties camp at the Lunch Counter, although

Mount Adams–Bird Creek Meadows Approach

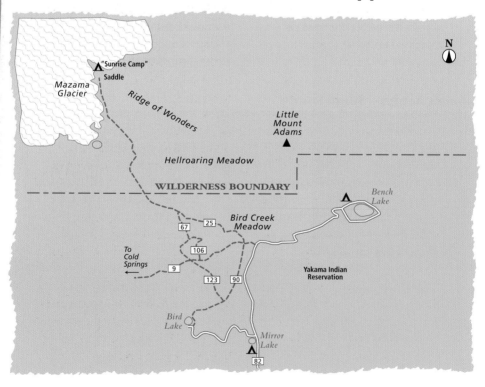

the round-trip is feasible from Cold Springs if you start early.

From the Lunch Counter, continue due north up steep snow or scree to the false summit, Piker's Peak, elevation 11,700 feet. Continue north across a divide to the summit.

The route is relatively easy, with no special difficulty or danger, except possibly avalanches in early season and an occasional stray boulder tumbling down the slope. Although the route does cross the summit ice cap, if you stay on the route, crevasses are not a problem. Bring crampons, an ice axe, and a short length of rope just in case.

Glissading is the most popular method of descent, but is also the leading cause of injuries on this climb. Don't glissade while wearing crampons, and make sure you have a safe runout, because sliding into rocks after a slip on snow is a common cause of injury here. Another leading cause of problems on this route is poor routefinding; if bad weather sets in, it is easy to get lost on the way down if you don't make note of features along the route as you ascend. Altitude sickness is another common problem for those coming from sea level and ascending too quickly to 12,000 feet.

Descent: Descend via the route of ascent. If you are ascending during poor visibility, wand key junctions along the ascent route to help you find your way back down.

Bird Creek Meadows Approaches

It is possible to hike from South Climb Trail 183 east on Round-the-Mountain Trail 9 to Bird Creek Meadows, but it is shorter to begin from Bird Creek Meadows. An approach from Bird Creek Meadows requires access to the Yakama Indian Reservation and a Tract-D Permit (available from the Trout Creek Ranger Station). Drive FR 8290 and FR 285 to Bird Creek Meadows Trail 20. From trail's end, continue cross-country to the head of the Hellroaring Creek drainage, then follow moraine slopes to the toe of the Mazama Glacier. Continue to the Mazama Glacier saddle (Sunrise Camp), the popular bivouac site.

2. Mazama Glacier
Difficulty rating: 1
Grade: II
Class: N/A
Time to summit: 4–6 hours
Objective hazards: Moderately prone to avalanching and exposed to rockfall

The Mazama Glacier flanks the South Spur on the east. It is a good, basic glacier climb and is modestly popular.

From Sunrise Camp the route ascends the right flank of the Mazama Glacier to join the South Spur. There are no special difficulties, although there is frequent rockfall from the

Mount Adams—Southeast Side

Photo Robert Webster

right side of the Mazama Glacier at about 9,000 feet. Crevasses can be a problem in late season, and cornices frequently form on Suksdorf Ridge. Avalanches are not uncommon on the glacier and headwall.

A direct finish can be made up the headwall to Piker's Peak. This involves a steep (60-degree) ice slope; ice tools and ice screws are recommended.

Descent: Descend via the route of ascent or the South Spur (South Climb) route.

3. South Klickitat Glacier
Difficulty rating: 4
Grade: III
Class: 3–4, AI2
Time to summit: 6–8 hours
Objective hazards: Highly prone to avalanching and exposed to rockfall and icefall

This route, formerly called Mazama Glacier Icefall, climbs the steep, narrow ice ribbon on what is now considered the south lobe of the Klickitat Glacier. It is a narrow ribbon of heavily fractured ice, with attendant icefall and some rockfall problems.

Descend from the Mazama Glacier saddle onto the South Klickitat Glacier and ascend the glacier directly through the icefall (60-degree-plus ice). The route reaches the south shoulder just below the false summit (Piker's Peak). Ice tools and ice screws/pitons are recommended; belaying may be advisable under icy conditions.

Another option is to climb the major headwall dividing the lobes of the Klickitat Glacier. This is a dangerous route except under perfectly frozen conditions. From Mazama Glacier Saddle, drop down as for the South Klickitat Glacier route, but ascend to the headwall. The first ascent party climbed the obvious snow/ice slopes and gullies to the false summit, crossing and ascending several rock ribs along the way. The route has loose rock and high rockfall and avalanche danger, but when frozen solid is said to be enjoyable and challenging.

Descent: Descend via the Mazama Glacier or South Spur (South Climb) routes.

4. Klickitat Glacier
Difficulty rating: 4
Grade: III
Class: 3–4, AI2
Time to summit: 6–8 hours
Objective hazards: Highly prone to avalanching and exposed to rockfall and icefall

The Klickitat Glacier descends southeasterly from the summit slope through a narrow icefall into a broad glacial valley. It is a technically challenging route, with serious objective hazards.

Descend from the Mazama Glacier saddle and traverse to the middle of Klickitat Glacier as crevasses permit, then ascend more or less directly up the narrow icefall. The exact route up the glacier depends upon crevasse conditions, but be wary of icefall on the left side and rockfall from The Castle on the right side. During optimal conditions this is a challenging, enjoyable route. In less than optimal conditions, climb a different route.

Descent: Descend via the Mazama Glacier or South Spur (South Climb) routes.

5. The Castle
Difficulty rating: 3
Grade: III
Class: 3–4
Time to summit: 10–12 hours
Objective hazards: Highly prone to avalanching and exposed to rockfall and icefall, extremely loose rock

The Castle is a prominent rock buttress at the head of Battlement Ridge, which divides the Rusk and Klickitat Glaciers. This route was first climbed in 1921 by Claude E. Rusk and party, who approached from Rusk Glacier via Avalanche Valley. The original route has been all but abandoned in favor of a later variation approaching from Sunrise Camp. The climbing route was not wiped out by the 1997 rockfall, but that event should be a reminder of the dubious nature of the rock here and elsewhere on Mount Adams.

Modern parties ascending this route approach via the Mazama Glacier saddle from Bird Creek Meadows Trail. Traverse laterally across the Klickitat Glacier and over the crest of Battlement Ridge. Continue via Rusk Glacier until it is feasible to regain the crest of Battlement Ridge. Continue to the base of The Castle on the left side. Traverse across snowfields (scree in late season) to a crumbly chimney on the northeast side, or take the original route, which climbs a loose gully system on the southeast side. Continue across The Castle and down to the Rusk Glacier, which is climbed to the summit.

Expect routefinding problems and loose rock. Large parties are not recommended here, as they tend to knock loose rocks down on each other. The route is infrequently climbed and not highly recommended, but it is historically significant and climbed more often than its quality merits.

Descent: Most parties descend via the Mazama Glacier route; some descend via the route of ascent.

North-Side Approach Routes

Approaches to most of the north and northeastern routes on Mount Adams begin on Killen Creek Trail 113. The trail begins from FR 2329 just south of Killen Creek Camp. Follow Trail 113 to the PCT junction, where High Camp Trail 110 leads to Killen Meadows. From trail's end, where you go depends upon which route you are climbing. Camping in Killen Meadows is popular but often crowded and environmentally destructive. Bivouacking higher up, on snow or ice, is suggested to reduce impacts on Killen Meadows. Most of the route descriptions begin from the trail junction at Killen Meadows. The Killen Creek approach is the most popular for reaching Wilson, Lyman, and Lava Glaciers and Lava and North Ridges.

More direct but longer hiking approaches to most east-side routes on Mount Adams can be made via Muddy Meadows Trail 13. From Muddy Meadows, hike about 4.25 miles southward to a junction with Trail 114, crossing the PCT at 2.5 miles along the way. Continue south on Trail 114 another 5 miles to Devil's Gardens (very close to Lyman Glacier) and another 2.5 miles to Avalanche Valley (easy access to Rusk and Wilson Glaciers). Because of the hiking distance, and because the Cascade Alpine Guide recommends cross-country approaches from Killen Creek Trail, few climbers use the east-side trail approaches. However, they do offer less cross-country travel and easier routefinding for those who dare to climb the rotten eastern headwalls of Mount Adams.

Mount Adams–Northern Approaches

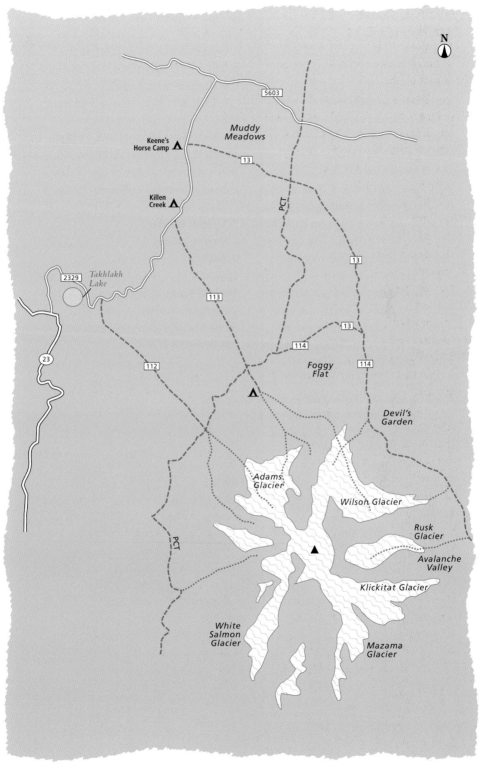

6. Wilson Glacier
Difficulty rating: 4
Grade: III
Class: AI2
Time to summit: 6 hours
Objective hazards: Highly prone to avalanching and exposed to rockfall and icefall

The Wilson Glacier flows down the northeast side of Mount Adams at the northern margin of Roosevelt Cliff in a steep, narrow icefall. It is a challenging route, with steep ice and crevasse difficulties and exposure to icefall from the summit ice cliffs.

Whichever approach you choose (Killen Meadows or Avalanche Valley), ascend the glacier's less crevassed northern flank to mid-height, then angle rightward to the base of the icefall and ascend as crevasses and seracs permit to the summit ice cap. Crevasse conditions will dictate the exact route of ascent. Ice tools and ice screws are recommended.

Descent: If you approached from the south, descend via the Mazama Glacier or South Spur (South Climb) routes. If you approach from the north, the North Ridge or Lava Ridge are recommended as descent routes.

7. Lyman Glacier
Difficulty rating: 3
Grade: III
Class: AI2
Time to summit: 6–8 hours
Objective hazards: Moderately prone to avalanching and exposed to rockfall and icefall

Mount Adams—Wilson and Lyman Glaciers

Victory Ridge

The Castle

Lyman Glacier

7

7

Rusk Glacier

Wilson Glacier

6

PHOTO CHRIS EARLE

The Lyman Glacier flows from the summit ice cap contiguous with the Wilson Glacier, but is cleaved off and again divided into two sections. It is a steep, heavily crevassed glacier, offering difficult glacier climbing. Approach from Killen Meadows, crossing the North Ridge and Lava Glacier, or via Trail 114 from Devil's Garden.

The usual route ascends the northern lobe of the glacier. From the toe of Lava Ridge, ascend obliquely across the glacier. Continue up the narrow icefall between the Lyman Cleaver and Lava Ridge. The route is consistently steep (45 to 60 degrees), and routefinding isn't usually a problem except in late season. Come before August for best conditions. This route is said to be the easiest and safest of the north-side glacier routes, but may still be subject to icefall, rockfall, and avalanches.

Descent: Descend via the Mazama Glacier or South Spur (South Climb) routes if approaching from the south or with arranged transportation, via North Ridge or Lava Ridge if approaching from the northwest.

8. Lava Ridge
Difficulty rating: 2
Grade: II
Class: 2–3
Time to summit: 6–8 hours
Objective hazards: Moderately prone to avalanching and exposed to rockfall

Lava Ridge divides the Lyman and Lava Glaciers on the north side of Mount Adams. It is a straightforward

Mount Adams—North Side

PHOTO JAKE WOODARD

climb with some rock and steep snow or ice. It is not as popular as the North Ridge due to a longer approach and more exposed climbing, but is usually less crowded.

Approach from Killen Meadows, crossing the North Ridge and Lava Glacier, or via Trail 114 from Devil's Garden. From the toe of Lava Ridge, ascend more or less directly up the ridge, staying on the Lava Glacier headwall side to avoid most obstacles. There is some exposure high up, and the route can be difficult when icy. Best earlier in the season to avoid loose rock and ice difficulties; it's not recommended in late season.

Descent: Most parties descend via the route of ascent or the North Ridge route. Some parties carry over the top and descend via South Spur (South Climb) with arranged transportation.

9. North Ridge

Difficulty rating: 1
Grade: II
Class: 2–3
Time to summit: 6–8 hours
Objective hazards: Exposed to rockfall, some approach variations more highly prone to avalanching

The North Ridge (or North Cleaver) of Mount Adams is a fairly direct and

Mount Adams—North Ridge

Photo Jason Broman/Mountain Madness

nontechnical route, but because of its length and loose rock in late season, it is not entirely recommended. It is believed to be the 1854 ascent route and still sees several ascents each year. It is more alpine in character and certainly less crowded than its south-side counterpart.

Access to the North Ridge is fairly easy and obvious from Killen Meadows. Hike to the base of the ridge or approach via one of the west-side snow basins in early season. In late season, stick with the ridge proper to minimize exposure to rockfall. Routefinding on the ridge is equally simple. Just climb the ridge as directly as possible, avoiding a few minor obstacles on the way to the summit shoulder. A long hike due south over the ice cap leads to the summit dome. This is a very long route, but without significant route-finding difficulties or extraordinary dangers under normal conditions.

Descent: Most parties descend via the route of ascent.

10. Adams Glacier
Difficulty rating: 3
Grade: III
Class: AI2
Time to summit: 6–8 hours
Objective hazards: Highly prone to avalanching and exposed to icefall

The Adams Glacier is the picturesque northwestern glacier descend-ing from the summit ice cap in an impressive icefall. It is highly regarded as a Mount Adams classic and is argu-ably the best route on the mountain.

From Killen Meadows, 1 mile of cross-country hiking leads to the lower slope of the Adams Glacier. The route is fairly straightforward from here, ascending whichever path you find through the steep crevasse jum-ble, where the angle remains between 40 and 50 degrees. Most parties begin on the right and finish on the left, although any route is possible so long as crevasses permit. Ascents prior to August are customary; the glacier becomes badly crevassed later.

Descent: Most parties descend via the North Ridge route or carry over the top via South Spur (South Climb) with arranged transportation.

11. Adams Glacier to Northwest Ridge
Difficulty rating: 3
Grade: III
Class: AI2
Time to summit: 6–8 hours
Objective hazards: Highly prone to avalanching and exposed to rockfall

A steep (averaging over 50 degrees), somewhat popular variation of the Northwest Ridge route, ascends from the base of the Adams Glacier icefall directly to the West Peak via con-tinuously steep snow and ice slopes. Rockfall has been reported, and the route ascends an obvious avalanche-prone slope. It is best climbed when

Mount Adams—Adams Glacier

West Peak

Piker's Peak

North
Ridge

9

White Salmon
Glacier

10

11

12

NW
Ridge

West
Ridge

Adams
Glacier

Pinnacle
Glacier

Photo Robert Webster

snow covered during stable snow conditions. A moderately challenging route, it is highly regarded by those who have climbed it.

Descent: Most parties descend via the North Ridge route or carry over the top via South Spur (South Climb) with arranged transportation.

12. Northwest Ridge
Difficulty rating: 2
Grade: II
Class: 3
Time to summit: 6 hours
Objective hazards: Moderately prone to avalanching and exposed to rockfall

This route is a good west-side option for those not prepared for the difficulties and exposure of the Adams Glacier routes. It is merely a long pumice and snow ridge leading to the West Peak without significant approach or routefinding difficulties. Approach as for Adams Glacier but continue traversing until you can gain the ridge, then climb the ridge directly. It's a mostly easy route; snow slopes near the top may be a problem when icy. Continue from the West Peak to the summit.

Descent: Descend via the route of ascent or the North Ridge route.

6.

Mount St. Helens

Mount St. Helens (8,365 feet/2,550 meters) hardly needs an introduction here. Present-day Mount St. Helens is a poor reminder of the once symmetrical cone rising above the placid waters of Spirit Lake. Though named for a friend of Captain George Vancouver, the native name Low-We-Lat-Klah or Low-We-Not-Thlat or Loowit, (meaning Throwing-Up-Smoke or Smoking Mountain) is more apt, especially following the mountain's 1980 eruption.

The formerly interesting summit climb, too, has been reduced to a strenuous tourist hike. The pre-eruption volcano rose to a height of 9,677 feet/2,950 meters and was first ascended by Thomas J. Dryer, founder of *The Oregonian,* and his party, in 1853. Post-1980 ascents were made prior to the opening of the "Red Zone," and a few parties were arrested and fined for their derring-do. The first post-eruption ascent was probably made during winter 1981–82; illegal ascents were certainly made during spring 1982 and after. The first legal post-eruption ascent of Mount St. Helens was not made until after the Red Zone was opened in 1987.

Most visitors to Mount St. Helens prior to 1980 thought impossible the eventual eruption that blew off over 1,000 feet of the mountain's summit and devastated the surrounding landscape. The mountain had not been active during the previous century, aside from a few long-forgotten outbursts of steam and ash, and there was no evidence to the casual observer that the mountain was not dormant. Geologists, however, had as early as 1975 predicted a possible violent eruption in the near future.

In March 1980 the mountain gave its first sign of awakening in 123 years with an earthquake measuring over 4.0 on the Richter Scale. The earthquakes continued, growing stronger and more frequent, until harmonic tremors occurred almost continuously. The mountain swelled and its crater opened. Mount St. Helens was poised and ready for a big eruption. Still, life went on. Geologists flew daily reconnaissance over the mountain, and Harry Truman refused to budge from his Spirit Lake lodge even after evacuation of the "Red Zone" was ordered.

"Where were you when the mountain blew?" In the quiet of early morning on May 18, 1980, an earthquake registering 5.0 on the Richter Scale caused an enormous landslide, as the north side of Mount St. Helens collapsed and slid toward Spirit Lake. This collapse literally uncorked the pressure that had built up within the mountain, causing upward and outward explosions of gas, ash, and pyroclastic projectiles that killed everything within a half-mile radius of the north side of the mountain (the "Eruption Impact Area") and shot an ash cloud 14 miles into the stratosphere. Pyroclastic material as hot as 1,600 degrees F poured down the mountain at speeds estimated at 100 miles per hour, cushioned by compressed air, burning everything

that was still intact after the eruption. Water from displaced lakes, mixed with ash, snow, ice, and assorted volcanic debris, generated catastrophic mudflows that wiped out bridges, logging equipment, and buildings.

This brief account of the events of May 18 and the days that followed hardly captures the eruption of Mount St. Helens in all its glory. If you wish to learn more about historical or geological Mount St. Helens, consult the bibliography and its references, visit the visitor center, view any of dozens of films chronicling the eruption, or better yet, visit the northern portion of the monument to get a firsthand look at the destructive legacy of the May 1980 eruption. If you

Mount St. Helens Crater Rim.
PHOTO ROBERT WEBSTER

visit the mountain, you will see that the barren wilderness created by the eruption is slowly coming back to life.

As noted previously, the route to the summit of Mount St. Helens is no longer challenging, but it is certainly much more popular. The USDA Forest Service estimated the number of post-eruption ascents at about 12,000 as of September 1987, and the pace hasn't slowed since. Permits are reserved months in advance for the climb. Don't expect solitude here.

While there are several possible ways to climb the mountain, the usual route is Monitor Ridge, which reaches the summit fairly directly. Other routes have been climbed since the eruption, and others may be possible, but none is truly technical in a mountaineering sense. Early-season ascents are recommended, as snow climbing is usually preferable to slogging up endless, steep pumice slopes. Tourists and casual hikers will probably want to wait until after the snow is gone before climbing the mountain, unless they are prepared for steep snow travel.

Climbers should be wary of the crater rim, which is quite unstable and prone to avalanching. More than one summit visitor has fallen into the crater. Keep back! Be sure to bring sun and wind protection. Gaiters and goggles will help keep ash out of your boots and eyes and a bandana or particle filter will help you avoid breathing the volcanic ash

whipped up by the wind. Ice axe, crampons, and ropes are advisable as conditions require.

Permits are required for all travel above timberline. From November 1 to March 31, simply register before and after your climb at Lone Fir Resort, 16806 Lewis River Rd., Cougar (on WA 503). Between April 1 and October 31, fee permits are required. After March 31 a quota of one hundred climbers per day is imposed. Permits can be obtained from approximately February 1 through October 31 through the Mount St. Helens Institute, and are available on a first-come, first-served basis. Permits must be obtained at least 24 hours prior to your climb, and they can go fast, so get yours early! Permits are valid for 24 hours. Climbers must sign in and check out.

Because Mount St. Helens has no technical climbing to offer, only two routes are described here. If you intend to try a different route, please do so when it is snow covered; late-season ascents will undoubtedly damage the fragile slopes of Mount St. Helens, and human-caused erosion should be minimized.

Don't forget that Mount St. Helens is an active volcano. Even though geologists can better predict eruptions, an eruption could still occur without much warning. The lava dome is still growing, and it has been blown off several times already. In the event of an eruption, descend

Mount St. Helens

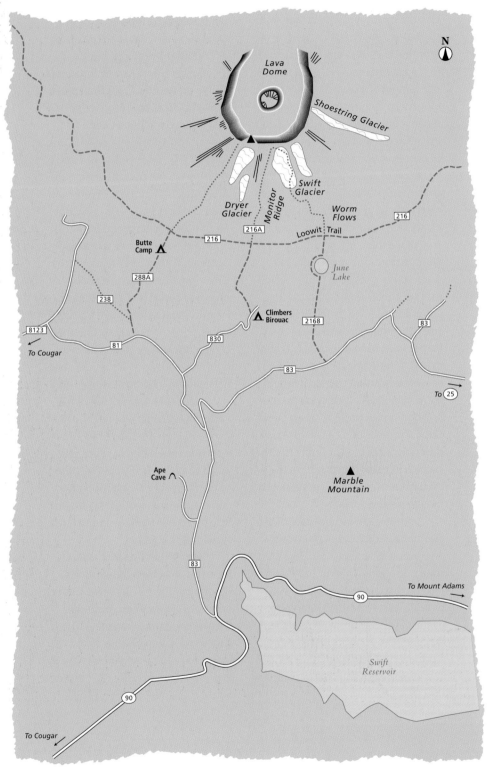

immediately, avoiding gullies and depressions, and breathe through a moist cloth if ash overwhelms you.

For more information about climbing Mount St. Helens, contact Mount St. Helens National Volcanic Monument, 42218 NE Yale Bridge Rd., Amboy, WA 98601, (360) 449-7800; Cascade Volcano Observatory, http://vulcan.wr.usgs.gov/Volcanoes/MSH/NatMonument/climb_msh.html; or Mount St. Helens Institute, http://www.mshinstitute.org.

Forest Roads to Mount St. Helens
To reach the routes, drive about 4 miles past Cougar on WA 90. Turn left onto FR 83 just after WA 90 bends

north to skirt Swift Reservoir. Drive about 3 miles to where the road forks and becomes unpaved. To reach Climbers Bivouac, stay left at the fork on FR 81, then turn right on FR 830. To reach the Marble Mountain Sno Park, stay right on FR 83.

1. Monitor Ridge
Difficulty rating: 0
Grade: I
Class: 1–2
Time to summit: 4–5 hours
Objective hazards: Unstable crater rim, cornices on crater rim

The Monitor Ridge route is the most popular route up the mountain. It is

Mount St. Helens—South Side

Monitor Ridge

1

2

Worm Flows Route
Winter Route

PHOTO LICENSED BY SHUTTERSTOCK.COM

a nontechnical "scramble" (i.e., pumice slog), taking an average of 6 to 9 hours for most climbers to complete round-trip. It is literally a "dog route"; you can bring your dog, although it is not recommended because the pumice is hard on dog paws and there is no water on the route.

Approach by driving to Climbers Bivouac at the end of FR 830. Overnight camping is allowed here with a climbing permit or Northwest Forest Pass. Hike up Ptarmigan Trail 216A about 2.2 miles to timberline at 4,800 feet. Continue upward, following Monitor Ridge, scrambling up lava flows and loose lava blocks, pumice, and ash. The route is posted to about 7,000 feet; the final 1,300 feet to the summit is not marked. Routefinding is usually easy—just follow everybody else. But during poor visibility it is important to stay on the "route" to avoid getting lost or wandering into dangerous terrain.

Be especially careful on the summit rim. Climbers have fallen through cornices or just wandered off the edge and fallen into the crater, to end up on the evening news in one fashion or another. Also be careful not to kick rocks loose as you climb, to protect those below you from rockfall.

Descent: Descend via the route of ascent.

2. Worm Flows Route
Difficulty rating: 0
Grade: I
Class: N/A
Time to summit: 4–6 hours
Objective hazards: Moderately prone to avalanching, unstable crater rim, cornices on crater rim

The Worm Flows Route is the most direct summit route in winter and is a popular ski climb and descent. Drive to Marble Mountain Sno Park, located on FR 83 near the June Lake trailhead. Follow Swift Ski Trail 244 to timberline, then cross to the west side of Swift Creek, just above Chocolate Falls. Follow ridges and open slopes more or less directly to the rim. The route is posted from timberline to about 4,800 feet, but is not marked the rest of the way.

As this is a winter climb to 8,300 feet over steep snow and mixed terrain, an ice axe, crampons, skis with climbing skins, cleated snowshoes, and wands are recommended. Avalanches are a possible hazard; be wary of cornices on the rim.

Snowmobiles are allowed on Mount St. Helens, so watch out for them during winter ascents. There is a snowmobile-free zone between Monitor Ridge and Worm Flows.

Descent: Descend via the route of ascent, preferably on skis.

Oregon

Successful climbers on the summit of Mount Hood.
PHOTO PETE KEANE/TIMBERLINE MOUNTAIN GUIDES

7.

Mount Hood

Standing at over 11,000 feet only 50 miles east of Portland, Oregon, Mount Hood (11,239 feet/3,426 meters) dominates the Columbia River Gorge and most of northwestern Oregon in the same way Mount Rainier commands the view from Puget Sound and Mount Shasta from northern California. Mount Hood is considered a dormant volcano, having not erupted since 1907, though it has active fumaroles in its crater. The mountain experienced some relatively minor eruptions within the past 200 to 300 years, but is not believed to have had any major volcanic activity for at least 1,000 years. The mountain is estimated to have once reached a height of just over 12,000 feet, but steady erosion, glaciation, and unstable composition have conspired to wear it down to its present height and form. Minor lava flows have occurred within the unrecorded past, but these were from lateral vents and not from the summit crater. Given its accessibility, Mount Hood's south side is an excellent geological field study, having numerous exposed volcanic and glacial features, including moraines, plug domes, flows and deposits of varying composition, and thermal vents.

Geologists agree that Mount Hood is among the most likely of the Pacific Northwest coast volcanoes to erupt in the future.

Mount Hood has a long and interesting climbing history. The first accepted ascent of Mount Hood was by W. S. Buckley, W. L. Chittenden, James Deardorff, H. L. Pittock, and L. J. Powell in 1857. Thomas Dryer, *Oregonian* editor and Mount St. Helens's first ascensionist, claimed the ascent in 1854, but faulty route descriptions discredited his claim. Whoever made the first climb, thousands followed. Climbing parties of more than 100 became common around the turn of the twentieth century. The Mazamas club of Portland, Oregon, was formed on the summit in 1894, when 193 climbers made the ascent. Although climbing parties of more than twenty are less common these days, it is not rare for more than one hundred climbers to visit the summit on early summer weekend days.

Because of its commanding position from Portland, the Columbia River Gorge, and most of north-central Oregon, Mount Hood is a much revered and sought-after summit. Although it has been called the most climbed glaciated peak in North America, Mount St. Helens likely has usurped that distinction since 1987, and South Sister, in central Oregon and also glaciated, is probably climbed more often. But Mount Hood is the most easily accessible of the "major" Cascade volcanoes. A year-round ski lift on its south slopes reaches to about 8,500 feet, and roads penetrate to timberline on two sides of the mountain, permitting hikes shorter than 1 mile to reach glacier ice. Some of the climbing routes involve less than 3 miles of hiking/climbing. Many of Mount Hood's routes can be climbed in an easy day from timberline. Because of easy access to the standard routes, one-day round-trips are common during late spring and summer. Because of its accessibility, Mount Hood's south

side is the site of thousands of annual ascents. Climbers vie for the honor of being the first on top for each new year. Mount Hood has reportedly been ascended by a woman wearing high heels, and a bicycle has been ridden along the summit crest. A gibbon reached the summit in 1964. Dogs are frequent summit visitors.

Belying its pedestrian nature, Mount Hood has claimed many lives. In July 1956 the "Youth Hostel Accident" claimed the life of one youth and seriously injured eleven others. In May 1986 eleven died in another highly publicized youth group accident. These and many other climbing accidents serve as reminders that Mount Hood is not an "easy climb" to be undertaken lightly. Some of its "easy" routes are quite technical and exposed even in good conditions.

Mount Hood. PHOTO TODD STAHLECKER

Still, many ill-prepared climbers and nonclimbers head off from Timberline Lodge bound for the summit. Fortunately, the summit is much farther away than it appears from Timberline, so most turn back. A few lucky fools do manage to reach the summit and return unharmed.

The culprit in most accidents on Mount Hood is the weather, which can be severe. Clear days often become cloudy, and storms can materialize with little warning. Cold temperatures, high winds, and poor visibility have contributed to many fatalities and near-fatalities on Mount Hood. As always, check the weather and avalanche reports before your climb, and heed rapid weather changes. Some parties have foolishly continued upward into a storm, becoming disoriented, lost, and hypothermic. Equally to blame in many Mount Hood accidents is inexperience. The summit climb is not a hike, as some apparently believe. An ice axe and crampons are bare necessities here no matter what the conditions, and even they may not be enough for a safe climb.

Most fatalities occurring on Mount Hood result from inexperienced climbers exercising poor judgment and underestimating their abilities and/or risks from effects of weather and other conditions. Proper planning, preparation, and experience could have prevented many of these deaths. Inexperienced climbers should not try to climb Mount Hood unless in the company of an experienced leader or guide. Casual hikers on Mount Hood's upper slopes are frequent accident victims.

During poor weather some climbers have become lost in the "Mount Hood Triangle" while descending the South Side to Timberline. Unable to distinguish landmarks they descended straight down, thinking they would come out at the lodge. Unfortunately, they found themselves far to the west, peering over the cliffs of Zig Zag Canyon. A simple compass bearing during the ascent can save much time and trouble later. This is not a frequent problem, but one that still causes some concern. The USDA Forest Service publishes a brochure that explains this phenomenon and provides other tips for staying on route during your descent. Read more about it at the day lodge before your climb.

As early as mid-July, Mount Hood's routes are subjected to increasing rockfall, a serious hazard that is prevalent on all routes. Mount Hood's rock is quite simply awful. After May, and on warm days, try to get out of harm's way before 10 a.m. There is very little solid rock on Mount Hood, making any route passing beneath or over its "rock" very hazardous. In winter and spring, avalanches are common, particularly on the steeper summit slopes, and summit cornices can present a serious hazard for the unwary.

Another hazard unrealized by a few climbers is the fumaroles. They smell pretty bad, like rotten eggs at best, so it's hard to believe anyone would want to get very close, but if you feel so inclined, think again. These vents lack oxygen, a fact found out too late by at least one climber, who suffocated before he could get away.

One final hazard of note is the year-round ski lift in operation from Timberline Lodge. The combined Palmer lifts climb just over 2,500 feet on snow and firn slopes between the Zig Zag and Palmer Glaciers. Wise climbers stay clear of the ski slopes after the lift operation begins for the day. Skiing is Mount Hood's biggest attraction, bringing thousands of skiers and millions of dollars to its three commercial ski areas. Summer skiing on Palmer Glacier is very popular, and if you bring skis to the summit, you can usually enjoy a very long run from the crater down to Timberline Lodge.

Most of Mount Hood and the surrounding area is wilderness, protected by the Wilderness Act of 1964. The original wilderness was expanded to its present size in 1978. The entire mountain is not within the wilderness boundary, as roads and ski lifts penetrate far up the mountain's south side. Climbers entering Mount Hood Wilderness are urged to use no-trace techniques to limit the visible signs of their use. Stay on snow whenever possible to protect fragile plant life and lessen erosion of loose pumice ridges. If staying overnight, pick a campsite that is sheltered from the wind, but be sure to use existing sites or camp on snow or ice. Don't displace rocks or soil to create new tent or bivouac sites. Human waste is a growing concern at high-use campsites; use minimum-impact human waste disposal methods. Don't switchback trails. Limit your party to no more than six climbers to lessen impacts caused by overuse. Come during the week to avoid overcrowding on popular routes. Clean up after yourself, and pack all refuse out.

Registration and permits are required year-round when climbing from Timberline and from May 15 to October 15 at other trailheads. Permits are free and self-issued at most trailheads. Permits and blue bags are available at the Wy'east Day Lodge at Timberline for ascents originating there.

Oregon law now requires climbers to carry a Mountain Locator Unit or cell phone while climbing Mount Hood. (Be sure to fully charge your cell phone before you climb.) If you fail to comply and a rescue becomes necessary, you will be held liable for up to $500 in rescue costs. Transmitters permit rescuers to pinpoint a lost or stranded climber's exact location on the mountain, saving valuable search and rescue time and resources. MLUs are available for rent from several local mountain shops.

Mount Hood–Vicinity

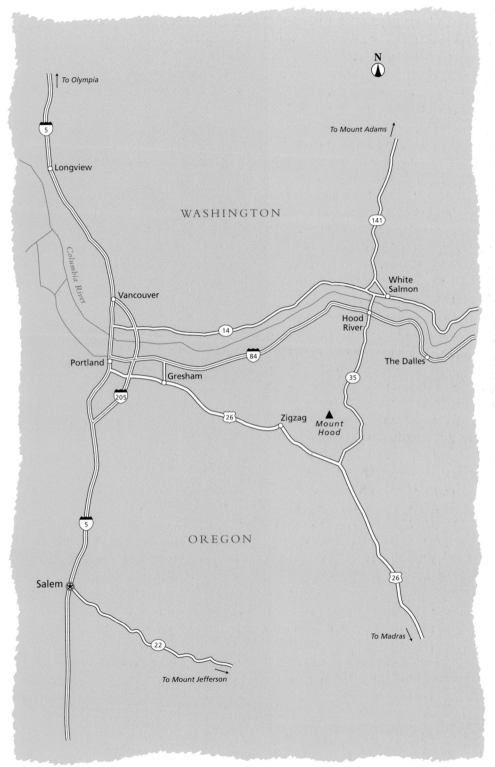

Mount Hood–Timberline Lodge

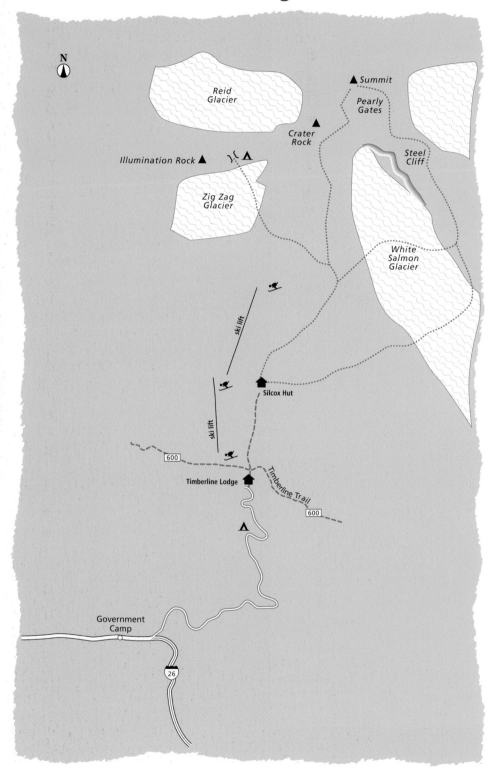

For further information, contact Zigzag Ranger District, 70220 E. Hwy. 224, Zigzag, OR 97049, (503) 622-3191; or Mount Hood Information Center, 65000 E. Hwy. 26, Welches, OR 97067, (503) 622-4822 or (888) 622-4822, www.fs.fed.us/r6/mthood/recreation/climbing/index.shtml.

Timberline Lodge Approach

Most of the south- and west-side routes on Mount Hood originate from Timberline Lodge. The Depression-era lodge is a leading tourist attraction that also serves as a base for skiers using the year-round Palmer Lift.

The road leading to Timberline Lodge is well marked, leaving US 26 only 0.5 mile east of Government Camp. Five curvy miles lead up to the lodge. Climbers are required to register at the Wy'east Day Lodge and obtain a permit (and blue bags); be sure to check out afterward. The climber registration "cave" provides route and other climber-oriented information. Camping is not allowed in the ski area parking lot; stay at the forest service campground just below.

1. South Side

Difficulty rating: 1
Grade: II
Class: 2–3
Time to summit: 4–6 hours
Objective hazards: Highly prone to avalanching and exposed to rockfall, summit ridge cornices

The South Side route (also known as the Hogback route) is the most accessible and direct and thus the most popular route on the mountain, ascending directly to the summit from

Mount Hood—South Side

PHOTO LICENSED BY SHUTTERSTOCK.COM

Timberline Lodge on the mountain's south slope. It is similar in character to the Avalanche Gulch route on Mount Shasta. Although straightforward and relatively short, this route deserves respect, particularly from inexperienced climbers. The route is often crowded, and slow parties regularly cause backups on the final slope.

Register at the day lodge, then hike "the Miracle Mile" from Timberline Lodge to the top of the Palmer ski lift via snowfields and pumice ridges, passing Silcox Hut and debris from the ski area. Guided climbers sometimes hire a snowcat for the ascent to about 8,500 feet. Riding the lift is a possibility, but it starts too late for most climbers, who are on their way down by the time the lift gets going. If you're interested in riding the lift, ask at the lift ticket booths across from the climber information cave at Wy'east Day Lodge. The ski area is an obstacle and danger to climbers; avoid it if you can, particularly on the descent. But then, if you brought skis or a snowboard, cowabunga!

From above the east side of the ski slopes, climb snow slopes and a pumice ridge just above White River Glacier into the summit crater between Crater Rock and Steel Cliff, passing left of smelly Devil's Kitchen. Climb the Hogback, a snow ridge located above and behind Crater Rock, going as high as possible before encountering the bergschrund. Two popular variations from the Hogback

include the Pearly Gates, two snow chutes on the right passing a crumbling rock buttress; and the Old Crater route, ascending the steep snow slopes farther left, directly above the crater. This variation is considered by some to be safer than the Pearly Gates during periods of rockfall danger, although the final summit ridge traverse is quite exposed. The Hogback has shifted west in recent years, prompting many climbers to stay left via the Old Chute variation. Another route passes Crater Rock on the west side to reach the Old Chute, but it is steep, with higher rockfall danger.

Beware of avalanches and rockfall below and in the Pearly Gates chute and surrounding rocks. Rockfall is the most common hazard here, especially after the sun hits the crater. The final slopes and gullies are steep and sometimes icy or slushy, making them quite treacherous. Stay out of the crater (oxygen voids that have caused at least one fatality). The crater and its vents are distinct. When descending in poor weather, be careful that you don't descend into the Mount Hood Triangle; take compass bearings on the way up so you can find your way back down to Timberline.

Because this route is heavily impacted, overnight camping is discouraged. The route takes only about 10 hours round-trip from the parking lot for most parties, so bivouacking should not be necessary except in emergencies.

Mount Hood—Crater Detail

"Old Crater" Route

Pearly Gates

Crater

Steel Cliff

Devil's Kitchen

Descent: Descend via the route of ascent.

2. Wy'east Route
Difficulty rating: 2
Grade: II
Class: 3–4
Time to summit: 6–8 hours
Objective hazards: Highly prone to avalanching and exposed to rockfall

Wy'east is a native name for Mount Hood. This route was attempted by Thomas Dryer in 1854 during his "first ascent." Begin as for the South Side route from Timberline Lodge, or more directly from The Meadows ski area.

From Timberline, ascend to about 7,600 feet, then traverse east across the moraine and onto the White River Glacier. Cross the glacier and ascend the snow or moraine slope above to a long moraine ridge. Continue up the moraine, then bear right around the top/back of Steel Cliff via scree and firn slopes above Newton Clark Glacier. Alternatively, from The Meadows, ascend beside the ski lift to Newton Clark Glacier; this is more direct than from Timberline Lodge. The final obstacle, a rock spur, is passed on the right. The summit ridge is gained via a loose traverse into a steep gully. The gully is very loose when empty of snow, and is prone to rockfall, especially after May.

Descent: Most parties descend via the South Side route du jour.

Cooper Spur Approach

Cooper Spur and several other routes on Mount Hood's north side are approached via Cooper Spur Road, which winds up from US 26 just south of Hood River. Cloud Cap Inn, a historic building, is located at timberline on Cooper Spur. Most of the routes originating from Cooper Spur were first climbed by the Langille brothers. Cloud Cap Inn is closed to the public, but

serves as headquarters for the Crag Rats climbing club (Hood River, Oregon).

To reach the inn and the Cooper Spur trailhead, drive OR 35 about 20 miles south from Hood River or about 18 miles north from the US 26/OR 35 junction to Polallie Campground. Take FR 3512 west to Cooper Spur ski area (well marked and paved). From the ski area, continue up the curvy, primitive road to its end at Cloud Cap Inn or Tilly Jane Campground. The Cooper Spur Road is snow free after July in most years. In winter there is a marked ski trail leading to the spur from the ski area.

Trails begin from road's end (Timberline Trail 600 from Cloud Cap Inn, Spur 600A from Tilly Jane

Mount Hood–Cooper Spur

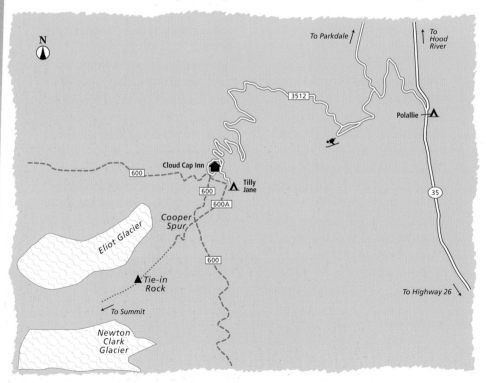

Campground), giving access to the Cooper Spur and North Face routes. The north side of Mount Hood is included in the Mount Hood Wilderness.

3. Cooper Spur
Difficulty rating: 2
Grade: II
Class: 2–3
Time to summit: 4–6 hours
Objective hazards: Highly prone to avalanching, highly exposed climbing

The Cooper Spur is the most straightforward route on Mount Hood. It was first ascended in 1897 by Will and Doug Langille, sons of Sarah Langille, who was the hostess of Cloud Cap Inn during its heyday. The Langille brothers frequently guided guests to the summit of Mount Hood around the turn of the twentieth century.

Begin from Cloud Cap Inn or Tilly Jane Campground to Tie-in Rock, a rock spur at about 8,000 feet. Continue straight up steep snow slopes (to 50 degrees near the top of the spur) to the summit.

This route has no technical difficulty, but is quite steep and exposed high up and has avalanche exposure. Although the route is not particularly difficult, it has a low margin for error. Falls from this route are common and often fatal. This is not to imply that climbers are regularly falling and dying on this route, but several rope teams have been dragged to their demise down the Eliot Glacier headwall during what would otherwise have been a survivable slip on snow. A few lucky climbers have survived the ride to the Eliot Glacier.

Mount Hood—North Side

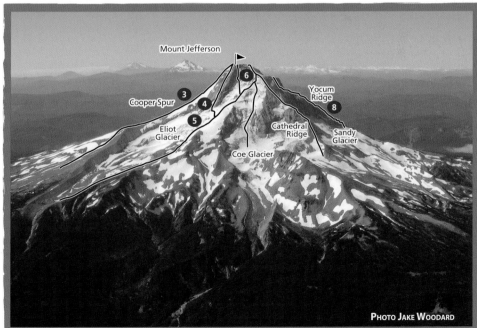

PHOTO JAKE WOODARD

Descent: Most parties descend via the route of ascent. Be extra careful during the descent, which is when a majority of accidents occur on Cooper Spur. Some prefer to carry over the top and descend the South Side to Timberline so as not to tempt fate.

4. North Face
Difficulty rating: 4
Grade: III
Class: 4–5, AI2–3 (couloirs)
Time to summit: 6–8 hours
Objective hazards: Highly prone to avalanching and exposed to rockfall, very loose rock

The North Face of Mount Hood has two prominent gullies and three rock ribs, which offer straightforward but challenging climbing routes. The rock routes are loose and not recommended; the gullies are avalanche and rockfall chutes except under optimal conditions.

Approach as for Eliot Glacier, staying left to meet the headwall wherever it appears easiest to pass the bergschrund. The long, narrow gullies on either side of the middle rock buttress are the more popular routes, offering good winter and spring climbing when snow filled and well frozen. Rockfall should be anticipated here, as well as avalanches. Ice tools and ice and rock protection are recommended.

All North Face routes (except the Northeast Spur) are commonly exited west of Cathedral Spire, a rotten pinnacle near the top of the headwall. Cathedral Spire may be ascended from the notch via rotten Class 4 rock, which is not recommended.

Mount Hood—Eliot Glacier and North Face

PHOTO PETE KEANE/TIMBERLINE MOUNTAIN GUIDES

Descent: Descend via Cooper Spur or Eliot Glacier—Sunshine Route, or carry over the top and down the South Side with arranged transportation.

5. Eliot Glacier—Sunshine Route
Difficulty rating: 2
Grade: II
Class: N/A
Time to summit: 6–8 hours
Objective hazards: Moderately prone to avalanching

This route ascends the Eliot Glacier to the summit ridge. It was first climbed solo by Bill Langille in 1892, and is popularly known as the Sunshine Route because it is usually in sunlight all day. It is a fine, nontechnical glacier outing that is very popular.

From low on Cooper Spur, descend to and traverse Eliot Glacier, ascending its right slope toward Horseshoe Rock (a small rock formation high up), which is most easily passed on the right. Continue up Cathedral Ridge to the summit. A late-season bergschrund often blocks passage beyond Horseshoe Rock; it can usually be skirted on the right. Several variations are possible; follow the route that looks most feasible or challenging to you, depending on conditions and your mood.

Descent: Most parties descend via the route of ascent or the Cooper Spur route. Some prefer to carry over the top and descend to Timberline with arranged transportation.

6. Eliot Glacier Headwall
Difficulty rating: 4
Grade: III
Class: 5, AI3/Mixed
Time to summit: 6–8 hours
Objective hazards: Highly prone to avalanching and exposed to rockfall and icefall

This is a challenging route that climbs through the Eliot Glacier icefalls and ascends the steep headwall rising above the upper Eliot Glacier. Before Yocum Ridge was climbed, Eliot Headwall was considered the most difficult route on Mount Hood. It is still a serious route, but is considered less dangerous and is much more popular than Yocum Ridge.

The route involves mixed rock and steep snow and ice (60 degrees, possibly Class 5 rock if not completely iced over), with considerable loose rock and rockfall hazard unless well frozen. During optimal conditions, the route receives considerable attention. The usual route climbs the headwall directly through a rock band on the right side. A variation ascends the left side of the headwall to the notch behind Cathedral Spire, then finishes up the last bit of the North Face.

Descent: Descend via Cooper Spur or Eliot Glacier—Sunshine Route, or carry over the top and down the South Side route to Timberline.

7. Sandy Glacier Headwall

Difficulty rating: 4
Grade: III
Class: 3–4, AI1–2
Time to summit: 8–10 hours
Objective hazards: Highly prone to avalanching and exposed to rockfall, glaciers are heavily crevassed

Ascending the Sandy Glacier Headwall on the mountain's west side is a somewhat popular route when in condition. A long and somewhat complicated approach makes it less popular than Leuthold Couloir, which is similar in character and much more readily approached, and thus more often climbed.

This and most of the other routes on the west side of Mount Hood are most often approached from Illumination Saddle, the prominent notch between Castle Crags and Illumination Rock. From Timberline Lodge, begin as for the South Side (Hogback) route, then traverse west toward the saddle across the Zig Zag Glacier at about 9,000 feet. If you start early enough, you can hike up beside the ski lift, then veer northwest from its top more directly to the saddle. Your route to the saddle will be obvious and straightforward, whichever way you go. Avoid the ski lift area during operation if you know what's good for you. Illumination Saddle is a popular base-camp site for west-side routes.

Illumination Rock, a crumbly spire, may be climbed by several routes, nearly all of which have moderate Class 5 climbing on shattered rock ("the best rock on Mount Hood"). A direct route climbs from the saddle directly up the East Arête or around to the west and up; a less-direct route climbs the West Arête from the Zig Zag Glacier. There are several other more or less difficult routes, but all routes on Illumination Rock have bad rock and are therefore not recommended.

Crevasses are rarely a problem on Zig Zag Glacier, though the glacier is crevassed. Roping up on the glacier is recommended but not often practiced. The descent to Reid Glacier is steep and avalanche prone at times. Crossing Reid Glacier can be complicated by heavy crevassing. It is recommended that you cross high to avoid the worst of the crevasses, although this leaves one exposed to greater avalanche and rockfall hazard from the headwall.

From Illumination Saddle, descend onto Reid Glacier and skirt around Yocum Ridge (carefully) to reach Sandy Glacier. It's not difficult if you are on route, but is exposed and requires careful routefinding. It is recommended that you not traverse Yocum Ridge during poor visibility or darkness, as any mistake in routefinding could be fatal.

Once across the traverse, ascend to the left side of Sandy

Glacier and climb the headwall via the most obvious gully (50-degree slopes), which gains Cathedral Ridge high up. Steep variations (up to 65 degrees) are possible near the top of the headwall. The route is best climbed when snow covered and well frozen, and during low avalanche danger. Otherwise, expect to climb volcanic mud and scree or be wiped out by a snow slide or rockfall. Ice tools and ice screws are recommended.

Descent: Descend via the South Side route to Timberline if you parked there. Cathedral Ridge is another option if you approached from the northwest side.

8. Yocum Ridge
Difficulty rating: 5
Grade: V
Class: 5, AI3–4/Mixed
Time to summit: 10–12 hours
Objective hazards: Difficult climbing on poor rock and ice with poor to nonexistent protection and avalanche, rockfall, and icefall exposure

> This route is extremely hazardous and is not recommended by the author or anyone else in his right mind.
>
> —*Ross Petrie, 1961*

Mount Hood—West Side

PHOTO LICENSED BY SHUTTERSTOCK.COM

Mount Hood–Yocum Ridge

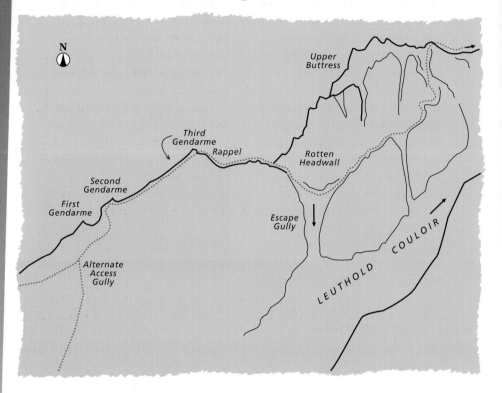

This extremely technical route on Mount Hood was first climbed by Fred Beckey and Leo Scheiblehner in 1959. Periods of cold weather with snow and rime ice cover are prerequisites for climbing this route. Climbers attempting the route during any other conditions should expect continuous, copious rockfall and Class 5 climbing on nightmarishly loose rock. Serious commitment, poor rock, and high exposure make it a poor choice for any but the most skilled climbers. Nevertheless, like many other "suicide" routes, it remains a popular pseudo-classic objective.

Approach from Illumination Saddle across the Reid Glacier to the base of the ridge, then ascend the ridge more or less directly past the third gendarme. A gully reaching the saddle above the third gendarme is commonly used to escape the ridge when the upper buttress is unclimbable, and as an alternate start to the upper buttress to avoid the lower ridge. An escape traverse to Sandy Glacier Headwall from the upper snow saddle has been done, but is not recommended any more than the final headwall. This route has abundant loose rock, extreme rockfall hazard, and bad protection. Take pitons and ice screws for luck if nothing else. If you are thinking of climbing this route, it would be best to consult every available reference and talk with someone who has climbed it before—so they can talk you out of it.

Descent: Descend via the South Side route to Timberline.

9. Reid Glacier Headwall— Leuthold Couloir
Difficulty rating: 2
Grade: II
Class: 3–4, AI1–2
Time to summit: 6–8 hours
Objective hazards: Highly prone to avalanching and exposed to rockfall, glacier is heavily crevassed

This route climbs a steep snow gully on the left side of the Reid Glacier Headwall. It is an excellent climb when conditions are good; otherwise it is an avalanche/rockfall funnel. Winter ascents are quite popular; summer ascents not so much.

From Illumination Saddle, cross the Reid Glacier and ascend the obvious snow chute through the left side of the headwall, angling left toward Yocum Ridge. Pass the Hourglass, a narrow spot in the couloir, and continue right at the couloir's end toward the summit. When the couloir is snow filled and the headwall well frozen, this is an excellent, popular route. Otherwise, expect copious rockfall or avalanches.

There are two prominent, narrow couloirs leading through the headwall to the right of the Hourglass, both of which offer steeper alternatives to the main couloir, with similar risks of avalanche and rockfall.

Descent: Descend via the South Side route to Timberline.

Mount Jefferson.
PHOTO LIZETTE MACLAURIN

8.

Mount Jefferson

Oregon's second-highest mountain is Mount Jefferson (10,497 feet/3,199 meters), a striking peak situated between Albany and Bend in north-central Oregon. Like Mount Hood, "Jeff" is a landmark of the Oregon Cascades. Smaller than Mount Hood, and certainly less accessible, Jefferson nevertheless is a popular climb, being a bit more rugged than Hood and offering a more traditional climbing experience than the typical up-and-down-in-a-day ascent of Mount Hood. Approach hikes are about 5 miles, and lakeside campsites in Jefferson Park are favorite bases for weekend climbing parties.

Mount Jefferson is an older volcano that has not been notably active in recent geologic history. Glaciers have worn down Jefferson's softer flanks, while the central vent and basaltic dikes and ridges have remained at least partly intact. Its volcanic history is relatively unimportant, except that it has very loose rock and a difficult summit pinnacle, which has withstood the ravages of erosion that have worn down its surrounding flanks. After the glaciers are finished with it, Mount Jefferson will become just another rotten central Oregon volcanic horn, like Mount Washington or Three Fingered Jack.

Although the mountain was reportedly first climbed in 1888, and had been climbed at least three times prior to the turn of the twentieth century, it was thought impossible by many climbers as late as 1905. Modern parties find few obstacles to success on the mountain, although the summit pinnacle still repels its share of climbers. Most of Mount Jefferson's routes involve minimally technical glacier and ridge climbing, usually with Class 3 and maybe a little bit of Class 4 or 5, but the summit pinnacle requires basic routefinding skills on its short, shattered Class 3, 4, and 5 rock pitches. Some climbers consider Jefferson the most difficult of the Cascade volcanoes, with no "easy" route to the summit.

SUMMIT PINNACLE ROUTES

From Red Saddle (the way most climbers access the pinnacle), there are several possible routes to the summit. For the most part, these routes consist of Class 3 and 4 climbing. In the words of Bill Soule of *Timberline Mountain Guides*:

They [the summit pinnacle routes] are short enough to make route-finding insignificant. The climbing consists of Class 3 or 4 with bad to nonexistent anchors on the worst rock imaginable. Don't get me wrong. Jefferson is a worthwhile climb, but the summit pinnacle is not the reason why. The standard summit pinnacle route from Red Saddle begins with an exposed, steep snow traverse on the west side all the way around to the north side, then climbs up loose Class 3 or 4 ledges to the summit. There is a direct route on the west side that gains the saddle between the two summit pinnacles, but this option is very loose and not recommended. Other more difficult variations have been done (Class 5.0 to 5.7 reported), but aren't much better. Any way you go, expect difficult, exposed climbing with plenty of loose rock.

Routes climbing the east flank of Mount Jefferson finish via a more direct but equally loose Class 5 route on the northeast side of the pinnacle.

Descents from Mount Jefferson are most easily made via Whitewater Glacier, East Face, or Southwest Ridge, depending upon where you parked your car.

Jefferson Park, the most popular area in the Mount Jefferson

Mount Jefferson—Summit Pinnacle

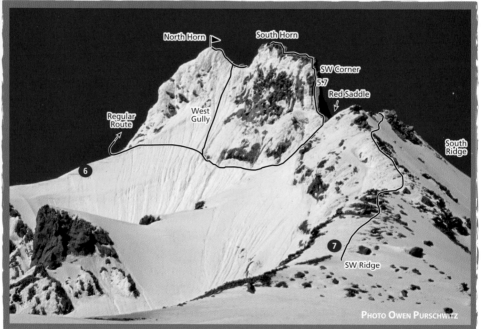

PHOTO OWEN PURSCHWITZ

Wilderness and the classic base camp for ascents of Mount Jefferson, is suffering from overuse. Please bring stoves instead of relying on natural fuel for cooking and heat, and make an effort to minimize your impact in this area. Self-issue permits are now required for day use of Mount Jefferson Wilderness. Overnight permits are not self-issue and must be obtained from a ranger district office or other outlet. Whitewater Glacier is on Warm Springs Indian Reservation land, but no special permit is needed unless you are going fishing. This could change, so check with the Detroit Ranger District office prior to your climb.

For information about permits and access, consult the Mount Jefferson Wilderness page on the Willamette National Forest website, or contact Detroit Ranger District, HC-73, Box 320, Mill City, OR 97360, (503) 854-3366, www.fs.fed.us/r6/willamette.

Jefferson Park Approach

Drive FR 2243 from Whitewater Campground (about 0.5 mile off OR 22, 6 miles east of Idanha). Continue 6 miles past the campground to road's end. Hike Whitewater Trail 3429 along Sentinel Creek 1.5 miles to its junction with Jefferson Park Trail 3373. Head east 2.5 miles to meet the Pacific

Central Oregon–Vicinity

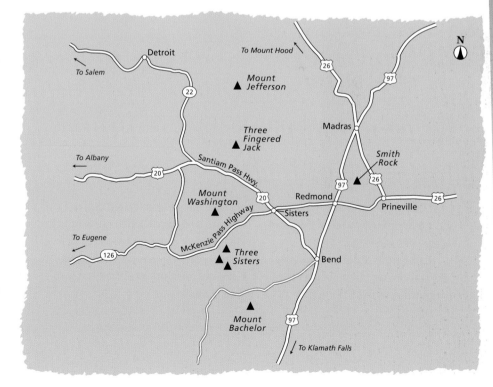

Mount Jefferson Western Approaches

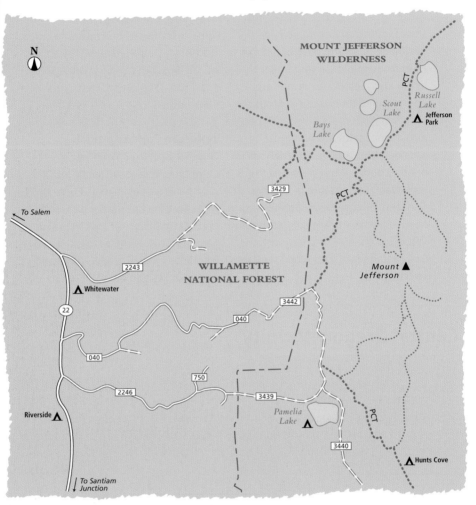

Crest Trail (PCT). Continue northeast another short mile to Scout Lake and lovely Jefferson Park.

Camping at Scout and Russell Lakes is popular, but there are many campsites in Jefferson Park that are now being rehabilitated due to overuse, and are closed to camping. Please check with the Detroit Ranger District office for road and trail conditions and campsite availability prior to your climb.

Mount Jefferson

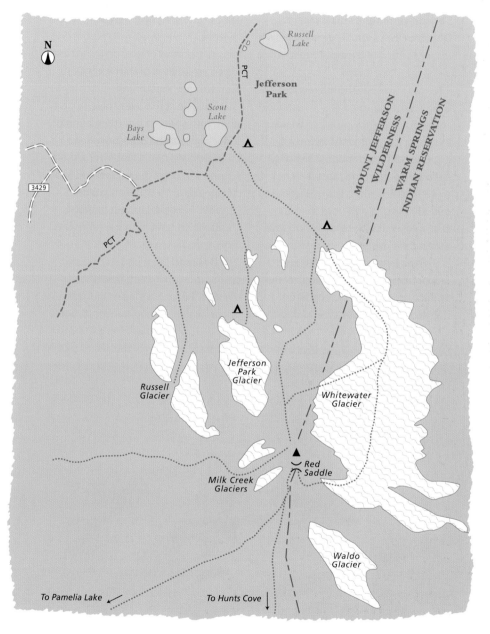

1. Whitewater Glacier

Difficulty rating: 3
Grade: II
Class: 4–5
Time to summit: 8–10 hours
Objective hazards: Moderately prone to avalanching and exposed to rockfall

This route ascends the Whitewater Glacier, a broad sheet of snow and ice on Mount Jefferson's eastern flanks. It is reportedly the most frequently climbed route on Mount Jefferson, although it is not the most direct route to the summit. The glacier is frequently skied to and from the southeast spur, which certainly would save time on the descent.

From Jefferson Park, hike south cross-country to the north flank of the Whitewater Glacier. Routefinding to the glacier can be difficult and time consuming for the uninitiated. If you have time the night before your ascent, scout the approach to the glacier, as it will save you time in the morning. If you camp higher, near the glacier, you'll save even more time. Some parties find themselves short of time on the ascent, so you are advised to start early if you want to reach the summit.

Once on the glacier, traverse south past the east face, then ascend snow slopes and a pumice ridge to the southeast spur. Climb over a short ridge and ascend the spur to Red Saddle (elevation 10,000 feet), a stone's fall away from the summit pinnacle. Climb the summit pinnacle route that most appeals to you.

Descent: Most parties descend via the route of ascent. Descending the West Rib or Southwest Ridge is an option with arranged transportation.

Mount Jefferson—North Side

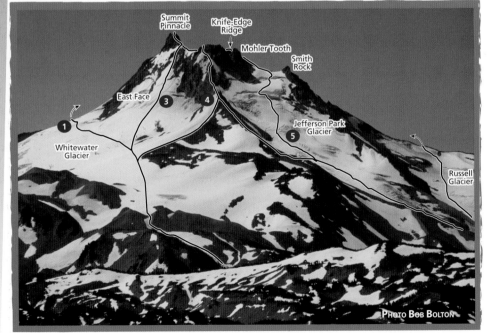

PHOTO BOB BOLTON

2. Whitewater Glacier— Warm Springs Couloir

Difficulty rating: 4
Grade: II
Class: 5, AI1–2
Time to summit: 6–8 hours
Objective hazards: Highly prone to avalanching and exposed to rockfall, loose rock

This route climbs a narrow couloir directly up the east face to the base of the summit pinnacle. Under perfect conditions this is a more challenging, direct snow and ice route to the summit. Under less than perfect conditions, it is an avalanche or rockfall funnel that should be avoided.

From the midsection of Whitewater Glacier, ascend the farthest left couloir (steep snow or ice) leading directly to the base of the summit pinnacle. Angle right to reach a snowfield that gives access to the upper East Arête. Continue up loose Class 5 rock to the summit.

Descent: Most parties descend via the Whitewater Glacier route.

3. East Face

Difficulty rating: 3
Grade: II
Class: 4–5
Time to summit: 6–8 hours
Objective hazards: Highly prone to avalanching and exposed to rockfall, loose rock

This route attains the North Ridge from the middle of Whitewater Glacier via steep snow slopes and gullies. Although said to be the shortest route to the summit from Jefferson Park, it

Mount Jefferson—East Side

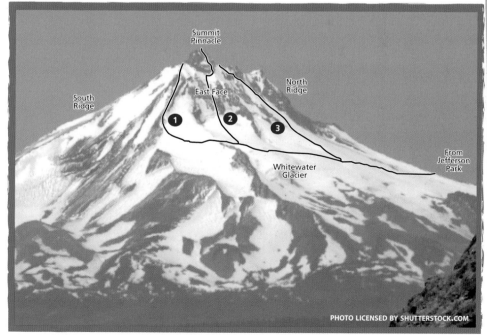

PHOTO LICENSED BY SHUTTERSTOCK.COM

is less popular than some of the other less direct routes.

Ascend to Whitewater Glacier to the base of the broad snow gully leading to the North Ridge. Ascend the snow slopes and pass a short rock band to reach the crest of the North Ridge. Once on the ridge, continue as for the North Ridge route. A variation reportedly climbs directly through the rotten upper rock buttress (loose Class 4), but is not recommended. East Face is best climbed in early season when the loose rock is snow covered and frozen in place.

Descent: Most parties descend via the Whitewater Glacier route, although descending the route of ascent is an option.

4. North Ridge
Difficulty rating: 3
Grade: II
Class: 4–5
Time to summit: 8–10 hours
Objective hazards: Exposed to rockfall, loose rock

> This is a difficult route over unsound rock, and should be attempted only by very experienced climbers.
> —John Biewener, 1955

This route ascends the north ridge directly from Jefferson Park; it was first ascended solo in 1903 by Sidney S. Mohler. The ridge is very

straightforward, and also very loose. It is not considered as difficult by today's standards as it was in 1955, and is barely more challenging than the East Face and Whitewater Glacier routes when the summit pinnacle is factored in. Nothing on the ridge is more difficult than the summit pinnacle, if that helps you decide whether or not to try it. Let's just say that most climbers choose a different route.

Approach from Jefferson Park as for Jefferson Park Glacier, but stay on the ridge crest. Some loose roped rock pitches may be encountered on the ridge unless snow permits easier climbing. The hardest part of the climb is gaining the upper ridge, then scrambling up ledges on the northwest side of the pinnacle reaches the summit. Like other volcanic ridges, it is best to climb this route when snow allows you to avoid some of the loose rock sections.

Descent: Most parties descend via the Whitewater Glacier route or another easier route, although descending the route of ascent is an option.

5. Jefferson Park Glacier
Difficulty rating: 3
Grade: III
Class: 4–5
Time to summit: 8–10 hours
Objective hazards: Highly prone to avalanching and exposed to rockfall

This is the second most popular route on Mount Jefferson, ascending a

Mount Jefferson—Jefferson Park Glacier

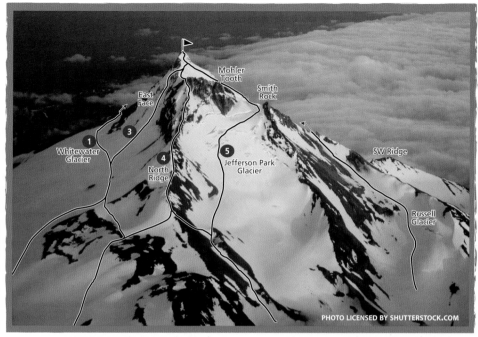

Mohler Tooth

Smith Rock

East Face

Whitewater Glacier

North Ridge

Jefferson Park Glacier

SW Ridge

Russell Glacier

PHOTO LICENSED BY SHUTTERSTOCK.COM

north-facing glacier and headwall. It is a steep and alpine route with some technical difficulty, making it very nearly a worthwhile route (except, of course, for the summit pinnacle).

Ascend from Scout Lake or the PCT junction to the east edge of Jefferson Park Glacier and continue more or less directly up the glacier to the bergschrund. Passing the bergschrund may present a problem; the best choice is to stay right, scrambling up a rock ridge, as going left subjects you to more frequent rockfall. A short traverse left above the bergschrund leads into a shallow cirque between the Mohler Tooth and Smith Rock formations, from where a narrow ridge crest behind

Mohler Tooth leads to the upper North Ridge. This ridge (the so-called Knife-Edge Ridge) has been variously reported as "scrambling" and "Class 5.1," but on fairly solid rock (compared to the summit pinnacle, though not all parties agree); expect some steep, exposed rock climbing on a narrow ridge crest. Other variations have been done here. However you finish, join the North Ridge route to the summit. The climb's difficulty will depend on the route taken and whether you are comfortable climbing exposed, loose rock unroped or feel the need to belay and place protection.

Descent: Most parties descend via the Whitewater Glacier or another easier route, although descending the route of ascent is an option.

6. West Rib
Difficulty rating: 3
Grade: II
Class: 4–5
Time to summit: 6 hours
Objective hazards: Moderately prone to avalanching and exposed to rockfall

The West Rib is a popular early-season snow route, one of the most direct routes to the summit. In late season it is not at all recommended due to loose rock.

A climber's trail follows Milk Creek from the PCT north of Pamelia Lake. Gain the West Rib on its north flank and ascend more or less directly to the summit pinnacle. The route is often climbed in a day, which is more

easily accomplished by those who ski down the route on the descent.

Descent: Descend via the route of ascent or one of the South Side routes.

7. Southwest Slope
Difficulty rating: 3
Grade: II
Class: 4–5
Time to summit: 8–10 hours
Objective hazards: Boredom, dehydration

There are two customary routes approaching from the southwest side to Red Saddle: the Pamelia Lake route (aka Southwest Ridge) and Hunts Cove route (aka South Ridge). These routes are technically the easiest but are by far the most tedious on Mount Jefferson. Bring extra water and

Mount Jefferson—West Rib

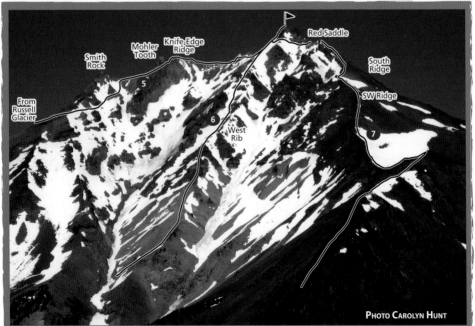

PHOTO CAROLYN HUNT

expect to take all day for your trip to the summit and back to high camp.

Pamelia Lake Trail is used to approach these and other west-side routes. To reach Pamelia Lake, take FR 2246 from OR 22 about 7 miles east from Idanha (2 miles north from Riverside Campground). Pamelia Lake Trail 3439 begins just before road's end, leading 2.25 miles to Pamelia Lake and junctions with the PCT and Skyline Trail 3440. Skyline Trail leads 3 miles south to Hunts Cove. Both Pamelia Lake and Hunts Cove are suffering from overuse, so minimize your impact in these overcrowded areas. Pamelia Lake is a Limited Entry Area requiring a special permit issued only at the Detroit Ranger District office. Check with the Detroit Ranger District for details if you plan to camp at or near Pamelia Lake.

This route is variously described as "a hot, dry climb," which is "the easiest but most tedious route" on Mount Jefferson. It is similar to the South Ridge of South Sister, but even longer and without a trail. From the PCT just north of Pamelia Lake, follow a climber's trail up steep cinder slopes to the crest of the southwest ridge and follow the open ridge to Red Saddle. The route from Hunts Cove is another "long, tedious climb." Beginning from Hunts Lake (south of Pamelia Lake), it climbs the south ridge directly to the southwest shoulder and ascends approximately due north to Red Saddle. Neither route is at all technical to Red Saddle. If you find the route to Red Saddle difficult, definitely stay off the summit pinnacle.

Descent: Descend via the route of ascent.

Mount Jefferson—South Side

PHOTO BOB BOLTON

Three Fingered Jack.
PHOTO USGS CASCADE VOLCANO
OBSERVATORY/W. E. SCOTT

9.

Three Fingered Jack

Oregon's Three Fingered Jack (7,841 feet/2,390 meters) is among the oldest high volcanoes in the Cascades. The complex internal structure of the now dormant volcano, along with the ravages of erosion by former glaciers, have combined to form the rugged summit of the present Three Fingered Jack. The mountain is believed to have undergone three distinguishable volcanic building phases, culminating in a basaltic intrusion into a

softer andesite cone. Over the epochs, glaciation has worn away the softer material, leaving only the erosion-resistant core. Mount Thielson and nearby Mount Washington share a similar geologic history.

Like Mount Washington, Three Fingered Jack has some very poor rock. So lowly regarded is the rock on Three Fingered Jack that the summit pinnacle is said to vibrate in high winds! The peak was first ascended

Three Fingered Jack–South Ridge Approach

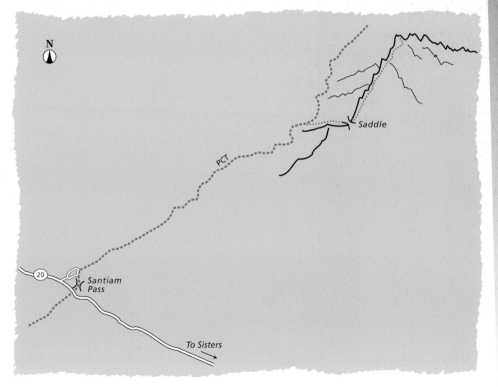

by the "Boys from Bend" in 1923 (as was Mount Washington). It is not a highly regarded climb, so only the standard route will be described. A full accounting of other routes on Three Fingered Jack, all of which are reportedly on very rotten rock, is contained in Jeff Thomas's *Oregon High*, for those so inclined. Just don't say I didn't warn you.

Potable water is scarce here, so bring plenty along. Also, when approaching and descending from the summit, take care not to cause any further erosion or exacerbate what has already been created by heedless herds of climbers.

Fill out a self-issue permit prior to entry into Three Fingered Jack Wilderness. A Recreation Pass is required to park at or near the trailhead.

For access and permit information, contact Sisters Ranger District, Pine Street and Highway 20, P.O. Box 249, Sisters, OR 97759, (541) 549-7700; or Detroit Ranger District, HC-73, Box 320, Mill City, OR 97360, (503) 854-3366; www.fs.fed.us/r6/willamette.

1. South Ridge
Difficulty rating: 3
Grade: II
Class: 5.2
Time to summit: 4–6 hours
Objective hazards: Loose rock, exposure to rockfall

Three Fingered Jack—Summit Ridge

Photo Owen Purschwitz

The easiest route up Three Fingered Jack, and the only "recommended" route, begins from Santiam Pass Highway (US 20) via the Pacific Crest Trail (PCT). The PCT trailhead is located a short distance west of Santiam Pass, on a well-marked loop road to the north. After about 5 miles of hiking north, the trail contours around a southern shoulder of Three Fingered Jack (Point 6961 on the USGS map), which now comes into full view. Within 0.5 mile an obvious climber's trail leads up the scree toward the South Ridge saddle.

From the saddle, scramble up the loose ridge toward the summit formation. At a point about 200 feet below the summit, a gendarme blocks easy progress. Traverse a narrow, exposed ledge (The Crawl) on the east side to pass the gendarme, and continue to the summit pinnacle. The traverse may seem frighteningly exposed and loose to some, but much of the loose rock has already been pulled or kicked off. Still, as Cascade volcanoes go, Three Fingered Jack is looser than most. Once across the traverse, a concave wall and shallow chimney give relatively solid access to the summit.

A rope and a few chocks are recommended for the gendarme traverse and the final pitch to the summit, both of which are very exposed Class 4 or easy Class 5 on less than perfect rock with more or less no protection for the leader. The climbing is easy enough that many experienced climbers proceed unroped, but the rock is friable in places, which has contributed to some long falls. This is definitely not a route for inexperienced climbers. A helmet might also be useful here.

Descent: Descend via the route of ascent. The descent involves rappelling off the summit pinnacle and downclimbing the Crawl.

10.

Mount Washington

Mount Washington (7,794 feet/2,376 meters), another rotten remnant of a former volcano, has a well-founded reputation for loose rock. Indeed, within ten years of the mountain's first ascent, the original route had disintegrated. The modern North Ridge route climbs slightly more stable rock closer to the ridge crest.

Mount Washington was first ascended in 1923, one of the last of the peaks included in this guide to be climbed. Up until that year, despite numerous attempts, Washington had repelled all comers. No one had been able to pass the first step of the upper North Ridge, which had been chosen as the most likely route to "go." The "Boys from Bend," perhaps undaunted by the mountain's reputation for hideous looseness and impenetrability, found a passage via a rotten ledge and even more rotten chimney. Ervin McNeal boldly led the exposed crux

Climbers approaching the North Ridge on Mount Washington.
PHOTO PETE KEANE/TIMBERLINE MOUNTAIN GUIDES

Mount Washington.
PHOTO MAX KESSLER

chimney, followed by Leo Harryman, Phil Philbrook, Armin Furrer, Wilbur Watkins, and Ron Sellers.

Although Mount Washington has numerous technical rock routes, these are not included in this guide, partly because few parties will (or even want to) climb most of the technical routes, which involve steep, exposed, loose rock. There are said to be some excellent free climbing pitches on Mount Washington, but these are situated between many pitches of ugly rock. Most users of this guide hopefully will prefer to reach the summit of Mount Washington by the easiest route possible rather than grapple with truly bad rock. With the recognition of nearby Smith Rock as one of the world's leading technical rock climbing areas, fewer ascents of Mount Washington's technical climbs will likely be made. Rock climbing specialists will undoubtedly prefer a 0.5-mile descent into the Crooked River Gorge than a dry 5-mile ascent of crumbly Mount Washington. However, if you are interested in climbing the technical rock routes on Mount Washington, *Oregon High* by Jeff Thomas lists them all. Have fun!

Potable water is scarce in Mount Washington Wilderness, so be sure to bring plenty along. Camping within the wilderness is typically hot and dry, and not recommended. Ascents are practical in one day, although some prefer to make an overnight trip despite limited water supplies and poor camping prospects.

Fill out a self-issue permit prior to entry into Mount Washington Wilderness. A Recreation Pass is required to park at the trailhead.

For access and permit information, contact Sisters Ranger District, Pine Street and Highway 20, P.O. Box 249, Sisters, OR 97759, (541) 549-7700; or Detroit Ranger District, HC-73, Box 320, Mill City, OR 97360, (503) 854-3366, www.fs.fed.us/r6/willamette.

1. North Ridge
Difficulty rating: 3
Grade: II
Class: 5.3
Time to summit: 5–6 hours
Objective hazards: Loose rock, exposed to rockfall

The North Ridge route is the easiest and most direct route to the summit of Mount Washington. Although it is not technically difficult as rock climbs go, it still involves challenging and exposed climbing on very poor quality rock.

Approach via the Pacific Crest Trail (PCT) from near Big Lake. Drive Santiam Pass Highway (US 20) to Hoodoo Ski Bowl and take FR 2690 south 2 miles to Big Lake. Just before reaching the lake, turn left onto the old Santiam Wagon Road (FR 500) and in 0.5 mile reach the junction with the PCT. (Alternatively, social trails south of Big Lake shortcut from Patjens Lake Trail to join the PCT after 1 mile, which is not much shorter really, and environmentally insensitive to boot.)

Hike south on the PCT for about 3.5 miles to where a cairn marks a climber's path heading east toward the north ridge of Mount Washington. The path contours onto the north ridge (just south of Point 6323) and

Mount Washington

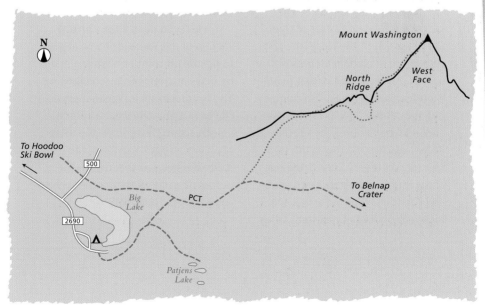

Mount Washington—North Ridge

North Ridge

The Nose

West Ridge

Descent to PCT

PHOTO OWEN PURSCHWITZ

continues along the east edge of the ridge until a westerly descent around the final pinnacles leads up a loose gully to the prominent saddle.

Most parties rope up at the saddle, as the next 75 feet of climbing to the top of The Nose (the first step) is the most difficult on the route. Scramble right 15 feet to enter a left-leaning chimney. The chimney peters out after 30 feet, where left-angling face climbing for another 30 feet reaches the top of the step. This section is easy Class 5; the rest of the route varies between Class 3 and easy Class 5 on loose volcanic rock with poor to nonexistent belay anchors. Party-caused rockfall is common on this route. Many parties unrope above The Nose, as the remaining climb is fairly straightforward except for a final short gully. If you feel you need a rope on any section of this route, don't be afraid to tie one on, although finding quality belay anchors can be challenging. This is not a route for inexperienced climbers. Definitely wear a helmet.

Descent: Descend via the route of ascent. Rappels may be made down the steepest sections on the descent, but check the anchors before committing to a rappel.

11.

Three Sisters

The Sisters are three prominent volcanoes situated just east of Bend, Oregon, each rising to just over 10,000 feet. The peaks are moderately glaciated, although these glaciers are mild and relatively uncrevassed in contrast to the glaciers on Mount Shasta and Mount Hood. Each of the three mountains can be climbed via relatively simple north–south ridges, except the summit pinnacle of North Sister, which involves loose rock climbing. It is not uncommon for climbers to traverse the entire group in a single long day (a "Three Sisters Marathon"). For those not up to a one-day marathon, it is more feasible to complete the traverse with a bivouac.

The Three Sisters have been named Faith, Hope, and Charity by some kindred, naive soul; more aptly, they would be Big Sister (South), Little Sister (Middle), and Ugly Sister (North). Boring, Dull, and Crumbly, which is what they are by their easiest routes, respectively, might be even more apt.

Fill out a self-issue permit prior to day-use entry into Three Sisters Wilderness. A Recreation Pass is required for parking at trailheads. Overnight stays in the Obsidian area require a Limited Access Permit from the Sisters Ranger District or Detroit Ranger District offices. There are camping and campfire setbacks in certain areas of Three Sisters Wilderness; be sure to check at ranger stations or trailheads for specifics.

For access and permit information, contact Sisters Ranger District, Pine Street and Highway 20, P.O. Box

Climbers make their way up the North Sister.
PHOTO CHRIS WRIGHT/TIMBERLINE MOUNTAIN GUIDES

249, Sisters, OR 97759; (541) 549-7700; Bend Ranger District, 1645 Hwy. 20 East, Bend, OR 97701, (503) 388-5664; McKenzie Ranger District, 57600 McKenzie Hwy., McKenzie Bridge, OR 97413, (503) 822-3381; or Rigdon/Oakridge Ranger District, 49098 Salmon Creek Rd., Oakridge, OR 97463, (503) 782-2291, www.fs.fed.us/r6/centraloregon/recreation/special/wilderness/threesisters.shtml.

NORTH SISTER

North Sister (10,085 feet/3,074 meters) is the oldest and most rugged of the Three Sisters group. The mountain's west flank is fairly moderate, but the east face is characteristically craggy and very unstable. North Sister once rose to an estimated height of over 11,000 feet. However, the mountain's construction was its downfall. The soft andesite cone has been erased, the crater is indistinguishable, and the remaining volcano has lost about one-third of its original mass to erosion. What is left is basically a big heap of loose volcanic rubble. North Sister, the "Black Beast of the Cascades," is a big, ugly mountain with two distinct pinnacles and numerous crumbly gendarmes decorating its scree-laden ridges. The higher horn is Prouty and a sub-summit is Glisan, named for venerated members of the Mazamas climbing club.

Because of the variable volcanic composition of the mountain, all routes involve climbing over remarkably unstable rock with high rockfall hazard. Massive rockfalls on the east and west faces are likely in the future; minor rockfalls are nearly constant on North Sister, except when the mountain is coated with ice. Any route climbing a couloir or gully on North Sister is a veritable shooting range (the main chute up Prouty is called the Bowling Alley). Thus, North Sister is a more serious objective

North Sister.
PHOTO LICENSED BY
SHUTTERSTOCK.COM

than Middle or South Sisters. Expect loose rock and copious rockfall no matter where you venture on this mountain, even under the best conditions. All things considered, this peak is not particularly safe by any route. You should come when the mountain is frozen and has some snow cover, so some of the loose rocks will be frozen in place during your climb. That said, some climbers prefer to climb North Sister in late season to avoid snow because climbing on mixed snow and rock can be even more hazardous than climbing on the bare, loose rock.

Three Sisters–Obsidian Trail Approach

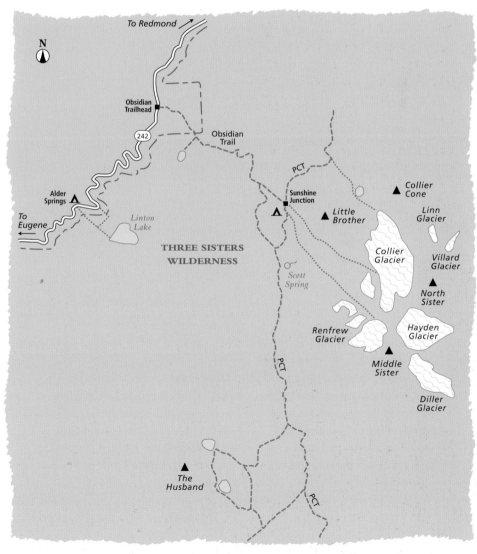

Three Sisters–East Side Approaches

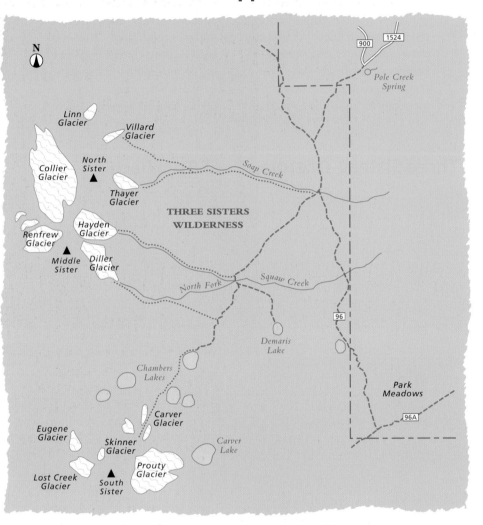

Because of rockfall, all routes on the east and west faces of North Sister are extremely dangerous, and none except the easier routes are often climbed. If you must climb North Sister, do so by one of the ridge routes, preferably the South or Southeast Ridges. Helmets should be considered mandatory for all routes on North Sister. Winter conditions may reduce rockfall hazard, but will by no means eliminate it completely.

North Sister—South Ridge

Prouty

Glisan

4

NW Ridge

Terrible
Traverse

Camel's Hump

SE Ridge

1

South
Ridge

PHOTO BOB BOLTON

1. South Ridge
Difficulty rating: 3
Grade: II
Class: 4–5
Time to summit: 6 hours
Objective hazards: Exposed to rockfall, loose rock, moderately avalanche prone

> The conquest of this mountain is probably one of the most brilliant feats ever attempted in America.
> —*Photo caption in 1905* Mazama

The South Ridge route was first ascended in 1910 by H. H. Prouty, the first member of a large Mazama party to surmount the summit pinnacle. It is the most popular route up North Sister, only because it is the most straightforward, but even so it is not entirely safe and thus not truly "popular."

This and other routes originating from the North-Middle Sister saddle begin from the well-signed Obsidian Trailhead 3528 just off OR 242 southwest of McKenzie Pass. Hike 3.5 miles to a junction. Take the left fork (Spur 3528A) another 1 mile to reach the former site of Sunshine Shelter and a junction with the PCT (known as Sunshine Junction or simply Sunshine). From Sunshine Junction a climber's trail continues southeast toward North Sister. Follow the climber's trail then continue with cross-country hiking for another 1.5 miles to the Collier Glacier. Cross the glacier and ascend snow or scree slopes to gain the South Ridge.

Once on the ridge the route is straightforward. Ascend snow and scree slopes directly up or closely right of the ridge crest to a point just below and south of the first big gendarme. Traverse below the gendarme on the left (west) side, then regain the ridge crest, passing another gendarme on the right (east) side, to a saddle just below the south Prouty horn. Here begins the "Terrible Traverse," a steep, exposed snow and/or scree traverse below the south horn, which is considered by many to be the most hazardous part of the climb. The traverse is considered best by some when completely snow covered, worse when just scree (although some prefer the traverse snow free), worst when patchy snow and scree. Some climbers cringe in terror while clawing their way across the shattered rock; others cruise right across. Once across, ascend the snow chute or rock gully (the Bowling Alley) splitting the Prouty horns. Ascend the gully to the gap between the Prouty horns, staying high and right at the top to avoid the worst of the loose rock, then scramble north to the summit over slightly more stable rock. When there is no snow in the gully, come

prepared for loose Class 4–5 and almost certain rockfall.

Variations include the Southeast Ridge, which has a longer approach from the east side and joins the South Ridge higher up; and the West Face, which leads more directly to the Bowling Alley via steep snow climbing but is more exposed to rockfall and avalanches depending on snow conditions. Routes also ascend directly up the West Face from Collier Glacier. Most parties stick to the South Ridge route, however, because it is the shortest route to the summit.

Descent: Descend via the route of ascent or the Northwest Ridge route; a rappel can be made down the last bit of the Bowling Alley if a good anchor can be found.

2. East Face—
Early Morning Couloir
Difficulty rating: 3
Grade: III
Class: 4–5, AI1–2
Time to summit: 6 hours
Objective hazards: Highly prone to avalanching and exposed to rockfall

> ROCK! A big one was lazily bounding down the fall line 2,000 feet above us. Nothing to do but move—quickly—crouch, wait.
>
> —Nicholas Dodge, during the first ascent in 1968

North Sister—East Face

Glisan
Pinnacle

East
Buttress

Camel's
Hump

1

SE Spur of
South Ridge

NE Arête

3

2

Villard
Glacier

PHOTO PETE KEANE

This route climbs the obvious couloir on the east face of North Sister leading directly to the base of Glisan Pinnacle. Being a couloir on a notoriously rotten mountain face, it is a natural rockfall and avalanche funnel. An enjoyable climb during stable snow conditions, it is recommended only in early season when well frozen. Expect rocks to start rolling down the couloir once the sun hits the upper slopes of the east face.

This and the Villard Glacier route are best approached from the east via Pole Creek Springs. From McKenzie Pass Highway (OR 242), head south on well-marked Pole Creek Springs Road (FR 1524); if coming from McKenzie Pass, drive south on FR 1018 to its junction with FR 1524. Follow FR 1524 to its end (about 3 miles from the junction). Pole Creek Springs Trail 96D leads about 1.5 miles to a junction with Three Sisters Trail 96, the main north–south trail east of Three Sisters. Cross-country hiking or skiing west from this junction, along or near Soap Creek, leads to North Sister's east face.

From the base of the east face, ascend steep snow to enter the couloir, then ascend directly to the headwall of Glisan. From here, either traverse right along the base of

Glisan to finish as for Villard Glacier or climb the rock shoulder of Glisan directly. The direct finish is reportedly up to 5.7 in difficulty, on varying degrees of loose rock depending on the route taken.

Descent: Descend via the Villard Glacier or South Ridge routes.

3. Villard Glacier
Difficulty rating: 2
Grade: II
Class: 4–5
Time to summit: 6 hours
Objective hazards: Highly prone to avalanching and exposed to rockfall

Of the east face routes on North Sister, Villard Glacier is the most straightforward and easiest, following moderately steep snow slopes directly to the summit ridge just north of Glisan.

Approach via Pole Creek Springs as for the East Face—Early Morning Couloir route. Ascend the glacier and snow slopes to the summit ridge just north of Glisan. Traverse around the west side to the saddle between Glisan and Prouty, then scramble over blocky rock to the summit. Villard Glacier is highly prone to avalanching in the spring; ascend only during stable snow conditions. The route's difficulty depends on which route you take to the summit and whether you climb Prouty or Glisan.

Descent: Descend via the route of ascent or the South Ridge route.

4. Northwest Ridge
Difficulty rating: 3
Grade: II
Class: 4–5
Time to summit: 8–10 hours
Objective hazards: Exposed to rockfall, loose rock

The Northwest Ridge is said to be the safest route to the summit of North Sister, but it is quite long and not nearly as popular as the South Ridge route.

Approach via the Obsidian Trail to Sunshine, then traverse cross-country to the Collier Glacier. Cross the glacier or moraines, passing Little Brother on either its north or south sides, to gain the Northwest Ridge. Alternatively, continue north on the PCT from Sunshine until it is feasible to hike cross-country to the ridge. Either approach is longer and more complicated than the South Ridge, which is probably the primary reason the route is not as popular.

Once you reach the ridge, ascend it more or less directly. Where the ridge becomes too narrow, drop down on the west side. A loose traverse around Glisan leads to the saddle dividing Glisan from Prouty. The final pitch up Prouty is very loose, and if you can climb snow instead of rock, do so. Glisan is an easier, safer climb from the gap and is recommended if your ego permits skipping the true summit. Alternatively, traverse around Prouty on the northwest side (scree or snow, rockfall hazard) to the Bowling Alley chute.

Descent: Descend via the route of ascent or the South Ridge route.

MIDDLE SISTER

Middle Sister (10,047 feet/3,062 meters) is a simple cone that has had some erosion on its east face. It is fairly unremarkable, with a few challenging routes on the east face. There are numerous possible routes climbing the south slope and southeast ridge via snow or scree, none of which involve technical climbing. Routes on the east face have rockfall danger and should be climbed only when well frozen.

5. North Ridge
Difficulty rating: 0
Grade: I
Class: 2
Time to summit: 2–4 hours
Objective hazards: Mildly prone to avalanching, possible rockfall

The North Ridge is the most direct route up Middle Sister, a straightforward snow or cinder hike. Almost any route on the north, west, and south sides of Middle Sister is similar in character, although the approaches are longer.

Approach approximately as for North Sister's South Ridge route, but bearing south toward the col, or approach more directly via Renfrew Glacier. From the col dividing North and Middle Sister, ascend the easy snow and cinder ridge to the summit. Most parties climb from the saddle to the summit in about an hour.

The route can be avalanche prone during periods of unstable snow, and climber-caused rockfall is a possibility, but it is generally a safe route under all but the worst conditions.

Middle Sister.
Photo Owen Purschwitz

Middle Sister

SE Ridge
6

North Ridge

5

7

Diller
Glacier

8

Hayden
Glacier

9

PHOTO OWEN PURSCHWITZ

Descent: Descend via the route of ascent unless traversing to South Sister.

6. Southeast Ridge
Difficulty rating: 0
Grade: I
Class: 2
Time to summit: 2–4 hours
Objective hazards: Mildly prone to avalanching, possible rockfall exposure

There are numerous possible routes climbing Middle Sister's south slope and southeast ridge via snow or scree, none of which involve technical climbing. The Southeast Ridge is the most popular of the south-side routes, ascending a gentle snow or pumice ridge from the Diller Glacier to the summit.

Approach from the east via Pole Creek Springs, or cross the col between North and Middle Sister and drop down and across Hayden Glacier to reach Diller Glacier. Beware of crevasses on Diller Glacier if you cross it approaching or descending the ridge. Follow the ridge to the summit, staying west of the crest where appropriate to avoid triggering a scree slide and falling down the east face.

Descent: Descend via the route of ascent or the North Ridge route.

7. East Face

Difficulty rating: 4
Grade: III
Class: 4–5, AI1–2
Time to summit: 6 hours
Objective hazards: Highly prone to avalanching and exposed to rockfall

This route ascends a snow gully through the Diller Glacier headwall rock bands more or less directly to the summit. Like other volcano headwall routes, this route has unsound rock and is subject to random rockfall, but it's a good climb when snow covered and well frozen.

Middle Sister's east face can be reached by hiking cross-country to Hayden Glacier from about halfway along Chambers Lakes Trail 96B, which is reached about 0.5 mile south from the Pole Creek Springs Trail junction. Alternatively, approach from the west to the North-Middle Sister col, descend from the col to Hayden Glacier, then traverse to Diller Glacier.

However you approach, ascend Diller Glacier to the base of the east face, directly above a prominent V-shaped moraine. Traverse to the base of the central gully, cut right above the bergschrund, and ascend the gully. A short rock band is the only difficulty. Finish the route before the sun hits it to minimize rockfall exposure. The route is avalanche prone, especially in spring, and should be climbed only during stable snow conditions.

Descent: Descend via either the North Ridge or Southeast Ridge routes.

8. East Arête

Difficulty rating: 4
Grade: III
Class: 5.6
Time to summit: 6–8 hours
Objective hazards: Loose rock, exposed to rockfall

This is a fairly technical route up the arête dividing the Diller and Hayden Glacier headwalls. It is said to be a good route during favorable conditions, but involves some climbing on rotten volcanic rock.

Approach from the east as for the East Face or from the west over the North-Middle Sister col to reach Hayden Glacier. However you approach, aim for the medial moraine between Diller and Hayden Glaciers and cross the glaciers to the base of the arête. Climb steepening snow, passing an obvious pinnacle on the right to the base of the first rock band. Pass the rock band just left of an obvious wide couloir, climbing a little more than one rope length of Class 4 rock. Continue up another rope length of steep snow to a second rock band, which may be passed via an obvious chimney just right of the arête. Ascend the chimney about 50 feet (5.6) and traverse right a few moves, then continue up another 50 feet to the crest of the arête. Continue up snow to where the arête meets the North Ridge, then on to the summit.

Descent: Descend via the North Ridge or Southeast Ridge routes.

9. Northeast Face
Difficulty rating: 4
Grade: III
Class: 5.6 or WI3
Time to summit: 4–6 hours
Objective hazards: Highly prone to avalanching and exposed to rockfall

This route ascends an obvious couloir and gullies directly through the Hayden Glacier headwall. It is an active rockfall funnel and avalanche chute, so beware!

Approach from the east or the west via the Hayden Glacier to the base of the obvious couloir. Ascend steepening snow, passing two bergschrunds, to where the couloir narrows. At about 500 feet above the glacier, the couloir terminates in a rock (or ice) wall. Pass the wall via about one rope length of steep, rotten rock or possibly a frozen waterfall. (The frozen waterfall is the preferred route.) Once above the crux wall, continue right along a steep snow traverse beneath

Hikers high on the South Sister Climber's Trail.

a rock wall to a snow rib that leads above the rock face. Easy snow slopes (avalanche prone during poor conditions) lead to a steep snow traverse left around another rock band. Gain the East Arête just below where it merges with the North Ridge and continue to the summit.

Descent: Descend via the North Ridge or Southeast Ridge routes.

SOUTH SISTER

South Sister (10,358 feet/3,157 meters) is the tallest of the Sisters group and rivals Mount St. Helens and Mount Hood as the most climbed glaciated volcanic peaks in North America. Its eruptive history is similar to most of the other Oregon volcanoes. Built atop a basaltic base, the mountain is composed of soft andesite topped by a harder basaltic cone. South Sister has a symmetrical form and a nearly perfectly preserved summit crater. More recent eruptions have been from basal or lateral vents, which have produced dacite and obsidian flows.

Most of South Sister's routes have little or no technical challenge, although a few routes pass through difficult rock bands. There are abundant stone windbreaks along the crater rim, providing breathtaking bivouac sites for those possessed by the desire to carry overnight gear up the mountain. After August a small lake (Oregon's highest) forms in the crater.

South Sister.
PHOTO USGS CASCADE VOLCANO OBSERVATORY/GENE IWATSUBO

South Sister Approaches

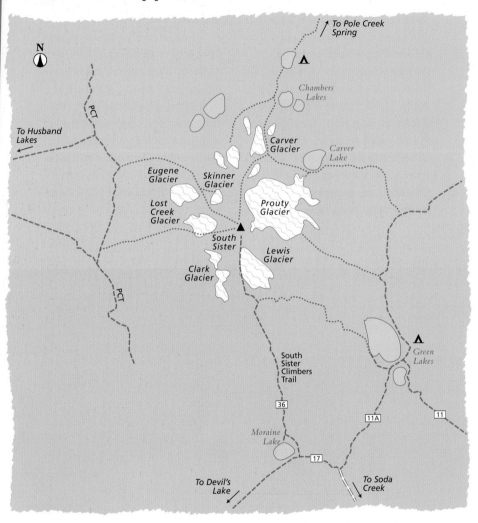

N

To Pole Creek
Spring

Chambers
Lakes

To Husband
Lakes

PCT

Carver
Glacier

Carver
Lake

Eugene
Glacier

Skinner
Glacier

Prouty
Glacier

Lost
Creek
Glacier

South
Sister

Lewis
Glacier

Clark
Glacier

PCT

South
Sister
Climbers
Trail

Green
Lakes

36

11A

11

Moraine
Lake

17

To Devil's
Lake

To Soda
Creek

10. South Sister Climber's Trail
Difficulty rating: 0
Grade: I
Class: 1
Time to summit: 4–6 hours
Objective hazards: Loose scree

South Sister Climber's Trail 36 begins from Devil's Lake and is the easiest, most direct, and most frequently used route to the summit of South Sister. The trail leads the whole way to the summit (5.75 miles one-way), providing snow-free access for adventurers of

South Sister—South Side

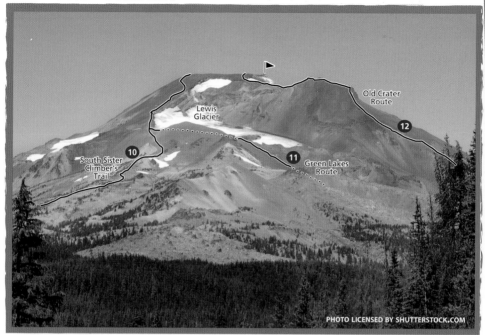

Lewis Glacier

Old Crater Route

South Sister Climber's Trail

10

11

Green Lakes Route

12

PHOTO LICENSED BY SHUTTERSTOCK.COM

all shapes, sizes, and species on summer weekends after July. The final 1 mile to the summit follows "the Mother of all cinder ridges," a breathtakingly horrendous scree slog. Bring plenty of water and don't be ashamed to take a rest break; everyone else does, if only to interrupt the sheer tedium of hiking up the ridge. It is a long, monotonous, crowded hike—great if you're a hiker, lousy if you're a climber. The views are worth the hike, but just barely.

This trail is badly eroded. In places, shifting pumice blocks make footing precarious and progress negligible. Take care with each step, not only for your sake but also for the safety of others. A fall could land you in some

very rough scree, and a dislodged rock could cause severe injury to those hiking below. Sturdy lug-soled boots are recommended for stability and foot and ankle protection.

Camping in the summit crater is semipopular among the masochistic crowd that enjoys lugging overnight gear and water up there.

Descent: Descend via the route of ascent.

11. Green Lakes Route
Difficulty rating: 0
Grade: II
Class: 1
Time to summit: 6 hours
Objective hazards: Mildly prone to avalanching

South Sister—East Side

PHOTO OWEN PURSCHWITZ

The usual route up South Sister before the Climber's Trail went in was the Green Lakes route. It ascends snow gullies and scree slopes and ridges from Green Lakes on the mountain's southeast side and is still a good alternative for those seeking a nontechnical climb without the crowds.

Approach via Green Lakes Trail, the usual approach for routes on the east side of South Sister. The trail begins from a well-signed trailhead just west of Soda Creek Campground on OR 46 west of Bend, at Sparks Lake, and leads 4.5 miles to Green Lakes. There are two trails,

Forest Service Trail 11 and the more scenic Trail 11A, which accesses Moraine Lake Trail 17. Some parties camp at or near Green Lakes and make a round-trip ascent the next morning. No campfires are permitted within 0.5 mile of Green Lakes, and campsites must be more than 100 feet away from lakeshores. This is a highly impacted area, so take care. A Limited Access Permit is required for overnight camping.

From Green Lakes, ascend directly to the head of the southeast drainage basin to reach the south ridge/slope. Don't climb the gully directly, but find a "trail" on the right (stay right, nearer the trees, to avoid unnecessary erosion of this heavily damaged slope). Continue up a steep climber's trail and snow slopes, then skirt around Lewis Glacier to join the South Sister Climber's Trail.

The Lewis Glacier offers a direct variation, avoiding the climber's trail, but it doesn't save much time on the ascent. It offers an enticing glissading shortcut on the way down, but the glacier is steep and may have hidden crevasses.

Descent: Descend via the route of ascent or the East Ridge—Old Crater Route.

12. East Ridge—Old Crater Route
Difficulty rating: 1
Grade: II
Class: 2
Time to summit: 6 hours
Objective hazards: Mildly prone to avalanching

The Old Crater Route is a straightforward, simple ascent—a tedious scree and snow hike by climbing standards—just like the South Sister Climber's Trail but without the trail or the throngs of day hikers.

Hike to Green Lakes, then ascend moraines to the base of the mountain's east ridge and continue up the gentle ridge directly to the summit, straying left (south) of the crest as necessary to skirt rotten rock. It is a long, tedious scree hike by late

season, better done in early season on snow. The final portion of the ridge is along the rim of one of South Sister's craters.

Descent: Descend via the route of ascent or the Green Lakes route.

13. Prouty Glacier
Difficulty rating: 2
Grade: II
Class: N/A
Time to summit: 6–8 hours
Objective hazards: Moderately prone to avalanching and exposed to rockfall

Prouty is the largest glacier on South Sister, residing on the northeastern flank of the mountain. It offers the only true glacier climb on South Sister.

From the northernmost point of Green Lakes, hike cross-country up an obvious low-angled gully toward a gap in Prouty Glacier's terminal moraine to reach the glacier's south flank. Ascend the glacier, passing the headwall via a broad snow chute and rock, closely right of the mountain's east ridge to reach the upper snow slopes. Variations climb the headwall more directly, but with increased exposure to rockfall. The main route has no technical difficulty, just snow or ice and crevasses.

Descent: Descend via the route of ascent or go up and over the East Ridge—Old Crater Route, Green Lakes, or South Sister Climber's Trail.

South Sister—North Side

PHOTO OWEN PURSCHWITZ

14. North Ridge
Difficulty rating: 2
Grade: II
Class: 3–4
Time to summit: 6 hours
Objective hazards: Loose rock, exposed to rockfall

The North Ridge is not a popular route because of its long approach and unworthy climbing, but is frequently ascended anyway because it is the fastest way to the summit of South Sister for those wishing to complete a Three Sisters Marathon.

If approaching from Green Lakes, contour past Prouty Glacier to Carver Lake to gain the obvious ridge. Alternatively, hike from Pole Creek Springs to Chambers Lakes (about 7 miles) and gain the ridge directly. Or, if you are doing a marathon, approach by traversing over Middle Sister.

Ascend a long cinder slope more than halfway to the summit until halted by a red rock buttress. A short, loose, mildly difficult traverse (unfavorably compared to the Bowling Alley chute on North Sister) eventually leads to the right flank of the buttress, where an easy snow or cinder slope ascends to the crater rim just below the summit. Rockfall from the buttress is a definite hazard.

Descent: Descend via the route of ascent or Prouty Glacier, East Ridge—Old Crater Route, Green Lakes, or South Sister Climber's Trail.

15. Silver Couloir
Difficulty rating: 4
Grade: III
Class: 4–5, AI2
Time to summit: 8–10 hours
Objective hazards: Highly prone to avalanching and exposed to rockfall

This is the leftmost and least technical of the two prominent couloirs on the north face of South Sister. Approach via either Green Lakes, Pole Creek Spring, or the PCT near Separation Creek (in that order of preference) to Skinner Glacier.

From the head of Skinner Glacier, ascend the couloir directly, avoiding or overcoming some short rock bands. The route is best if snow covered and well frozen; rockfall is likely at any other time. Silver Couloir is avalanche prone like any other couloir route.

Descent: Descend via the Prouty Glacier route or one of the other nontechnical routes, whichever gets you back to your car the quickest.

16. North Face Couloir
Difficulty rating: 4
Grade: III
Class: 4–5, AI2
Time to summit: 8–10 hours
Objective hazards: Highly prone to avalanching and exposed to rockfall

This is the other prominent couloir on the north face, on the right. It is a bit more difficult than Silver Couloir.

Approach as for Silver Couloir but traverse farther right (west) and ascend the right-hand couloir on snow or ice, passing through several loose rock bands. Follow the narrowing couloir as it pinches down to chimney size at the last rock band. Like other rockfall-prone volcanic headwalls, this route is best climbed when well frozen, when ice permits easier climbing over rock bands and frozen snow holds loose stuff in place. If you hit it during prime conditions, it is mostly snow and ice climbing with very little rock. Come prepared for steep, difficult ice with possible verglas over loose rock.

Descent: Descend via the Prouty Glacier route or whichever of the other nontechnical routes gets you back to your car the quickest.

Broken Top Approaches

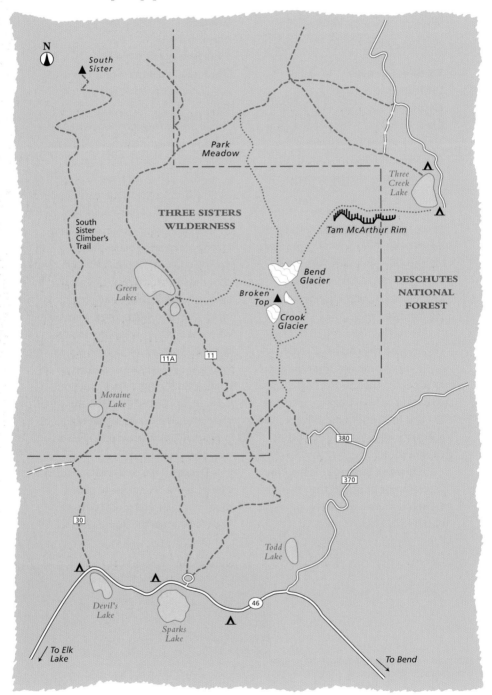

12.

Broken Top

Broken Top (9,175 feet/2,797 meters) is a craggy volcanic remnant with two glaciers situated at the eastern border of Oregon's Three Sisters Wilderness, directly north of Mount Bachelor. Broken Top has had a violent eruptive history, including a massive hot avalanche that devastated an estimated 200-square-mile area, including what are now suburbs of Bend. The mountain was significantly higher at one time, but the combination of being blown up and worn down by glaciation took a lot off the top. Interestingly, climbers can view the former interior of the volcano, including its stratification, which has been revealed by erosion.

The routes all involve rock of varying degrees of difficulty, inconsistency, and instability. Rockfall is a real danger on all Broken Top routes, and helmets should be considered mandatory. Like North Sister, no route on Broken Top is really recommended. If all you want to do is summit, take the Northwest Ridge route. The Northwest Ridge also is the fastest and safest descent for all routes on Broken Top. There are several difficult routes on the north face that have a reputation for being death routes, but are actually quite popular and enjoyable winter ascents during perfectly frozen conditions. The rock on Broken Top is some of the worst on any of the Cascade volcanoes, making all but two of the routes on the mountain not even worth considering when not encased in firmly frozen snow.

For access and permit information, contact Sisters Ranger District, Pine Street and Highway 20, P.O. Box 249, Sisters, OR 97759, (541) 549-7700; Bend Ranger District, 1645 Hwy. 20 East, Bend, OR 97701, (503) 388-5664; McKenzie Ranger District, 57600 McKenzie Hwy., McKenzie Bridge, OR 97413, (503) 822-3381; or Rigdon/Oakridge Ranger District, 49098 Salmon Creek Rd., Oakridge, OR 97463, (503) 782-2291, www.fs.fed.us/r6/centraloregon/recreation/special/wilderness/threesisters.shtml.

Broken Top.
PHOTO BOB BOLTON

1. Northwest Ridge
Difficulty rating: 2
Grade: I
Class: 3–4
Time to summit: 3–4 hours
Objective hazards: Loose rock, exposed to rockfall

This route is not the best route up Broken Top, but is the most direct and easiest way to the summit and back down, and thus the most popular.

Approach via Green Lakes Trail, which trail begins from a well-signed trailhead just west of Soda Creek Campground on OR 46 west of Bend, at Sparks Lake, and leads 4.5 miles to Green Lakes. There are two trails, Forest Service Trail 11 and the more scenic Trail 11A—both reach Green Lakes. Hike cross-country due east and ascend to an obvious saddle on the Northwest Ridge. Tedious scree slopes lead directly up the ridge to a point just below where it abuts the summit block. Pass a very short rock band (loose Class 4) to reach the base of the summit block. A ledge traverse right leads to a very loose but easy scramble to the summit. A more direct rock pitch (easy Class 5) is more solid.

Northwest Ridge

NW Ridge ①

Eleven O'Clock Couloir Exit ③

Nine O'Clock Couloir Exit ②

Broken Top—Summit Detail

PHOTO MATT STAMPLIS

Descent: Descend via the route of ascent.

CROOK GLACIER— CRATER WALL ROUTES

There are several routes ascending the crater wall above Crook Glacier, all but one of which is recommended only in winter or early season when snow covered and well frozen, as they are rockfall and avalanche funnels at any other time.

Approach via rough but scenic Todd Lake Road 370 (about 2 miles east of the Bachelor Butte turnoff on OR 46). There are some monster potholes along the way, so watch out! At about 4 miles, take a left turn on FR 380 (not FR 378, which ends in a loop much farther south of Broken Top). From road's end, Crater Gulch Trail 10 leads about 0.5 mile to Crater Creek. Follow the creek north (cross-country) to Crook Glacier.

The crater wall routes should not be climbed or descended unless well covered with snow and frozen solid. They are avalanche prone, requiring stable snow conditions, and are not at all recommended after the snow has melted away, except the South Gully route, which can be climbed in late season. Expect very loose rock and high exposure to rockfall on all routes. Once sunlight hits the crater wall, rockfall tends to increase, so climb early before the daily thaw begins.

Broken Top—Crater Routes

Crook Glacier

The rock on the crater rim and wall is some of the worst imaginable; if you can't find solid rock to climb on, try another route. Descend via the Northwest Ridge route and hike back to the trailhead via Green Lakes.

2. Nine O'Clock Couloir
Difficulty rating: 2
Grade: I
Class: 4–5, AI1
Time to summit: 3-4 hours
Objective hazards: Highly prone to avalanching and exposed to rockfall

Ascend the leftmost of the two obvious gullies in the crater's west wall to the lowest gap in the crater wall.

The last bit to the gap is via a narrow snow gully. This is an enjoyable snow climb (less so in late season). Don't try to climb the rotten ridge crest above the gap; stay west of the crater rim on scree or snow slopes, traversing to join the Northwest Ridge for the final climb to the summit pinnacle.

Descent: Descend via the route of ascent or the Northwest Ridge route.

3. Eleven O'Clock Couloir
Difficulty rating: 3
Grade: II
Class: 4–5, AI2
Time to summit: 3–4 hours
Objective hazards: Highly prone to avalanching and exposed to rockfall

The next obvious couloir to the right of Nine O'Clock Couloir is a more direct climb up a longer, steeper snow gully to the notch just west of the summit formation. This route should only be climbed during stable snow conditions when well frozen; do not climb it after the snow has melted out. As on Nine O'Clock, do not attempt to climb the rotten ridge crest above the gap; stay west of the crater rim to join the Northwest Ridge route to the top.

Descent: Descend via Nine O'Clock Couloir or the Northwest Ridge route.

4. High Noon
Difficulty rating: 4
Grade: III
Class: 5, AI3
Time to summit: 4–6 hours
Objective hazards: Loose rock, highly avalanche prone and exposed to rockfall

High Noon is the most direct and serious of the crater routes, climbing straight up the crater wall to the summit pinnacle. The gully angles right to the base of the summit rock bands, where a left-leading snow/ice ramp continues to the summit. This route should only be done when snow covered and frozen solid, to avoid rockfall and avalanche hazard. The final pitches are steep and exposed. Try to avoid being on the face when the sun hits. It may be possible to escape from below the rock bands to the crater rim east of the pinnacle and descend the South Gully route should conditions warrant. Ice tools, ice screws, and other snow/ice protection are recommended.

Descent: Descend via the Nine O'Clock Couloir, Northwest Ridge, or South Gully routes, whichever you are most familiar with and depending on snow conditions.

5. South Gully
Difficulty rating: 3
Grade: II
Class: 4–5
Time to summit: 4–5 hours
Objective hazards: Highly prone to avalanching and exposed to rockfall, loose rock

This is the only south-side route that can be safely climbed when not snow covered, although it still has loose rock and rockfall exposure. From the crater floor, ascend east to a broad gap in the crater rim, then scramble up the crater rim to the summit pinnacle. The final ascent to the summit involves some steep, loose rock climbing.

Descent: Descend via the route of ascent or the Northwest Ridge or Nine O'Clock Couloir routes, depending on snow conditions.

13.

Mount Bachelor

Mount Bachelor (9,065 feet/2,763 meters), erstwhile Bachelor Butte, is a high, uniform cone located immediately west of Bend on OR 46. Bachelor is best known for its skiing, and has perhaps the most popular ski area in central Oregon. It also has a glacial remnant on its north slope. Geologists have speculated that the mountain is between eruptive cycles. North-slope

Mount Bachelor.
PHOTO **USGS CASCADE VOLCANO OBSERVATORY/GENE IWATSUBO**

Mount Bachelor

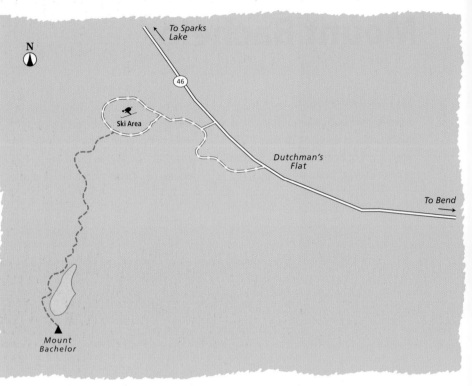

fumaroles, which reportedly sometimes melt snow and trap unwary
skiers, give a clue that the mountain is
still active.

For more information, check the
Mount Bachelor hiking web page:
http://www.mtbachelor.com/
summer/services_activities/activities/
hiking.

1. Mount Bachelor Trail
Difficulty rating: 0
Grade: I
Class: 1

Time to summit: 3–4 hours
Objective hazards: None

The summit trail begins from the ski
area parking lot near the base of the
Sunshine Express chairlift. Drive to the
Sunshine Lodge parking area at Mt.
Bachelor Ski Resort. Hike to the base
of the lift, follow a cat track for about
100 yards right from the lift, then
turn left along a singletrack trail, and
continue switchbacking up the ski
run to the top of the chairlift, where
a green hiker sign marks the hiking

Mount Bachelor Trail

Ski Area

trail leading the rest of the way to the summit. This trail is open only when the ski area is closed. In early season the trail may be obscured by snow; just hike up the snow to the top of the lift and then follow the trail or snow slopes about 3.1 miles to the top. When in doubt, hike uphill.

Descent: Hike back down the trail.

South Central Oregon

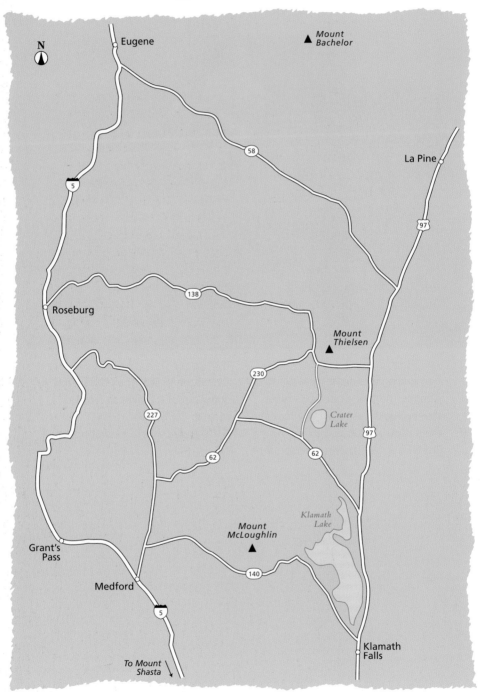

14.

Mount Thielsen

> It gives one almost the same feeling as if one were perched high on a swaying tree; it seems as if the steep rock might suddenly collapse in a puff of wind.
> —*Jamieson Parker, describing the summit of Mount Thielsen in 1921*

Mount Thielsen (9,182 feet/2,799 meters) is known as "The Lightning Rod of the Cascades," not only because its summit horn stands so high but also because Thielsen's summit is struck by lightning seemingly more often than any other Cascade peak. Reasons for this are speculative, but there is ample evidence of lightning strikes on the summit area. Fulgurites (lightning-caused deposits similar to obsidian) found on the summit are of interest to rock collectors and geologists. Like Mount Washington, Thielsen's summit horn is a remnant of basaltic intrusions in the later stages of the volcano's growth. This erosion-resistant plug intruded

Climbers on winter ascent of Mount Thielsen.

Mount Thielsen
Photo USGS Cascade Volcano
Observatory/W. E. Scott

Mount Thielsen Approach

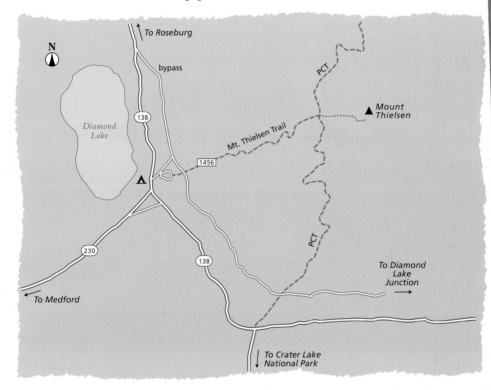

on softer material, which has eroded away, leaving a sharp peak.

As a climb, Thielsen's standard route is not difficult enough to discourage nonclimbers, though difficult enough that maybe it should. The only unusual hazard here is that, during stormy weather, the summit is almost certain to be struck by lightning. If a thunderstorm rolls in, descend immediately if you know what's good for you.

As with Mount Washington and Three Fingered Jack, there are other more technical route possibilities on Mount Thielsen, but most climbers will be content with reaching this impressive summit by the easy route.

For access and permit information, contact Fremont-Winema National Forest Headquarters, 1301 South G Street, Lakeview, OR 97630, (541) 947-2151, or Chemult Ranger District, 110500 Highway 97 N, Chemult, OR 97731, (541), 365-7001. To report an accident or other emergency, dial 911 or call Crater Lake National Park, (541) 594-3100.

Mount Thielsen

Class 3-4

Scree

PHOTO OWEN PURSCHWITZ

1. West Ridge
Difficulty rating: 3
Grade: II
Class: 5.1
Time to summit: 4–6 hours
Objective hazards: Loose scree on approach, avalanche-prone slopes, exposed to rockfall

Oregon's Mount Thielsen sits east of Diamond Lake, which is reached via OR 138 off US 97 south of Bend. Approach from the Diamond Lake parking area, where Mount Thielsen Trail 1456 leads 3 miles east to the Pacific Crest Trail (PCT). Cross the PCT and hike cross-country up the West Ridge to the base of the summit horn. From tree line, two routes are popular. One ascends more or less directly up the ridge (Class 3–4); the other traverses to easier scree slopes to the south and up. The scree slopes consist of sometimes frighteningly unstable blocks and "dinner plates" that threaten to slide out from underfoot, which can be unnerving and create potential rockfall hazard to those climbing below. Climb carefully whichever way you go. Aim for a notch on the southeast side of the summit horn. From the southeast base of the horn, a short pitch of exposed, but fairly solid rock reaches the summit.

Small parties are recommended because there isn't much room on the summit (one source suggests twelve persons could fit comfortably, though that number seems a bit high if comfort is one of your criteria). Although many climbers make this ascent without a rope or protection, it is recommended that you bring a rope and a few chocks in case you change your mind about the final pitch.

Descent: Descend via the route of ascent.

Mount McLoughlin.
PHOTO MIKE GOFF

15.

Mount McLoughlin

Mount McLoughlin (9,495 feet/2,894 meters) is a relatively unknown volcano to those not living in its shadow. It is briefly visible from I-5 west of Medford, Oregon, but is otherwise an unassuming peak that goes largely unnoticed among the higher glaciated giants that are more visible from populated urban areas. Although it is the highest peak between Mount Shasta and South Sister and the sixth-highest summit in Oregon, it is largely ignored by climbers. Like Mount Bachelor it has a trail leading to its summit, giving it little appeal as a climbing objective, but making it a popular ascent with hikers and peak baggers, and a popular winter ski descent.

Mount McLoughlin Trail

Mount McLoughlin is similar to other Cascade volcanoes in at least one respect—its eruptive history. Like nearby Mount Thielsen, it underwent numerous stages of building. However, unlike Thielsen, its summit has been much less dramatically eroded, leaving a less rugged, more uniform profile that is relatively uninspiring compared with Oregon's other high volcanoes.

For access and permit information, contact Fremont-Winema National Forest Headquarters, 1301 South G Street, Lakeview, OR 97630, (541) 947-2151, or Klamath Ranger District, 2819 Dahlia Street, Suite A, Klamath Falls, OR 97601, (541) 883-6714.

1. Mount McLoughlin Trail
Difficulty rating: 0
Grade: I
Class: 1
Time to summit: 3–4 hours
Objective hazards: None

To reach the trail, drive 3 miles west from Lake of the Woods (33 miles east from Klamath Falls on OR 140) to Four Mile Lake Road 3650, which leads 2.5 miles north to Mount McLoughlin Trail 3716. This trail crosses the PCT and climbs strenuously to timberline, where the path becomes less distinct and much steeper. The trail is rocky and steep; sturdy lug-soled boots are recommended for support and foot and ankle protection. The entire trip to the summit is about 6 miles one-way. Routefinding is relatively easy except during poor weather.

Descent: Hike down the trail.

California

Mount Shasta.

PHOTO LICENSED BY SHUTTERSTOCK.COM

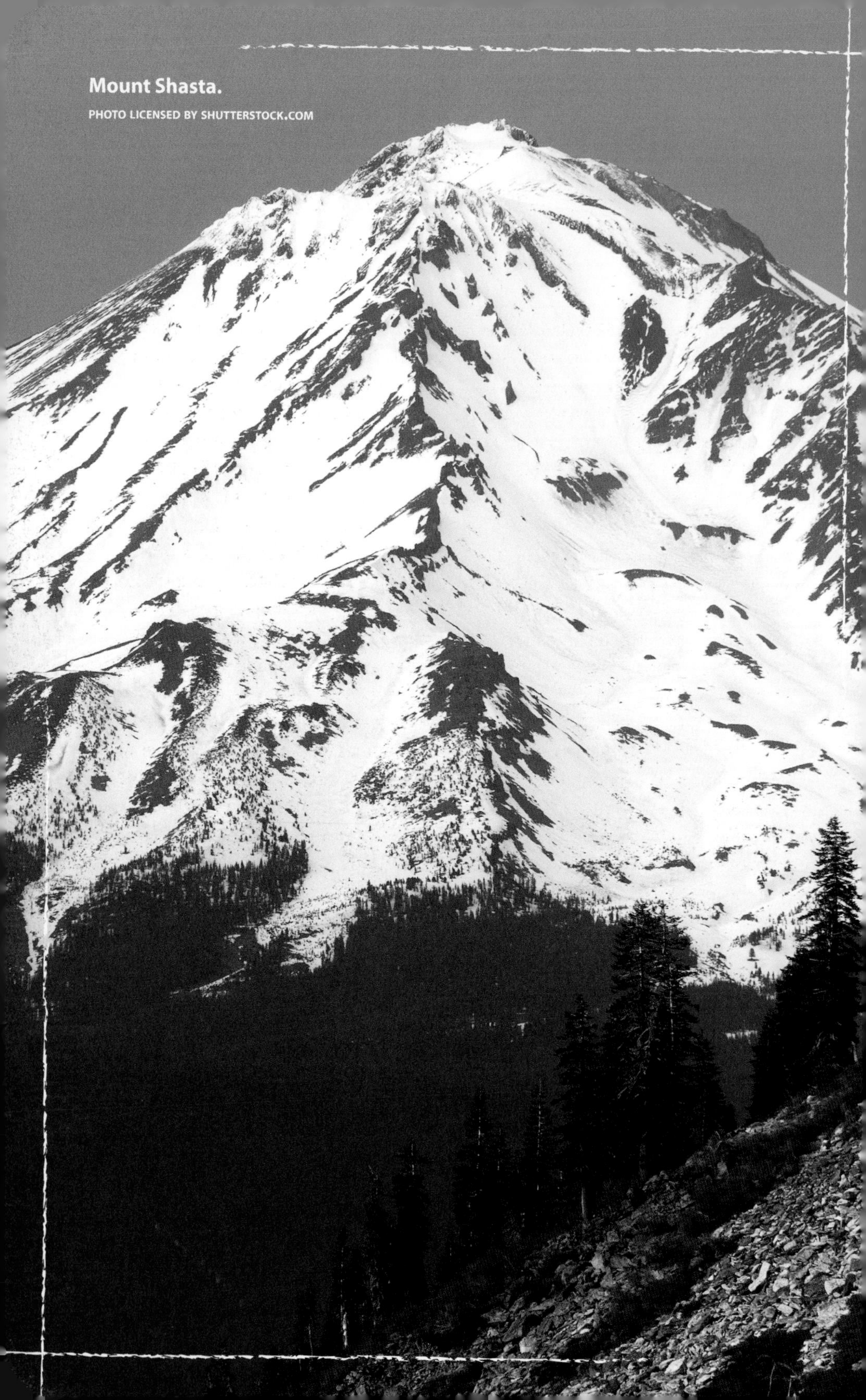

16.

Mount Shasta

Mount Shasta (14,162 feet/4,317 meters) is the second highest of the Cascade volcanoes, and the center-piece of the Mount Shasta Wilderness, established in 1984. Like its relatives farther north, Shasta was formed by various eruptions over the last half million years or so. Intermittent erup-tions have built up the main peak, and a lateral vent eruption around the time of the last ice age (or possibly more recently) resulted in present-day Shastina, a parasitic cone. More recent activity has built up the summit to its present height, and hot springs just below the summit serve as fair warning that the mountain is merely napping. Mount Shasta appears to be a youthful volcano, as it is relatively unscoured by glaciers and lacks many of the features that are commonplace on volcanoes farther north.

Although it rises more than 10,000 feet above its base—the larg-est base-to-peak rise of any mountain included in this guide—Mount Shasta is a "gentle giant" compared with some of the northern volcanoes, such as Mount Baker and Mount Rainier. Shasta's glaciers are typically not heavily crevassed until late season, its slopes are not too steep nor very

seriously eroded, and few routes to its summit involve truly technical rock or ice climbing. However, this does not mean that Shasta's routes are never serious undertakings. Weather and season often determine difficulty. Mount Shasta's weather is similar to that of Mount Rainier, although it receives much less annual rainfall and snow accumulation. Voluminous lenticular clouds frequently cap the mountain, foretelling the coming of storms. High winds and heavy snows are not uncommon, even when not expected or likely. Like Rainier, Shasta sometimes creates its own weather. When lenticular clouds begin to settle in over the summit, a storm is likely close behind, and a hasty descent is none too cautious.

Shasta has seven named glaciers, which have been in retreat for many years. The present ice volume of all Mount Shasta glaciers is close to that of the Emmons and Winthrop Glaciers on Mount Rainier. The Whitney Glacier, a narrow ice river 2 miles long, is Cali-fornia's largest. Mount Shasta's glaciers remain active on the northern side of the mountain. Avalanche Gulch and Cascade Gulch were formerly occu-pied by Pleistocene glaciers.

Local Indians considered Mount Shasta the center of their universe and an inspiring summer hunting ground. When it spewed smoke, however, they ran, afraid for their lives. A possible sighting of Mount Shasta was recorded in 1817 by Fray Narcisco Duran, a Spanish explorer who named the mountain Jesus Maria. The 1841 Wilkes expedition named the mountain Shasty Peak. Captain John Fremont called it Shastl. The origin of the name has not been pinpointed. Tshastal (Russian for "pure" or "white") has been suggested, although "chaste" (French for "pure") or an obscure Indian word are other possible sources. Shasta was also believed to be the name of an Indian tribe living near Yreka.

The first recorded ascent of Mount Shasta was made in 1854 by Captain E. D. Pearce, a Yreka sawmill foreman. Clarence King climbed the mountain a few years later, spending a night in Shastina's crater. John Muir also climbed the mountain and wrote eloquently of it. Like other Cascade volcanoes, Mount Shasta is a magnet for hikers, climbers, and skiers. Many come to Shasta to commune with nature in the presence of this wonderous mountain, and a few religious sects worship Shasta as a "magic mountain." There are astonishing legends of tunnel networks and great telekinetic races living within the mountain. As at Mount Rainier, UFO sightings are regularly reported.

Natives still consider Mount Shasta a sacred place. Local devotees, fanatics, and kooks also worship Mount Shasta in varying degrees.

Climbers familiar with Mount Shasta should not assume that northern volcanoes are similar climbing objectives. Although similar in size to Mount Rainier (bigger actually), Shasta is more comparable to Mount Hood in climbing terms, in that only a few routes are technically difficult or greatly committing. Each mountain certainly has its difficult routes, but most are, overall, fairly pedestrian (i.e., climbers of all abilities can and do make routine ascents without incident). Generally, the easier routes up Mount Rainier are about as committing as the more difficult routes up Mount Shasta. This is obviously a slightly biased and generalized statement, since there are routes on Shasta that involve serious and technical climbing. However, the differences in latitude, topography, climate, and ice volume between the two giants should be evident to even the least experienced observer. This is not to minimize the seriousness or commitment of Mount Shasta. Ascents of Shasta are strenuous and can be serious, especially if weather or other conditions conspire against you. Climbing any mountain has its rigors and dangers. Mount Shasta, at over 14,000 feet, has more than most.

Approaches to many of the routes begin on trails or abandoned roads (closed with the formation of the wilderness area), but eventually the trails peter out and cross-country hiking leads to the glaciers. The network of logging roads surrounding Mount Shasta Wilderness is quite complex and confusing, making driving to trailheads a troubling aspect of routefinding for visitors. The lower slopes of Mount Shasta are fairly open, making the approach hikes straightforward, a stark contrast to the dense forests of the northern volcanoes. However, the Mount Shasta landscape is much more fragile than the evergreen forests surrounding, say, Mount Baker. Take care to minimize your impact when not following established trails.

The Mount Shasta Wilderness Plan became effective during the summer of 1990. The plan focuses on finding a balance between recreational use and preservation of the wilderness area. Climbing is recognized as the main recreational attraction of the Mount Shasta Wilderness, and it is doubtful that climbing will be restricted except where necessary to preserve the visual and environmental integrity of the mountain and its surroundings (for example, Avalanche Gulch). The USDA Forest Service hopefully will continue to improve roads to make approaches easier, which will spread climbers out, away from the heavily used Avalanche Gulch route.

Mount Shasta Vicinity

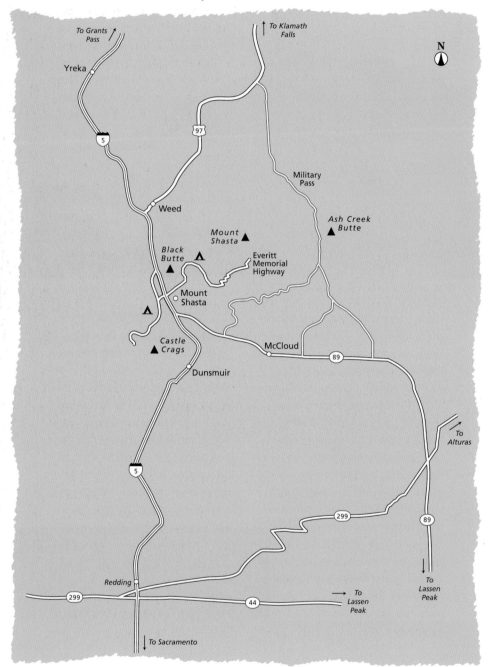

The town of Mount Shasta is located 60 miles north of Redding on I-5, and is the hub of all nonclimbing activity in the area. Everitt Memorial Highway heads north from town toward the mountain. Other approach routes are discussed with individual routes. Mount Shasta has all services and accommodations, making a pancake breakfast at Jerry's the morning of your ascent almost feasible.

Climbers are required to have a Wilderness Permit, Summit Pass, and Human Waste Pack-out Bags. All of these are self-issued and can be obtained at all trailheads or at the Mount Shasta Ranger Station. One-trip Summit Passes (fee) are good for three days. Annual Summit Passes are available from the Mount Shasta and McCloud Ranger Stations during business hours, at The Fifth Season and Shasta Base Camp in Mount Shasta, and at various REI stores in the Bay Area and Sacramento. Reservations are not required. Group size in Mount Shasta Wilderness is ten people; no dogs are allowed.

For further information, contact Mount Shasta Ranger District, 204 W. Alma St., Mount Shasta, CA 96067; (916) 926-4511.

Climbing information, equipment, and equipment rentals can be obtained from The Fifth Season, the local climbing shop (426 N. Mount Shasta Blvd., Mount Shasta, CA 96067; 916-926-3606). The Fifth Season also has a 24-hour weather and climbing condition hotline, (916) 926-5555. The *Mount Shasta Climber's Review* (The Fifth Season) is a poster-size guide to climbing and skiing on Mount Shasta. *The Mt. Shasta Book* (Wilderness Press, 1989) is a concise guide to all recreational activities within Mount Shasta Wilderness, including hiking, climbing, and skiing. The author gratefully acknowledges the acquiescence of Wilderness Press and The Fifth Season, and the contributions of Michael Zanger and Leif Voeltz, in preparing this chapter.

The Mt. Shasta Climber's Guide website at www.climbingmtshasta .org has additional information and links to current climbing conditions.

1. Avalanche Gulch (John Muir Route)
Difficulty rating: 1
Grade: II
Class: 3
Time to summit: 8 hours
Objective hazards: Highly prone to avalanching and exposed to rockfall

This straightforward and simple route was that taken by Captain E. D. Pearce on the first ascent in 1854, and remains the route of choice for a majority of Mount Shasta's climbers.

Most climbs of Mount Shasta begin from the Sierra Club Alpine Lodge. The simplest approach to the lodge is from Bunny Flat via Everitt Memorial Highway, where a trail leads

Mount Shasta South Side Approaches

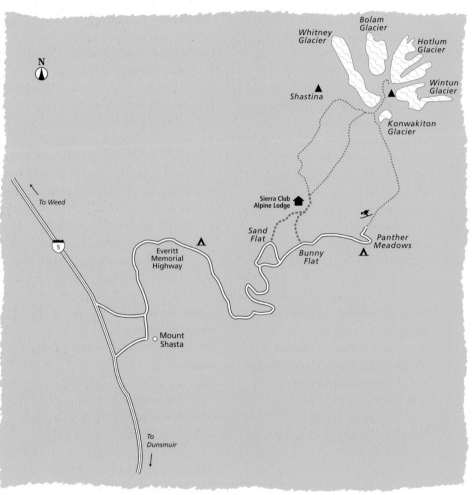

about 2 miles northwest to the Sierra Club Alpine Lodge and Horse Camp, a heavily used campsite offering a good view of the climbing route. An alternate approach is via Sand Flat; however, this approach is not recommended during early season unless you are skiing in. New quotas may limit camping at or near the lodge and higher on Mount Shasta.

Olberman's Causeway, a stone pathway, leads toward the route from the lodge. Many parties camp at Lake Helen, a moraine lake at 10,440 feet, to get a higher start on summit day. There are more than fifty campsites at

Mount Shasta—Avalanche Gulch

PHOTO CHRIS CARR/SHASTA MOUNTAIN GUIDES

Lake Helen, and the area is overused. Sanitation has been a major problem; fortunately, the mandatory use of blue bags has mitigated this problem significantly.

From Lake Helen, ascend snow slopes (scree in late season) closely right of Casaval Ridge, eventually contouring right across the upper gulch toward Thumb Rock saddle, the broad saddle at the head of Sargents Ridge, skirting beneath the obvious Red Banks cliff band near the top of the slope. From the saddle, continue upward to Misery Hill, a final steep slope leading to the summit col. Traverse the summit col and circle around to the northeast side for a short Class 2–3 scramble to the often crowded summit.

There are several possible variations of this route. The Red Banks route is the most popular—in fact, more parties take this variation than the route previously described because it offers a shortcut through the cliff band when snow conditions allow easier climbing. Usually you can follow the footsteps of others up one of the broad chimneys. Crampons and a belay may be necessary, as the chimneys are often icy and unnerving for less experienced climbers. Rockfall is possible in the chimneys, although less so in early morning when the route is snow covered and frozen. Helmets are recommended.

Because of the relative straightforwardness of this route, it is attempted by many ill-prepared and inexperienced climbers. The route should not be taken lightly. Beware of avalanches and rockfall, especially while crossing Avalanche Gulch toward Thumb Rock saddle, when climbing below and through the Red Banks, and on the summit formation. Rock avalanches on this route have caused several fatalities here, particularly in late season. It may also be necessary to pass a bergschrund above Thumb Rock saddle. Some parties make the round-trip in a long day from the lodge, although bivouacking at Lake Helen improves your chances for success. Early-season ascents are recommended; late-season ascents can be interminably tedious scree slogs with the added hazard of climber-induced rockfall.

Descent: Descend via the route of ascent or an easier variation. Ski descents are popular, as are long glissades down the snow slopes when snow conditions are good.

2. Cascade Gulch
Difficulty rating: 1
Grade: II
Class: 2–3
Time to summit: 8–10 hours
Objective hazards: Highly prone to avalanching and exposed to rockfall

Cascade Gulch is the westernmost south-side route on Mount Shasta, ascending the broad V-shaped gully dividing Shasta and Shastina. It is a good alternative if the Avalanche Gulch route is too crowded, though it's a bit longer, and is the standard route for those ascending Shastina.

Approach via the Sierra Club Alpine Lodge (most parties camp at Horse Camp). From the lodge, ascend west around the toe of Casaval Ridge, bearing toward an "obelisk-like rock" visible from the lodge. Once around the corner, ascend directly up the gulch to Shastina Saddle, the saddle dividing Shastina from the Mount Shasta summit. From the saddle, continue east up the snow or scree ridge to the summit crest and scramble to the top. The route can be difficult when icy, is prone to avalanches when covered in wet or unconsolidated snow, and is fairly tedious when snow free.

From the saddle it is easy to climb Shastina. It is also possible to drop down to the upper Whitney Glacier from about 300 feet up the ridge from the saddle, to finish via that route's upper snow/ice slopes. Alternatively, you can find the obvious snow gully (the Hidden Valley route) ascending the broad snow slope/gully immediately left of Casaval Ridge, which gives direct access to upper Shastina Ridge and is about as difficult as the Red Banks.

Descent: Descend via the route of descent or the Avalanche Gulch route.

Mount Shasta South Side

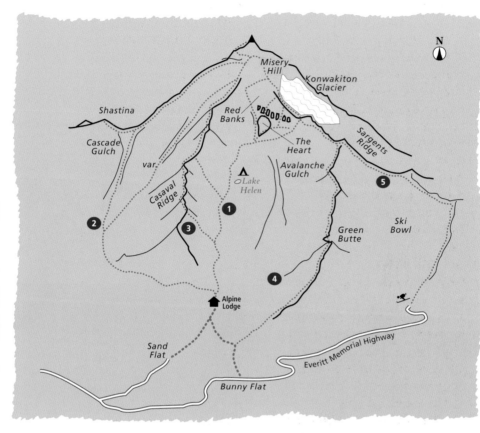

3. West Buttress—Casaval Ridge
Difficulty rating: 3
Grade: III
Class: 3–4
Time to summit: 8–10 hours
Objective hazards: Avalanche-prone slopes approaching the ridge, some loose rock

This is the obvious ridge dividing Cascade and Avalanche Gulches. It is an enjoyable climb with moderate mixed climbing, and is recommended as a good winter route, generally safe from avalanches and rockfall.

Approach from the Sierra Club Alpine Lodge to the west side of the ridge and ascend the ridge as directly as possible, staying on snow as much as possible. A few obstacles on the ridge are fairly easily bypassed. You may encounter some Class 3 scrambling, and at a few spots a rope might be desirable. Alternatively, it

Mount Shasta—South Side

Misery Hill

1

Thumb Rock

var.

Red Banks

Casaval Ridge

2

The Heart

Avalanche Gulch

var.

3

1

Cascade Gulch

4

Green Butte Ridge

Lake Helen

is possible to access the ridge from either of two "windows" from Avalanche Gulch, both of which also offer an escape from the ridge except in high avalanche conditions. Without snow cover this route is a tedious, loose rock scramble and is not recommended. Most parties wisely descend Avalanche Gulch, except during periods of snow instability.

Descent: Descend via the Avalanche Gulch route or easiest variation.

4. Green Butte Ridge
Difficulty rating: 2
Grade: II
Class: 3–4
Time to summit: 8 hours
Objective hazards: Moderately prone to avalanching and exposed to rockfall

A popular variation of the Avalanche Gulch route, this route ascends the obvious long ridge from Green Butte to the crest of Sargents Ridge and on to the summit. It is a recommended winter ascent due to relatively low avalanche and rockfall hazard. By late season it is a tedious scree slog.

Approach as for Avalanche Gulch, but angle right and up the ridge to Green Butte, where the narrow ridge leads upward to join Sargents Ridge just below the Thumb Rock saddle. Stay on the west side of Thumb Rock to reach the saddle. Join the Avalanche Gulch route to the summit.

This route has no major difficulties. The ridge is relatively safe from avalanches, but slopes below the ridge are exposed and there may be cornices. Moderate rock scrambling is required depending on the route taken, with some loose Class 3–4 sections possible on the upper portion of the ridge.

Descent: Descend via the Avalanche Gulch route or easiest variation.

5. Sargents Ridge
Difficulty rating: 2
Grade: II
Class: 3
Time to summit: 8–10 hours
Objective hazards: Moderately prone to avalanching and exposed to rockfall

This fine route ascends the obvious ridge to the east of Avalanche Gulch, directly above the Ski Bowl parking area. It is a recommended winter ascent due to relatively low avalanche and rockfall hazard. By late season it is a tedious scree slog.

From Ski Bowl, the route is straightforward and not particularly difficult to Shastarama Point (elevation 11,135 feet). Continue along the upper ridge to Thumb Rock saddle, staying on the west side of Thumb Rock to reach the saddle. Join the Avalanche Gulch route to the summit.

This route has no major difficulties, although early-season

Mount Shasta East Side Approaches

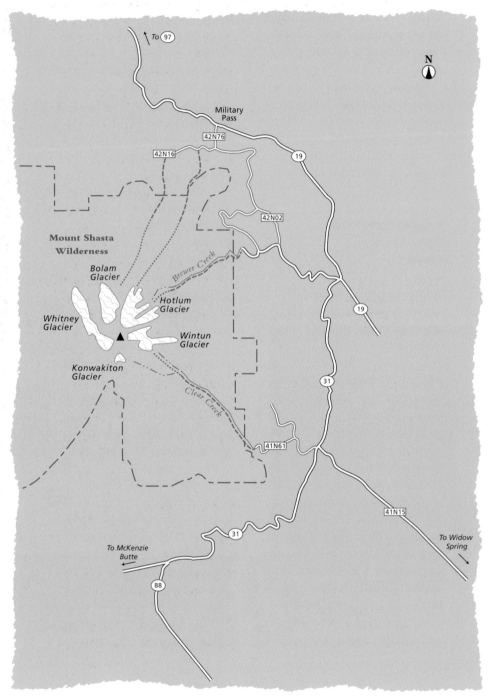

approaches can be troublesome because of avalanches slopes and indistinct terrain. The ridge is relatively safe from avalanches, but slopes below the ridge are exposed. There is moderate rock scrambling depending on the route taken, with some Class 3–4 sections possible on the upper portion of the ridge.

Descent: Descend via the route of ascent or the Avalanche Gulch route.

6. Wintun Glacier
Difficulty rating: 2
Grade: II
Class: 3
Time to summit: 8 hours
Objective hazards: Moderately prone to avalanching and exposed to rockfall

The Wintun Glacier is the easternmost of Mount Shasta's north-side glaciers. It offers a variety of climbing situations on its various glacier sections and bordering ridges.

Brewer Creek Trail is commonly used to access the Wintun and Hotlum Glacier routes. There are several possible ways to reach the trailhead, and any attempt to give directions would be confusing. The drive to the trailhead is usually well marked, so just follow the signs or refer to a map.

Follow Brewer Creek Trail to its end, then drop south into Wintun Canyon to Ash Creek. The descent over the moraines to Ash Creek is loose and unstable. Pick the safest-looking route and be careful. Follow Ash Creek up to the northern lobe of the Wintun Glacier. Rope up here.

The route ascends the glacier directly to the south shoulder. The lower portion of the glacier is often badly crevassed, and there are some perpetually hidden crevasses higher up. Once past the crevasses, the route to the summit shoulder is relatively straightforward.

A variation ascends Wintun Ridge, the long snow/scree ridge directly south of the glacier that forms the east ridge of Mount Shasta. Wintun Ridge can be approached directly from Clear Creek Trail on the southeast side of the mountain, or by traversing south from Ash Creek below the lowest lobe of Wintun Glacier. It is a straightforward ascent with no technical difficulty, and a decent climb when snow covered; otherwise it is an interminable scree slog.

Descent: Descend via the route of ascent or carry over the top and down the Avalanche Gulch route.

7. Wintun-Hotlum Route
Difficulty rating: 1
Grade: II
Class: 3
Time to summit: 8 hours
Objective hazards: Mildly prone to avalanching and exposed to rockfall

This route ascends the gentle ridge separating the Wintun and Hotlum

Mount Shasta—Aerial View

Bolam
Glacier

10

Wintun
Ridge

6

Shastina

Cascade
Gulch

Casaval
Ridge

Sargents
Ridge

5

11

2

3

4

Whitney
Glacier

1

Green
Butte

Avalanche
Gulch

PHOTO **USGS** CASCADE VOLCANO OBSERVATORY/MIKE DOUKAS

Glaciers. It is not so much a ridge as a scree line between the glaciers, but it offers a fairly straightforward and enjoyable line of ascent to the summit.

Approach via Brewer Creek Trail, hiking cross-country from trail's end north to and then alongside Brewer Creek. Follow snowfields left (east) of Hotlum Glacier, then either traverse left across the upper Wintun Glacier to the south shoulder finish, mindful of crevasses, or else ascend the Hotlum-Wintun Ridge to the crest just northeast of the summit. This route is not particularly difficult, although there are more difficult ridge finish variations, up to Class 4

and/or technical ice, leading to the summit shoulder.

Descent: Descend via the route of ascent or an easier variation.

8. Hotlum Glacier
Difficulty rating: 3
Grade: III
Class: 3–4 up to 5.8 depending on variation taken to summit
Time to summit: 8–10 hours
Objective hazards: Highly prone to avalanching and exposed to rockfall

Hotlum Glacier is a popular north-side climb, ascending a broad glacier to a steep headwall. The headwall can be bypassed at the top, but

Mount Shasta—North Side

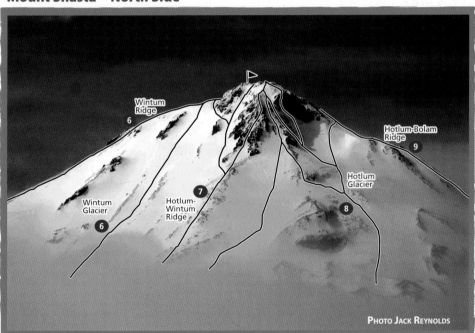

PHOTO JACK REYNOLDS

Mount Shasta North Side Approaches

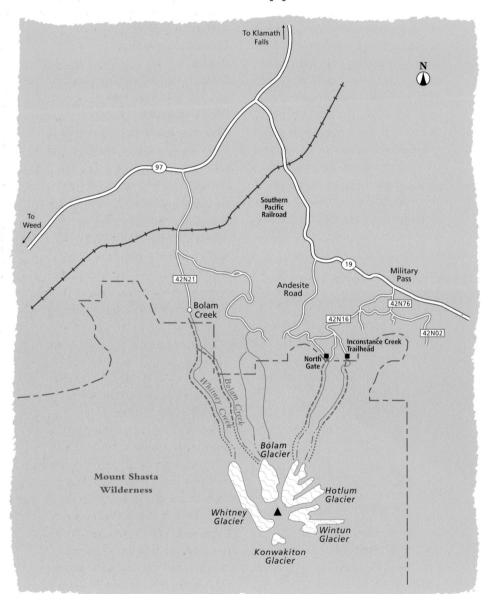

offers some of Mount Shasta's most challenging climbing.

This route may be approached either from Gravel Creek or Brewer Creek (better) as for the Wintun-Hotlum Route. Ascend the glacier fairly directly to 13,000 feet (as directly as permitted by the crevasses, which can become troublesome by late season), then finish via one of several possible variations up or around the headwall. The most popular variation ascends the ridge on the south side of the headwall or a snow finger on the headwall side of the ridge. Another variation is the headwall directly via much more difficult 5.8 rock and/or ice. Yet another variation ascends an ice gully on the far right (north) side of the headwall, which is recommended as a late-season ice climb but otherwise not popular or recommended. The route has moderate avalanche danger and some rockfall exposure beneath the headwall. Crevasses can be troublesome in late season.

Descent: Descend via the route of ascent or an easier variation.

9. Hotlum-Bolam Ridge
Difficulty rating: 1
Grade: II
Class: 3–4
Time to summit: 8 hours
Objective hazards: Moderately prone to avalanching and exposed to rockfall, loose rock

This route ascends between the Hotlum and Bolam Glaciers via a gentle ridge forming Mount Shasta's true north ridge. The route is popular in all seasons, although by late season it has some tedious scree climbing.

Approach via the North Gate Trail. The roads approaching this trail are complex and confusing. Begin from Weed on US 97 to Military Pass Road, which is followed about 7 miles to Military Pass. Turn off Military Pass Road to a prominent fork (see a map for details, since directions would be confusing here). Staying left reaches Inconstance Creek Trailhead, an alternate approach to Hotlum Glacier; the right fork reaches North Gate Trailhead and more direct access to the Hotlam-Bolam area—this is also the recommended approach by some for the Whitney Glacier as the ascent via the Graham/Whitney Creek trail is a slog by comparison. Follow the map and signs.

Ascend from timberline to the ridge across a broad, flat lava flow that is straightforward and enjoyable when snow covered but not so much when bare of snow. Stay west to avoid the worst of the pumice and scree. Once on the ridge, ascend to a prominent step at about 13,000 feet, where options include contouring around to the right (west) to join the Bolam Glacier route; ascending a lobe of the glacier and snow slopes to bypass the steepest part of the ridge; or continuing directly up the blocky ridge, staying west of two prominent rock towers (Class 3–4). Although this route is regarded as the safest and most reliable north-side route, there have been fatalities here. The ridge finish has some loose rock, the glacier has crevasses, and the upper slopes can be avalanche prone. This route is often used as a descent from other north-side routes.

Descent: Descend via the route of ascent.

Whitney Creek Approach

Whitney Creek Road is the common approach to Whitney Glacier and can be used to access Bolam Glacier as well. Bolam Creek Road gets you closer, but has more difficult auto access (four-wheel drive only) and is not recommended. Whitney Creek Road begins about 12 miles from Weed on US 97 and is followed all the way to Graham Greek Trailhead. The trail forks; go right to Whitney Creek, left to Bolam Creek. Social trails and cross-country hiking leads to the glaciers. While this approach is more direct in a strict sense, it is more tedious than the North Gate trail approach.

10. Bolam Glacier

Difficulty rating: 2
Grade: II
Class: 3
Time to summit: 8 hours
Objective hazards: Moderately prone to avalanching and exposed to rockfall

Bolam is a broad glacier on the mountain's north flank. There are several possible routes, depending on approach and glacier conditions.

Approach via either North Gate Trail (longer, but recommended) or Bolam or Whitney Creek Trails. Climb either the east or west upper lobes of the glacier, depending on your route of approach, to the summit crest. The easterly version ascends a lobe of the glacier and snow slopes to join the north ridge near 13,000 feet, above the steepest part of the ridge; the west route stays on the glacier proper and does not join the ridge until very near the summit. Overall, this is a straightforward and enjoyable route, although crevasses can be a problem in late season and the headwall slopes can be avalanche prone.

Descent: Descend via the route of ascent or the Hotlum-Bolam Ridge route.

11. Whitney Glacier

Difficulty rating: 2
Grade: III
Class: 3
Time to summit: 10–12 hours
Objective hazards: Moderately prone to avalanching and exposed to rockfall and icefall (depending on variation)

Whitney Glacier is the longest glacier in California and the most impressive on Mount Shasta. It extends for about 2 miles and is narrow and quite active, with a substantial icefall.

Mount Shasta—North Side

Hotlum-Wintum Ridge

7

Hotlum Glacier

8

9

Bolam Glacier

10

11

Stastina

Whitney Glacier

PHOTO DAVE STEPHENS

Approach via either North Gate Trail (longer, but recommended) or Whitney or Bolam Creek Trails. The traditional route gains the eastern portion of the glacier's terminus and ascends as crevasses dictate to the head of the glacier and on to the summit crest. Keep your distance from Shastina's flanks due to rockfall hazard. This route is long and time consuming, but is recommended.

A variation ascends left of the glacier on snow or pumice slopes (the Bolam-Whitney Divide), never touching glacier ice. This route is okay during early season, but in late season can seem like an eternal scree slog. The icefall can be climbed directly in early season when stable, but is usually only used for ice climbing practice on the seracs, and is not recommended during warm weather.

Descent: Descend via the route of descent or the Hotlum-Bolam Ridge route, or carry over the top and down the Avalanche Gulch route.

Lassen Peak.
PHOTO STEVE PIERCE

17.

Lassen Peak

A minor volcano compared with the glaciated giants farther north, Lassen Peak (10,457 feet/3,188 meters), the southernmost of the Cascade volcanoes, is included in this guide even though its only official route is a trail leading to the summit.

Lassen Peak (also called Mount Lassen) is a significant plug-dome remnant of a former 11,000-foot-high stratovolcano, Mount Tehama (or Brokeoff Volcano). Mount Tehama collapsed and was nearly erased by ice age glaciers, but Lassen Peak, a dacite dome, extruded itself from Tehama's remains some 11,000 years ago. In May 1914 Lassen awoke, and a year later it began spilling lava, snow, and mud across its slopes. On May 22, 1915, the mountain erupted violently, shooting hot gasses and ash into the stratosphere. A simultaneous lateral blast and *nuée ardente* (meaning "glowing cloud," a hot pyroclastic flow) devastated the northwestern part of the present-day park. This eruption, and the presence of fumaroles and 200-degree F mud pots nearby, signal that the mountain is far from dormant.

Mount Lassen, the "largest plug dome in the world," is the centerpiece of one of California's less crowded national parks, Lassen Volcanic National Park, and is located in northeastern California about 180 miles north of Sacramento. The park may be reached via CA 44 east from Redding in 45 miles, or via CA 36 east from Red Bluff, also about 45 miles, or west from Susanville via either CA 36 or 44, in about 70 miles. North from Mount Shasta, CA 89 runs south directly through the park.

Lassen Peak is not the only volcanic peak within the park. Cinder Cone (6,907 feet/2,105 meters) is located just northeast of Lassen, as is Prospect Peak (8,338 feet/2,541 meters), a shield volcano. These and other volcanic peaks within the park may also be ascended without technical difficulty.

A fee is charged to enter Lassen National Park. Numerous reasonably priced campgrounds are found within the park; for reservations, call (877) 444-6777. Backcountry camping requires a permit, which may be obtained upon entry to the park.

For further information, contact Lassen Volcanic National Park, Box 100, Mineral, CA 96063; (530) 595-4480; www.nps.gov/lavo/planyourvisit/hiking_lassen_peak.htm. In case

Lassen Volcanic National Park

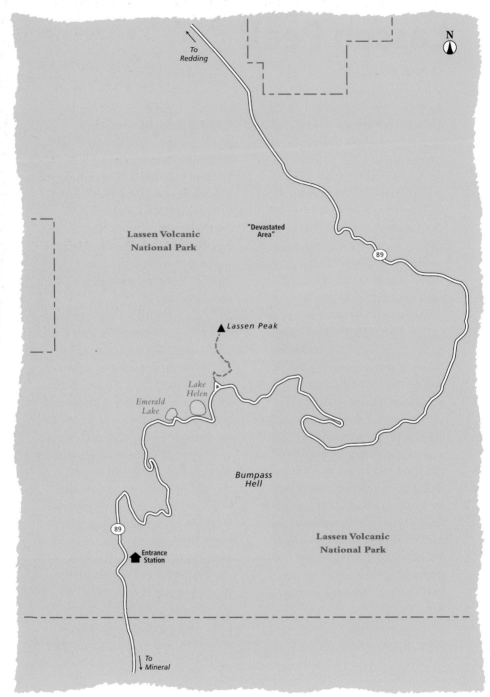

of an emergency, dial 911. The nearest hospital is Seneca Healthcare District, (530) 258-2151.

1. Lassen Peak Trail
Difficulty rating: 0
Grade: I
Class: 1
Time to summit: 2 hours
Objective hazards: None

Drive about 8 miles inside the park from the southern entrance, just beyond Lake Helen, to where the well-marked Lassen Peak Trail begins. Hike steeply 2.5 miles to the summit. This is a heavily traveled tourist trail, and park rangers lead guided hikes to the summit. There are usually no special dangers or difficulties, assuming you stay on the trail and have no health problems. Obtain a map and brochure upon entry to the park for directions.

In winter, snow routes and ski descents on all sides of the mountain are possible. Although the National Park Service prefers no off-trail hiking to preserve the fragile landscape, winter and spring climbs on snow do no harm and offer something different.

Descent: Hike back down the trail.

Appendix

Websites

If you are planning an ascent of any of the Cascade volcanoes, you can find detailed route information, trip reports, topos, photos, and current route and access information on one or more of the following websites:

Cascade Climbers

Discussion forum, trip reports, photos, and more
www.cascadeclimbers.com

Climbing Washington

General information, current access information, topos
www.climbingwashington.com/ccv.html

Mount Rainier

The most current information about Mount Rainier climbing available
http://mountrainierclimbing.blogspot.com

Mt. Shasta Climber's Guide

All Mount Shasta, all the time
www.climbingmtshasta.org

Peak Bagger

Route information, trip reports, photos
www.peakbagger.com

Skiing the Cascade Volcanoes

Detailed climbing and ski route information for all Cascade volcanoes and then some
www.skimountaineer.com/CascadeSki/CascadeSki.html

Summit Post

Route information, trip reports, photos
www.summitpost.org

Traditional Mountaineering

Route information, news, trip reports, photos for Oregon volcanoes and more
www.traditionalmountaineering.org

Guide Services

The following guide services provide climbing instruction and guided ascents of one or more of the Cascade volcanoes. This information is provided for reference only, without endorsement or warranty except that each of these guide services is accredited by the American Mountain Guides Association (the guides in the United States anyway). For information about these or other guide services in your area, contact the AMGA at (303) 271-0984, http://hireaguide.amga.com/.

Alpine Ascents International

109 W. Mercer St.
Seattle, WA 98119
(206) 376-1927
www.alpineascents.com

American Alpine Institute

1515 12th St.
Bellingham, WA 98225
(206) 671-1505
www.aai.cc/

Canada West Mountain School
47 W. Broadway
Vancouver, BC V5Y 1P1
(888) 892-2266
www.themountainschool.com

Mountain Madness
3018 SW Charlestown St.
Seattle, WA 98126
(206) 973-8389 or (800) 328-5925
www.mountainmadness.com

Rainier Mountaineering, Inc.
30027 SR 706 East
P.O. Box Q
Ashford, WA 98304
(888) 892-5462
www.rmiguides.com

Shasta Mountain Guides
P.O. Box 1543
Mount Shasta, CA 96067
(530) 926-3117
http://shastaguides.com

Timberline Mountain Guides
P.O. Box 1167
Bend, OR 97709
(541) 312-9242
http://timberlinemtguides.com

Mountaineering Clubs
The British Columbia Mountaineering Club
P.O. Box 2674
Vancouver, BC V6B 3W8
(604) 286-9502
www.outdoorvancouver.com/clubs/
british_columbia_mountaineering_
club.aspx.html

The Cascadians
P.O. Box 2201
Yakima, WA 98907
http://cascadians.org

The Mazamas
527 SE 43rd Ave.
Portland, OR 97215
(503) 227-2345
www.mazamas.org

The Mountaineers
7700 Sandpoint Way NE
Seattle, WA 98115
(206) 521-6001
www.mountaineers.org

The Obsidians
P.O. Box 322
Eugene, OR 97440
www.obsidians.org

The Sierra Club
85 2nd St., Second Floor
San Francisco, CA 94105
(415) 977-5500
www.sierraclub.org

Washington Alpine Club
P.O. Box 352
Seattle, WA 98111
www.wacweb.org

Bibliography

Printed References and Books of Interest

American Alpine Journal, 36:475, 39:310, 46:44, 49:143, 219, 50:121, 54:23, 57:1–28, 58:78–81, 59:301, 305, 60:114–16, 121, 61:336; 61:360, 62:204, 63:469–71, 64:169–70, 65:407, 66:126–28, 366–67, 67:384–86, 69:305, 338–39, 71:228, 340, 349, 72:113–14, 74:141–42, 76:441, 79:182–84.

Avalanche Echoes (B.C.), 64:4, 68:4–5, 69:4–5, 10/73:3, 12/74:7, 11/79:3, 6/80:4, 4/83:6, 2/84:2, 10/84:2.

Baldwin, John, *Exploring the Coast Mountains on Skis,* 1983.

Bauer, Jack, "The North Face of Mount Rainier," *The Mountaineer No. 27,* 1938.

B.C. Mountaineering Club Newsletter, 7/25:6, 6/44, 11/55, 4/66, 8/71, 9/80, 11/82:15, 6/84:30–43, 11/85:12, 12/87:5–6, 8/88:1, 42.

Beckey, Fred, *Cascade Alpine Guide, Climbing and High Routes, Columbia River to Stevens Pass,* 2nd ed., Seattle: The Mountaineers 1987; *Cascade Alpine Guide, Climbing and High Routes, Stevens Pass to Rainy Pass,* Seattle: The Mountaineers 1981; *Cascade Alpine Guide, Climbing and High Routes, Rainy Pass to Fraser River,* Seattle: The Mountaineers 1987; *Mountains of North America,* San Francisco: Sierra Club Books 1982; *Challenge of the North Cascades,* Seattle: The Mountaineers 1977.

Bien, Vic, *Mountain Skiing,* Seattle: The Mountaineers 9/82.

Biewener, Jack, "A Climber's Guide to Mt. Hood," Portland: *Mazama 56:28;* "A Climber's Guide to Three Sisters, Mt. Washington, and Three Fingered Jack," *Mazama 55:16.*

Brugman/Post, "Effects of Volcanism on the Glaciers of Mount St. Helens," *USGS Bulletin 1981.*

Canadian Alpine Journal, 08:205–10, 11:175–76, 12:140, 32:90–91, 37:107–11, 57:73–74, 71:68–69, 72:71–72, 81:64–65, 86:53.

Climbing (Magazine), 5/82:13 (Little Tahoma Peak), 12/87:52–56 ("Willis Wall" by Gary Speer), 4/91:81 ("North Ridge of Mount Baker" by Alan Kearney).

Coleman, Edmund, *The first ascent of Mount Baker, Bellingham,* Washington: Shorey 1966.

Crandell, Dwight, "Recent Eruptive History of Mount Hood, Oregon, and Potential Hazards from Future Eruptions," *USGS Bulletin 1980.*

Crandell/Mullineaux, Donal, "Volcanic Hazards at Mount Rainier, Washington," *USGS Bulletin 1238.*

Culbert, Dick, *Alpine Guide to Southwestern British Columbia,* 1974.

Dodge, Nick, *A Climbing Guide to Oregon,* Beaverton, Oregon: The Touchstone Press 1975; *A Climber's Guide to Oregon,* Portland: The Mazamas 1968.

Fairley, Bruce, *Climbing & Hiking in Southwestern British Columbia,* Vancouver: Gordon Soules Book Publishers 1986.

Foxworthy, B. L./Hill, "Volcanic Eruptions of 1980 at Mount St. Helens: The First 100 Days," Geological Survey Professional Paper 1249, 1984.

Gillette/Dostal, Ned/John, *Cross-Country Skiing,* 3rd ed., Seattle: The Mountaineers 1988.

Grauer, Jack, *Mount Hood: A complete history,* 1975.

Haines, Aubrey, *Mountain Fever, Historic Conquests of Rainier,* Salem: Oregon Historical Society 1962.

Hall, "In Oregon It's Mount Jefferson," *Off Belay* No. 11, 10/73.

Harris, Stephen, *Fire Mountains of the West: The Cascade and Mono Lake Volcanoes,* Missoula: Mountain Press Publishing Company 1988.

Hazard, Joseph, *The Glacier Playfields of Mount Rainier National Park,* Seattle: Western Printing 1920.

———, *Snow Sentinels of the Pacific Northwest,* Seattle: Lowman & Hanford Co., 1932.

Hildreth, Wes/Fierstein, Judy, "Mount Adams: Eruptive History of an Andeside-Dacite Stratovolcano at the Focus of a Fundamentally Basaltic Volcanic Field," *USGS Open-File Report 85–521 1985.*

Hill, M., "Volcano History and Geology," *Off Belay* No. 8, 4/73.

LaChapelle, Ed, *The ABC of Avalanche Safety,* Seattle: The Mountaineers 1986.

Lowe, Don and Roberta, *62 Hiking Trails—Northern Oregon Cascades,* Beaverton, Oregon: The Touchstone Press 1979; *60 Hiking Trails—Central Oregon Cascades,* Beaverton, Oregon: The Touchstone Press 1978.

Macaree, Mary and David, *103 Hikes in Southwest British Columbia,* Seattle: The Mountaineers, and Vancouver: Gordon Soules Book Publishers 1987.

Majors, H. M., *Mount Baker: A Chronicle of its Historic Eruptions and First Ascent,* Bellingham: Northwest Press 1978.

Manning, Harvey/Spring, Ira, *50 Hikes in Mount Rainier National Park,* Seattle: The Mountaineers 1975.

Martinson, Arthur, *Wilderness Above the Sound: The story of Mount Rainier National Park,* Seattle: Northland Press 1986.

Mathews, W. H., *Garibaldi Geology, A popular guide to the geology of the Garibaldi Lake area,* Vancouver: Geological Association of Canada 1975.

Mathews, Daniel, *Cascade - Olympic Natural History, a trailside reference,* Portland: Raven Editions 1988.

Matthes, Francois, *Mount Rainier and its Glaciers,* 1928.

Mazama (Club Journal): 00:1–40, 00:203–7, 03:143–47, 164–75, 05:201–34, 07:5–26, 67–69, 12:6–20, 13:1–20, 36–38, 14:1–27, 37–38, 54–62, 69–77, 15:1–24, 16:1–28, 17:127–45, 180–86, 19:301–18, 339–42, 20:3–16, 26–54, 21:9–11, 19–27, 46–47, 22:21–35, 23:21–24,

69–75, 24:32–39, 25:25–66, 32:7–23, 33:7–29, 34:29–32, 35:36–37, 36:36, 41–43, 38:13–17, 39:9–11, 53:31–36, 54:5–11, 31–36, 55:16–25, 56:28–34, 57:32–34, 58:79, 60:42–44, 52–53, 64:12–22, 65:43, 66:51–52, 67:28–30, 67–70, 68:54–56, 69:16–20, 41, 47–49, 70:28, 71:13–15, 21–23, 72:26–30, 74–77, 73:17–19, 83:30–31.

McCoy, Keith, *The Mount Adams Country—Forgotten Corner of the Columbia River Gorge,* White Salmon, Washington: Pahto Publications 1987.

Meany, Edmund, *Mount Rainier: A Record of Exploration,* Portland: Binfords & Mort 1916.

Miles, John, *Koma Kulshan: The Story of Mt. Baker,* Seattle: The Mountaineers 1984; "Mount Baker - 1868," Off Belay No. 28, 8/76.

Miller, C. Dan, "Potential Hazards from Future Eruptions of Mount Shasta Volcano, Northern California," *USGS Bulletin 1980.*

Mitchell, "Arctic Mountaineering on the 47th Parallel," *Off Belay* No. 2, April 1972.

Molenaar, Dee, *The Challenge of Rainier,* Seattle: The Mountaineers 1987.

Mountaineer (Club Journal): 12:37, 18:49, 20:46–47, 24:57, 30:22–24, 31:12, 56–58, 33:14, 34:5, 35:3–7, 37:23, 48:50, 53, 49:1–4, 55, 54:67–68, 56:38–54, 122, 58:96–99, 101–2, 59:105, 60:76, 61:97, 99–100, 62:91–92, 98–99, 63:87–89, 64:131, 66:203–4, 68:205, 69:112, 70:108–9, 71:72–74, 75:102, 77:72, 106, 78:104.

Mountaineers, The, *Mountaineering: The Freedom of the Hills,* 4th ed., Seattle: The Mountaineers 1982.

Nadeau, *Highway to Paradise,* Tacoma: Valley Press 1983.

Naragon, Janice and Mason, Christopher, *Best Foot Forward,* Woodinville, Washington: GrizzlyWare [c] 1990; interviews 10/91, 12/91.

National Geographic (Magazine), 5/63 ("Mount Rainier: Training Ground for Everest").

National Park Service, *Mount Rainier National Park Wilderness Management Plan; Backcountry Trip Planner;* Mount Rainier National Park press releases, photo, and historical archives; miscellaneous records and publications.

Off Belay (Magazine): #1:22–26, #2:30–36, #13:4–9, 51, #18:2–9, #24:10–15, #29:2–5, #34:9–23, #35:21–25, #36:5–12, #42:2–9. #1:10–13, 42, #2:7–11, 48–49, #8:41, #9:37, #12:30–35, #16:33, #17:2–10, 20–25, #20:33–35, #26:31–35, #27:51–55, #39:33, #40:31–32, #44:20–27, 30–31, #49:32, #55:22. Citations of particular interest: "Mount Adams—A History," "Mountaineering on Mount Adams," 6/72; "Mount Washington, Oregon's Outlaw," 10/72, "In Oregon, It's Mount Jefferson," 10/72, "Boom!," 6/80.

Prater, Gene, *Snowshoeing,* 3rd ed., Seattle: The Mountaineers 1988.

Ream, Lanny, *Northwest Volcanoes, A Roadside Geologic Guide,* Renton: B.J. Books 1983.

Reid, H. F., "Three-Fingered Jack—A directory and some comments," Mazama 1929.

Richard, Terry, *The Oregonian*, "Five Oregon Peaks That could Use Some Glue," 2007, http://blog.oregonlive.com/terryrichard/2007/09/five_oregon_peaks_that_could_u.html.

Roper, Steve, "Climbers' Guide to Mount Shasta," *Ascent* No. 2, 1968.

Roper, Steve/Steck, Allen, *Fifty Classic Climbs in North America*, San Francisco: Sierra Club Books 1979.

Rusk, C. E., *Tales of a Western Mountaineer*, Boston and New York: Houghton Mifflin Company 1924 (reprinted 1978 by The Mountaineers with new photos, biography of C. E. Rusk, by Darryl Lloyd).

Seattle Post-Intelligencer, 1/17/91:F1–2.

Seattle Times, 6/10/91:A1–2.

Selters, Andy, *Glacier Travel and Crevasse Rescue*, Seattle: The Mountaineers 1990.

Selters, Andy/Zanger, Michael, *The Mt. Shasta Book*, Berkeley: The Wilderness Press 1989.

Shane, Scott, *Discovering Mount St. Helens*, Seattle: University of Washington Press 1985.

Snow, Ray, *Mount Rainier: The story behind the scenery*, Las Vegas: K.C. Publications Inc. 1988.

Spring, Ira/Manning, Harvey, *100 Hikes in the Glacier Peak Region*, Seattle: The Mountaineers 1988; *100 Hikes in the North Cascades*, Seattle: The Mountaineers 1988; *100 Hikes in the South Cascades and Olympics*, Seattle: The Mountaineers 1985.

Summit (Magazine): 1/57:10–11, 5/62:6, 1/63:30–35, 6/64:9–11, 4/65:18–25, 5/66:15–18, 7/66:8–11, 3/67:4–7, 9/69:10–13, 9/71:16–17, 5/72:6–8, 5/73:2–7, 12/82:23, 3/85:8–10, 7/85:8–13, 9/85:28–31, 1/86:10–13, 3/86:12–21, 7/86:4–15, 3/87:30, 11/87:21–25, 5/88:1–21.

Thomas, Jeff, *Oregon High*, Portland: Keep Climbing Press, 1991.

Tolbert, C. L., *History of Mount Rainier National Park*, Seattle: Lowman & Hanford 1933.

U.S. Forest Service: "Guide to the Mt. Baker District," Mt. Baker-Snoqualmie National Forest; U.S. Forest Service: "Climbing Mount Hood, A guide to south side routes"; *Wilderness Management Plans for Mount Shasta, Three Sisters, Mount Jefferson, and Mount Washington wilderness areas;* TRIS.

Varsity *Outdoor Club Journal*: 60:11, 27, 61:10, 65:9, 23, 68:59, 69:17, 56, 106, 71:60, 72:13–14, 73:60, 74:16–18, 39–41, 50–52, 65–66, 75:25, 42, 44–46, 76:27–8, 78:39–40, 79:26–27, 83:71–72, 87:11–13, 88.

Washington Geologic Newsletter, Vol. 15 No. 4, October 1987.

Wilkerson, James, *Medicine for Mountaineering*, Seattle: The Mountaineers 1986.

Wilkerson, James/Bangs, Cameron/Hayward, John, *Hypothermia, Frostbite and other Cold Injuries*, Seattle: The Mountaineers 1986.

Williams, Chuck, *Mount St. Helens National Volcanic Monument*, Seattle: The Mountaineers 1988.

Index

Index

About the Author

Jeff Smoot is a climber, hiker, lawyer, and the author of six other FalconGuides, including *Backpacking Washington's Alpine Lakes Wilderness, Hiking Washington's Alpine Lakes Wilderness, Adventure Guide to Mount Rainier, Climbing the Cascade Volcanoes,* and *Climbing Washington's Mountains.* He is based in Seattle, Washington.

PROTECTING CLIMBING **ACCESS** SINCE 1991

ACCESS FUND

| JOIN US |
WWW.ACCESSFUND.ORG

Jonathan Siegrist, Third Millenium (14a), the Monastery, CO. Photo by: Keith Ladzinski